COURAGE
IS A
THREE-LETTER
WORD

COURAGE
IS A
THREE-LETTER
WORD

WALTER ANDERSON

RANDOM HOUSE   NEW YORK

Grateful acknowledgment is made to *The New York Times*
for permission to reprint an excerpt from the obituary
of Joseph Lubin by Walter H. Waggoner, April 6, 1983.
Copyright © 1983 by The New York Times Company.
Reprinted by permission.

Library of Congress Cataloging-in-Publication Data
Anderson, Walter, 1944–
Courage is a three-letter word.

1. Security (Psychology) 2. Anxiety. 3. Success.
I. Title.
BF575.S35A53   1986   152.4   85-25711
ISBN 0-394-54656-3

Manufactured in the United States of America
24689753
First Edition

For Loretta,
with love

If one tells the truth, one is sure sooner
or later to be found out.

—OSCAR WILDE

I was gratified to be able to answer
promptly, and I did. I said I didn't know.

—MARK TWAIN

CONTENTS

COURAGE
IS A
THREE-LETTER
WORD

Chapter 1

WHAT WILL I DO WHEN THEY FIND OUT I'M ME?

It was Good Friday, April 17, 1981, and I had just asked John Ehrlichman why he had not committed suicide.

He sat across from me at a small table in a rear corner of Danny Stradella's Restaurant on East Forty-sixth Street in Manhattan. We had walked there from my office, which was only a half-block away. Our conversation was polite, correct. As we spoke I wondered whether I had made a mistake by agreeing to meet this former presidential aide, a character I remembered from the Watergate hearings in 1973 as arrogant, contemptuous—frankly, to my mind, a man who had threatened my country.

Yet, there he sat, now bearded and bespectacled, only inches from me.

"My life is different today," he offered. An understatement, I thought, as I noticed that he spoke tentatively and not with the pompous self-assurance that had alienated millions of his fellow Americans who watched him on television defending Richard Nixon. I noticed something else, too. His bearing. No longer the mighty bull, he was more a calf stepping out of the barn into the sunshine for the first time. His steps were hesitant. He spoke softly, leaning away.

I did not order a drink.

He did not order a drink.

I ordered an appetizer.

He ordered an appetizer.

I ordered the special.

He paused. "The special," he told the waiter.

"John," I said, "as editor of *Parade* magazine, I have a responsibility to readers in more than twenty million homes. . . ." He nodded quickly, assuring me, "I understand."

"Good," I said, "because some of what you will hear from me will be painful. If you are to write for *Parade,* though, I need to know first who you are, who you really are."

Again he said softly, "I understand."

Released from Swift Trail Federal Prison Camp in Arizona on April 27, 1978, three years to the month before this lunch, John Ehrlichman had already written two successful novels about the presidency, including *The Company,* which became a popular TV movie, *Washington Behind Closed Doors,* starring Jason Robards, Jr. His prison time behind him, divorced and remarried, he was trying to expand his range as a writer and, with a young family dependent on him, he needed to earn more money. His indomitable literary agent, Mort Janklow, had arranged our meeting, although I warned Mort, "He will have to answer some tough questions."

"Walter, my friend," Mort replied, "John Ehrlichman has answered tough questions. Please meet with him and let me know what you think."

What I thought was that John Ehrlichman had lived my darkest nightmare; he had been shamed before an entire nation—ridiculed and stripped. How, though, could *his* experience be *my* nightmare? We seemed to share so little. He was a convicted criminal, a former high government official who had been ostracized by many of his countrymen; I was the editor of the largest-circulation magazine in America, the chairman of the board of a fine college, a respected citizen in my community. Yet, although I had broken no law, I found myself asking, What if I, like John Ehrlichman, lost everything? My concern, though groundless, was nonetheless real to me. I was groping with an important difference, as you'll discover later, between fear and anxiety.

"There's not a city you can enter," I said, eye to eye with the man across the table, neither Ehrlichman nor I eating, "not a cab, a hotel, a school, a theater, a store you can visit in which someone might not hold you in contempt. Your very name can inspire revulsion in almost every nook and cranny from coast to coast. How can you live with this?"

I took a breath. "Why have you not taken your life?"

Deep down I knew I had asked the question not for the readers of *Parade,* not for journalism, not for history, but for me. I wanted to understand how any person could survive such terrible public shame. John Ehrlichman, after all, had been a trusted aide to the President of the United States. His fall—going from the White House, where he wielded enormous power, to the prison in which he served his time— had been steep, complete and humiliating. What, I wondered, kept him alive?

"I thought about dying," he said. "Actually, I thought about it a lot. My name is John Ehrlichman and I know better than anyone else that what you say is true. I had to decide for myself whether to live or to die. That was the choice. No one else could pull me out of self-pity. If I couldn't live with the truth that many people will never accept me as a person, if I have to depend on others for my self-esteem, then I must choose death. If I wanted to live, I had to quit my depression. I had to say my life had value, and I had to mean it. I chose life."

John Ehrlichman's voice had been soft until his last sentence: "I chose life." I'll never forget those words or the voice in which he spoke them.

"I have one more question."

"Please ask," he said, softly again.

"Would you accept an assignment?"

During the last few years I have had the rare and wonderful opportunity to come to know many extraordinary people, some of whom you'll find in these pages. I begin this book with John Ehrlichman, a man scorned, because in his ordeal we can see a person grasping for dignity —a struggle each of us lives through in our own way every day even without having committed any crime. In this book you'll also meet a prince and an astronaut, two men whose challenges are considerably different from John Ehrlichman's. You'll be introduced to the presidents of some important corporations and a sculptor, a Nobel Prize winner and an Olympic athlete, a comic genius and a courageous priest, several acclaimed actors and actresses, writers, photographers and artists, people of exceptional power and apparent confidence, people who I once believed were without the fears you and I share. But in this book you'll find that they often feel insecure, that they have failed, that many of them fear that others will discover their inadequacies. Even more important, though, you'll see how these successful men and women have learned to do more than simply cope with their most agonizing fears by actually turning those feelings into assets. You'll learn how they, and you, can summon courage, once you understand what courage really is. But I promise you no easy formulas. This book is about real life, real people, real problems. I'm sure that many names will be familiar to you, but most of the stories, many of which are personal and intimate, will be new. I hope they will touch you as they have touched me. I have published many of these talented people, been their editor and their friend, have been privileged to see their minds at work and, sometimes, the secret places of their hearts revealed.

Hundreds of times I have looked into the eyes of a successful person and asked, "When it is dark and you are alone, do you ever say to yourself, What will I do when they find out I'm me?" I've never failed to make a friend with the question. And I've never failed to get a nod. It was as if I knew who they were, that I understood and, because I understood, I could be trusted. I've seen the cool, disciplined, practiced composure of some of America's toughest business leaders melt.

What about me? How did I, a boy raised in a tenement on the outskirts of New York, an adolescent who quit high school at sixteen to join the Marines, become editor of America's most widely read magazine before I was thirty-six? This book, as you'll soon see, is that journey too. I know now that making the decision to tell my story was as difficult as it was to write it. Why? What was it I had been afraid —and in many ways still am—that others might discover?

That I am inferior.

That I am vulnerable.

That I deserve to be rejected.

How about you? When it's dark and you're alone in your most troubled moments, do you worry that someone will find out that you're not good enough, that you can be hurt, that you don't belong? If so, read on. Your fears, my fears are shared by millions of sane people. We are not alone. Truth be told, it is we who are the majority, and it is we who are normal. Fear, once you understand it, can be OK. In fact, sometimes it can save your life.

John Ehrlichman leaned back in his chair at Danny Stradella's Restaurant. Our "special," a mixture of pasta and seafood, had grown cold.

"Yes," he said, "I want to write for you, but what do you have in mind?"

"John," I began, "you must find a white family in Appalachia, a black family on the south side of Chicago, a Chicano family and an American Indian family out West—"

"Why?" he interrupted.

"—and they must all be poor. Why? Because I want you to meet these people—folks whose names I don't even know—and tell our readers how, despite their poverty, they manage to live with dignity. I want you to report their struggles and their victories over hard times. As I said, I don't know their names, but I know that they're there and I know that you will find them."

"Why me?" He asked the question gently.

"Because," I told him, "I know no one else who will search as hard as you will for the members of these courageous American families and who will understand what they have overcome." If I'm wrong, I realized, he'll fail more than this assignment; he'll fail himself. John Ehrlichman *needed* to find dignity, maybe more than anyone else I'd known. Would he try?

"I'd like to start immediately," he volunteered, leaning forward.

"Can we eat first?" I asked.

. . .

Fear is what kept our primitive ancestors alive in a hostile world. They had no time to wonder or ponder. They had a minute, maybe two, to make the life-or-death choice: "Should we fight or should we run?" Adrenaline flooded their bloodstream, adding speed, energy and strength. Their veins and arteries simultaneously constricted to slow the bleeding if they were wounded. Their pulses quickened, their bodily defenses stiffened. This physical response to a clear and present danger is fear, the fear that we depend on to save our lives.

Today, most of what we call fear is something else. It is anxiety, a response not to danger itself but to anticipated danger. The cave dweller was rightly concerned about being some creature's breakfast on the spot. What he felt was real fear. When we worry about something that might happen later—when we say, "I just know I'm going to fail!" —that's anxiety. When the brakes in your car stop working on a hill or a mugger demands your money, what you feel is fear. When you worry over what you'll say at a meeting next Tuesday, that's anxiety— and anxiety is a lot more agonizing than fear. Fear usually ends with the event: the car stops, the mugger is arrested, the fear's over. Anxiety can be endless.

Why do I emphasize the distinction?

I do because your body often does not.

Have you ever noticed how your body responds when you're anxious? Quickened pulse. Sweaty palms. Dry throat, just as if you were face-to-face with a creature who wanted to gobble you up for breakfast! Anxiety is so frustrating. All that energy and nothing to do with it. You can't run or fight, because there's nothing to run from, nothing to fight. You sit with a knot in your stomach, anticipating danger.

We all know that anxiety can produce symptoms ranging from mild discomfort, like the uneasiness I felt when I first began talking to John Ehrlichman, to psychological and physical incapacitation and death. Yes, anxiety can kill you—or it can ruin your day. That depends on you. Because in many of the stories you are about to read I use the word "fear" when "anxiety" would be the better choice, we'll have to remember the difference: anxiety is a response to *anticipated* danger.

And nothing can arouse that anticipation more quickly in nearly everyone I know than a simple request: "Will you stand up before our group?" My most vivid memory of this kind of fear goes all the way back to my seventh-grade class at Immanuel Lutheran School in Mount Vernon, New York.

I had turned thirteen only a few months before, and I believed all eyes were on me, burning right through to the back of my neck as surely as if they were spotlights. I wanted to scream or cry or die. My heart beat so loudly in my ears I was sure that others nearby could hear it too. As I look back over my life, despite thousands of other mistakes and embarrassments, this was my most humiliating moment.

Our teacher had ordered me to remove my shirt and stand at my desk. What bothered him was that I had my shirt collar up, an adolescent style in the fifties. He was going to make me an example before my classmates.

"Take off your shirt!" he ordered.

I promised not to do it again.

"I've caught you twice," he said, striding to my desk. "Take it off!"

He had me and he knew it. Mount Vernon—four square miles of seventy-five thousand people living just beyond the Bronx, the northernmost borough of New York City—is a town with a tear in its belly, a railroad cut right down its middle. I lived deep in the south side of town in a tenement on a street where kids often wore motorcycle jackets, greased their hair, talked hard and tried to look unafraid, a neighborhood where the corner, however violent, was safer than the explosive tension at home—my home. Immanuel was deep in the north side—the right side of the tracks—in a section called Fleetwood, which might just as easily have been halfway across the world. It had prosperity and it had peace. I crossed the tracks to go home every night, home to a block where kids wore their collars up.

"Take it off!" the teacher ordered again, hovering over me.

He was a tall man and his body blocked any chance I might have had to run. Somebody giggled.

"Please . . ." I pleaded.

"Now!"

I unbuttoned the front of my shirt.

"Hurry up!"

I opened my cuffs and slipped the shirt off, draping it behind me on my chair. My undershirt had holes. Several people giggled.

"Stand up!"

I stood up.

The phenomenally successful British author H. G. Wells, who wrote *The Time Machine* and *The War of the Worlds,* is reported to have shuddered with fright one night during the Blitz of England in the forties. But, he told a visitor, "It's not the bombs; it's the dark. I've been afraid of darkness all my life." Logic has it that it was the bombs and not the darkness he should have feared. But what he feared was the darkness. What is *our* darkness? It is the fear of all we do not know. Knowledge, then, is the first step to making fear a friend.

We human beings share a universal experience that can be described in a word, a word that applies to the child born two thousand years ago or the child yet to be conceived. It is true of every culture, every tribe that has ever existed or will ever exist—all people, all races, all languages. The word is *struggle.* From the first slap on your behind until your last heartbeat, you struggle. We all do. And we all survive, we all endure until that last heartbeat. A few, a rare and precious few, seem to do more. They *prevail.* It is from their stories we can learn how to do more than live with anxiety. We can learn how to live better *because* of it.

Yes, better because of it. Throughout this book you'll share tender moments with some people from whose experiences you'll be able to gain greater insight into your own life. This, though, is a working book. It needs your effort.

There's an often-told story in the Far East about the Chinese grandfather who, each day of his life, rose early, climbed to the top of the nearby hill that blocked the early-morning sunlight, picked up a small stone, walked back down the hill and dropped the pebble on the other side of a stream near his home. His son and grandson joined him in this task. "Why do we do this?" the grandson asked.

"As long as you continue to do this and teach your children and grandchildren to carry the pebbles," the grandfather promised, "we're going to move this hill." The boy persisted, "But, Grandfather, you'll never see the hill moved."

The old man nodded: "Yes, but I *know* that someday it will be moved."

The spirit of this book is hope, the certain knowledge that you and I are not helpless. As small as our first steps may be, let's take them: Find a pebble, carry it, save it as a reminder that you can, when you set your mind to it, move a hill—or a mountain—of fear.

The teacher, who had been standing beside my desk, marched back to the front of the classroom. He had been bullying me all year. I thought then and understand now that it was because I was different, or at least seemed different. My clothes *were* unlike what the other students wore; mine were familiar in my neighborhood, but unfamiliar in that school. Having forgotten to turn my collar down, I had given him what he had been looking for.

I stood alone.

"Turn to page . . ." he said, ignoring me.

I heard my heart beat even louder in my ears; the heat at the base of my neck was becoming unbearable. For that thirteen-year-old boy, his worst secret had been revealed. The undershirt with its holes for all to see proved I was poor, proved I was a south-sider, unworthy of the north-siders in the room.

Maybe it was seconds, maybe it was minutes, before I reached for my shirt. It seemed a long time.

"I didn't tell you to move," the teacher said from the front of the class.

I ignored him as I buttoned my shirt and sat down. The bell rang for recess before he got to me.

"Wait!" he ordered. Everyone stopped.

"Just Walter," he amended.

One or two students hesitated by the door, hoping to hear what he was going to say. "Move," he told them.

"You are going to learn to listen to me," he said. I was silent.

"Go to recess."

I walked to the door, turned back to the teacher and called out his name.

"Yes?"

"Why don't you go to hell," I said, my eyes filling with tears.

From the depths of my anxiety I had found the right response. It was not my words, which, because of the provocation, were deliberately disrespectful. It was that I had asserted myself. In that moment I discovered the roots of my own dignity. I had dared to be myself. My mother, though she certainly did not condone my behavior, understood it, and stood by me when I was threatened with expulsion. The following night she pleaded with the school board to allow me to remain as a student until June, when—she promised the members who patiently heard her plea—she would transfer me elsewhere.

"Anywhere," she was advised.

Vindicated, the teacher for the most part stopped the bullying; I quietly finished the school year.

In my anxiety that I would be seen as inferior to my classmates, I found the courage to face down a bully. Anxiety can help you. That is the message of this book. Living with the endless crises of everyday life, we often see anxiety as the problem, rarely as a solution. But to claim our dignity and to find our courage, we need anxiety to help us. Dignity is the courage to be yourself. Courage is acting *with* fear, not without it. Courage is a three-letter word—and that word is *yes*. Yes, as you will see in the lives of others, you *can* dare to be you.

John Ehrlichman called me Tuesday morning, September 15, 1981. His article had appeared the previous Sunday. Entitled "Chronicles of Courage Among America's Poor," it had been warmly received by readers and was one of the most popular articles *Parade* had published in years. Above his byline had appeared this message: "Poverty has a human face. Every day, real people cope with diminishing means in order to survive. But some prevail. These are their stories, written by a man who searched for a lesson."

"Walter," he said, his voice strong and excited, "these people genuinely inspired me. I want to thank you again. If there's anything more I can do . . ." he volunteered.

"How about another assignment?" I asked.

He didn't hesitate. "I'd love to!"

I paused. "I have an idea," I said, "but, my friend, it could be the toughest assignment you've ever accepted."

"What is it?"

"The questions will never stop," I began, "until you share with the American people what you've experienced, what, in fact, you've learned from the Watergate experience. Americans are fair-minded, John. If you tell them the truth, they'll respond to you. Some will even forgive. Once, just once, you've got to tell it all. Otherwise it will hang like a dark cloud over you for the rest of your days. Say it and be done with it."

He was silent.

"This is very hard for me," he said, finally.

"I understand."

"Can I think on it," he asked, "and call you back in a few days?"

"Of course," I said.

What will I do when they find out I'm me?

As much as each of us might resist revealing to someone else who we really are, we must. To live our lives successfully, we need other people. We need their respect and their goodwill. Change your hairstyle or clothes, purchase a new pair of glasses or a hat—how important to you is the first person to comment? If today you heard a hundred words of praise and one word of criticism, which would be on your mind tonight?

Me too.

It *was* the most difficult assignment John Ehrlichman had ever accepted. He would later tell me, "It was the toughest writing—no, more accurately, it was the toughest job of opening up and saying how it was, to myself—that I had done since I walked along an Oregon beach in 1973 and admitted to myself that everything I'd valued in life was gone."

John Ehrlichman, in an article *Parade* published on September 26, 1982, candidly discussed his own role in the Watergate scandal, his shame, his deep regret and a vow he had made to himself: "I intend never again to abdicate the moral judgments I am called upon to make. I hope I succeed. Nothing I've learned is more important to me."

Months later he told me that the admission had become for him "a rite of passage," and he confided, "Since it was published, I have rarely looked back."

Nevertheless, for this book I asked John Ehrlichman to reflect one more time.

"When you asked me to tell my story," he wrote to me in a letter on October 31, 1984, "I hated the idea of re-opening the closed chapters of my life. I was getting fairly comfortable. The more time passed, the more the hurt seemed to subside. Deep down, though, I knew you were right. People deserved to hear it from me once and for all, as clearly and simply as I could say it. As you write your book, Walter, perhaps you can help your readers recognize that, as hard as it is to believe, there can be blessings in the most painful of experiences, even at the vortex of a scandal or the break-up of a marriage. In the midst of the turmoil, everything looks bad. Helpful friends may assure you that it's always darkest before the dawn, but when you're living with pain, optimism seems impossible. Yet everyone needs and deserves these assurances, because the assurances are true. Even the most horrible experience can be big with blessings."

We need each other, and it is for the sake of that need that I have selected the stories for this book. In succeeding chapters you'll read how others have overcome personal fears, sometimes to achieve remarkable success, and you'll probably find among the questions they've had to answer some you've had to ask yourself:

Who am I?
Do I belong?

Must I worry?

What if I make a mistake?

Why am I so angry?

Can I begin again?

When must I say good-bye?

Why me?

Am I ready?

Let me share with you a fable once told to me by the distinguished former editor of *McCall's* magazine Herb Mayes, who was trying to help me understand the value of experience. It's about a boy who wanted to study gems and who sought lessons from his city's master gem merchant:

"No," the master told the boy, "I can't teach you."

"Why not?" the boy asked.

"You lack the patience to learn."

"I don't," the boy persisted, "I don't! Please, please give me a chance."

The master studied the boy.

"No," he said.

"Please don't turn me away," the boy pleaded.

The master looked directly into the boy's eyes, reflected, then said, "Be here tomorrow."

The next morning the master put a jade stone in the boy's hand and instructed him to hold it, then continued his own work of cutting, weighing and setting gems. The boy sat quietly and waited.

The boy returned the following morning and again the master placed the jade stone in his hand and told him to hold it. And, again, the boy obeyed.

On the third, fourth and fifth days the master repeated the exercise and the instruction.

During the morning of the fifth day the boy could stand the silence no longer. "Master," he asked, "when will I learn something?"

"You'll learn," the master replied and, as he had on each previous morning, went about his business of cutting, weighing and setting gems.

Two more times the boy endured and the master repeated the lesson.

Finally, on the morning of the eighth day, the boy decided he'd had enough. The master would waste no more of his time, he promised himself. He was going to tell the master what he thought. By the time he arrived at the door he had himself in quite a state.

The master seemed hardly to notice and, before the boy could say anything at all, he placed a stone in his hand.

"This is not the jade stone!" the boy, whose face was red with anger, said immediately, not even glancing at the gem in his hand.

"You have learned," the master said.

Just as the boy held the jade stone and turned it in his hand day after day, so you should turn the stories you're reading. Turn them, weigh them, consider them, make them a part of you. Our challenge is to live with anxiety, to remind ourselves that it is an asset to our well-being. It can be our ally.

As you explore the intriguing lives and experiences of others, I'm confident you'll see yourself reflected in many of the stories you're about to read. Some are profoundly sad, even as they are inspirational. Others are joyous. All share a distinctive quality: they're true. To gain the most from this book, I'd recommend that you underline paragraphs, write notes in the margins, fold pages that you find particularly meaningful, *live* this book with me. Thus, together we can begin to answer the question "What will I do when they find out I'm me?"

Chapter 2

WHO AM I?

It was during the evening of May 12, 1983, when a slight, delicate woman thrust into my hand the Nobel Peace Prize she had been awarded six years earlier.

"The prize is the people's," Mairead Corrigan Maguire told me. "Here, hold it . . ."

"I can't," I protested, drawing my hand away.

"Yes, you can," she said, reaching toward me to clasp my left hand with her right. She turned my palm up and pressed the gold medal into it. I stared at the disk in my hand and was speechless. I was holding the Nobel Peace Prize; I was holding history.

A few minutes earlier Mrs. Maguire had had to stand on a milk crate to reach a microphone in the dining room of the College of New Rochelle in New York. There stood a person, a diminutive dark-haired woman in a simple patterned dress, who, I had to remind myself, had been only thirty-three when she was asked to share with Betty Williams the Nobel award in 1977 for a campaign to seek peace in Northern Ireland by encouraging the combatants—Protestants and Catholics—to protest the violence in their homeland. Her voice was light and lilting, and as she spoke, many in the audience seemed unconsciously to lean forward in their chairs. It was not her celebrity that gripped us;

it was her passion. Her emphasis, her intensity, even the words themselves were like crystal pins, fixing the attention of the nearly fifty
people with whom she was sharing dinner, a fund-raiser for her beloved
Community of the Peace People, a group that had invited me, as editor
of *Parade*, to attend.

"You feel it every day," she had said. "If you really want to see how
people live their sorrow in Northern Ireland, come to Belfast . . ."

Her tone was soft, the pattern of her speech halting. The audience
seemed to lean toward her even more.

"Our graveyards," she said, "are overpacked—everyone knows a
family who has lost a child to violence! Come to Belfast. People say that
two thousand five hundred deaths isn't much! But in a place that small!
Plus all those maimed and damaged by bombs, all those grieving, the
children never knowing peace or a normal childhood. Everyone's been
touched by it, everybody has someone in prison or dead or in a hospital.
The grief is too deep. It has to end."

I felt, as Mairead Corrigan Maguire spoke, that I understood, that
I had shared a special understanding from my own early years and their
often random violence. One incident in particular came to mind, alive
and aching even after a quarter of a century. It occurred in the bedroom
of my childhood.

I had been deep in sleep when the first slap shocked me awake.
Instinctively I cringed, covering my face with my hands, drawing my
body away from the blows. I smelled whiskey in the darkness. Wavering
before me was my father, his face red, his eyes narrowed in rage, his
fists clenched high to strike me again, his voice bellowing, "You can't
fool me! You think I was born yesterday? I know what you're going to
do—"

He struck my arms away as if they were paper. "—and I'll make sure
you don't"—his voice became even louder—"I'll beat you until I get
the truth!"

Although I could not have been more than twelve years old, I knew
not to cry out, not to protest that I was being beaten for something
I *might* do, some accusation I could not defend myself against, some
transgression boiling in my father's mind at 2:00 A.M.

He lifted his right fist higher; I drew my knees to my chest and in a futile gesture tried to tuck in my face. He drove his hand through my knees, grabbed my undershirt and the flesh of my chest, squeezed and started to lift me when my mother burst into the room shouting, "You leave that boy alone!"

Twenty-six years later, Mrs. Maguire's words stayed with me as I held her prize.

"I sometimes carry it in my purse," she told me, "so I can share it with others. Peace, and this award, are meant to be shared, enjoyed, touched. It doesn't have any value if it doesn't bring joy, Walter, and it has no value if it's locked away."

The Nobel Peace Prize still wonderfully in my hand, I considered the searing tragedies this fragile young woman had experienced. Her torment began on August 10, 1976. On a street in Belfast, Northern Ireland, her younger sister, Anne, had been pushing a baby carriage in which lay her six-week-old baby, Andrew. On top sat John, who was two. Holding on was Joanne, who was eight, and walking alongside was Mark, who was seven. Then, in a horrible instant, life exploded in the agonizing blur of war. Two members of the Irish Republican Army riding in a car provoked a gunfight with British soldiers, who fired back, shooting the driver in the head. The car sped out of control, off the road and smashed into Anne and her children, three of whom died. Anne herself was placed on a life support machine and, for the moment, survived.

The day following the tragedy Mairead Corrigan learned of a Protestant woman named Betty Williams who was organizing a rally against violence. Mairead, a Catholic, decided to join Mrs. Williams, a Belfast housewife. They held a peace rally at the place where the children had died, and thousands of Catholic and Protestant women joined them, all demanding an end to the violence. In the weeks and months that followed, Mairead campaigned harder, only to be physically and verbally abused, the Protestant paramilitary calling her an IRA dupe, the IRA calling her a British agent, the British dismissing her as naive. As her sister, Anne, seemed to grow stronger she, too, joined the peace movement, but her losses finally overcame her. Anne committed suicide on January 21, 1977, after hearing the beginning of a public inquiry into the killing of her children. Mairead continued, more intent than ever, seeing even more clearly the need for peace.

Can there be any wonder why I hesitated to hold the award Mairead Corrigan Maguire had earned? To me, she was a champion of incalculable courage who strode unarmed amid streets of sudden violence. I was humbled in the presence of a woman whom I could probably hold in one hand, yet she may be the strongest person I've known.

"Thank you," I said.

"Thank *you*," Mairead Corrigan Maguire replied and she smiled. I smiled too, and with a certain knowledge I passed the Nobel Peace Prize to a woman standing nearby.

"Oh, no, I can't . . ." she said.

I begin here with a moment of sharing and a moment of personal trauma, to explore the wonder of who we really are. Mairead Corrigan Maguire found her true character in a place of violence. In a different sense, so did I. Some of what you are reading remains painful to me, but I share the experience to provide an insight to help you and me know ourselves better.

The first question each of us must answer if we're to govern our own lives is, "Who am I?"

My father dropped me back on the bed, ready to turn his rage on his wife. With one hand she seemed to be trying to wipe her eyes awake, while with the other she clutched her cotton bathrobe tightly closed.

"What do you think *you're* going to do?" he demanded, his voice hoarse and challenging. He glared at my mother, who was barely five feet three inches tall. His eyes blinked slowly, and his body, which was as thick and muscular as a professional wrestler's at five feet ten and nearly two hundred pounds, weaved slightly from side to side.

"Well what are you—" he started, his words coming slowly and slurred.

"Now, honey," she interrupted, her voice soft and gentle.

"I don't care about you either," he told her, his voice not as loud, but still belligerent. "You don't mean nothing to me . . ."

Her voice stayed gentle and she coaxed him as you would a puppy, "Come on, honey, let's go in the kitchen so I can make you something to eat."

"I'm not hungry," he argued.

"Sure, you are," she said softly, moving herself between him and my bed. "You've been working hard all day and you're hungry."

Our apartment was on the second floor of the four-story apartment building at 159 South Eleventh Avenue in Mount Vernon, New York. It was a railroad flat, four square rooms lined up like the cars of a train. The kitchen had three doors: one to the main hallway—and the other apartments—which led down a flight of stairs to the front entrance; one to the back fire escape, which overlooked a screened garbage shack where the metal cans sat askew, filled with litter; and one to a bathroom the size of a linen closet in which a toilet, a bathtub and a sink no bigger than a spaghetti pot were stuffed. A fourth doorway with no door led to my room, which opened through another empty doorway into my parents' bedroom, which led—also doorless—into the living room. My brother, Bill, who was thirteen years older than I, and my sister, Carol, who was almost seven years older, were both married and no longer lived with us.

My mother squeezed my father's forearm lightly, urging, "Come on, honey . . ."

When he turned and stepped back into the doorway to the kitchen, my mother quickly glanced toward me and shook her head, signaling to me to be quiet. The storm had passed.

I quietly slipped back under the covers and lay motionless on my back, every sense alert, my breathing shallow.

I heard their voices on the other side of the wall, but the words didn't register until I heard my mother say, "You're tired, honey. Let's go to sleep."

My father mumbled and, as she helped him through my room to theirs, I lay as if paralyzed. I heard my father's body fall onto their bed, then silence.

A few minutes later my mother threaded through the darkness to my bed, sat at my side and placed her palm lightly on my forehead.

"I was really scared, Mom," I whispered.

"It's all right now," she whispered back. In the darkness I couldn't see her tears, but I knew they were there.

"How do you feel?" she asked.

"I'm OK, Mom," I answered.

"I love you," she told me, and kissed me on the forehead.

She left my side and padded without stirring a sound to the next room. Again, silence. I stared dry-eyed up and into the night. I rubbed my chest, which had begun to throb. My neck ached.

When my father rose a few hours later, he remembered nothing.

"What are you doing today?" he asked as we sat at the kitchen table. I watched him pour a shot glass of Four Roses whiskey into black coffee.

"School, Daddy," I said.

"Yeah, school," he said. "Well, you better hurry up."

Three factors determine who we are. Heredity, environment and, most important, our response to both.

You are the only you who will ever live. In front of a mirror or in front of a microphone, you are who you are, and accepting this plain truth can be both the toughest and the most rewarding challenge of your life.

There has never been anyone quite like you, or me.

My friend Dr. Carl Sagan, the distinguished scientist, scholar and Pulitzer Prize–winning author, has given me permission to share with you an observation from his book *Cosmos*:

> Were the Earth to be started over again with all its physical features identical, it is extremely unlikely that anything closely resembling a human being would ever again emerge. There is a powerful random character to the evolutionary process. . . . For example, consider our hands. We have five fingers, including one opposable thumb. They serve us quite well. But I think we would be served equally well with six fingers

including a thumb, or maybe five fingers and two thumbs. There is nothing intrinsically best about our particular configuration of fingers, which we ordinarily think of as so natural and inevitable. We have five fingers because we have descended from a Devonian fish that had five phalanges or bones in its fins. Had we descended from a fish with four or six phalanges, we would have four or six fingers on each hand and would think them perfectly natural.

Given that the odds would be astronomical that human beings should look precisely the way they do, I asked Dr. Sagan to calculate the chances of a particular individual being born, period.

"One thing to consider," he advised, "is how many spermatozoa exist in a single ejaculation. Let's say it's three hundred million. That's three hundred million *possible* human beings. Next, there are questions of physiology of both parents—and timing. The three hundred million spermatozoa represent only one sexual act at a particular time." You *are* unique.

The arithmetic helps us to understand just how special we are. Imagine more than 300 million chances to be you! Consider that your mother had 300 million chances to be precisely who she was, that your father had another 300 million. It could be argued that the odds against your being born are 300,000,000 multiplied by 300,000,000 multiplied by 300,000,000 multiplied by whatever the chances would be that your folks would meet in the first place and create you when they did. You are indeed a long shot, my friend—the winner, the day you're born, against odds of billions to one.

Can you imagine, though, what your life might be like if there were two of you? If you had a double, how would you answer, "Who am I?"

That's what I hoped to learn one rainy morning in the late fall of 1984, when I visited a man who had been my friend for more than a dozen years. His name was Fred Kleisner. Only five days younger than I, he had recently been appointed the vice president and general manager of the renowned Waldorf-Astoria. I had watched his career progress from general manager of the Rye Hilton, in Westchester County, to Washington, D.C., as general manager of the Capital Hilton, and then to Manhattan, where he took the helm of the world's preeminent hotel. His spine was straight as a career soldier's as we settled into a couch in his office, a long rectangle of a room decorated with nautical precision, masculine with brass and glass mementos and furniture of various periods and countries, all crafted of hard dark woods. His white shirt, I noticed, had been precisely tailored and, like his charcoal-gray wool suit, it had been flawlessly pressed. His maroon silk patterned tie had been properly knotted with a center dimple that was a *center* dimple. His black shoes glistened. Even his socks, unlike mine, did not crumple about his ankles. He was a measured man, precise and calm. I wasn't surprised that he paused before answering what was a most difficult question; I had asked him how, with an identical twin, he had achieved his own identity.

"Ted and I," he replied, "were born within a few minutes of each other—he's the older—and we were raised in the suburbs of Chicago. By the time we were in the ninth grade I think we both started to feel, I am somebody; I am not part of someone else. But we did not discuss those feelings with each other. Conflicts sometimes flared instead. Until our sophomore year in high school we were regarded more as a unit than as individuals. We dressed alike and we even answered to the name 'Twin,' because no one could tell us apart. Our parents, wisely and with a lot of foresight, asked us that year, 'Who would like to go away to school?' I secretly prayed, God, please let Ted go. I did not want to leave home. Ted volunteered enthusiastically. He *wanted* to go. On my own that year I tried out for the varsity debating team and I made it. That, I guess, was really the beginning of our growing separately."

"Did you cry when he left?" I asked.

"No," he said, "because deep down I felt it was a good idea. I somehow knew we'd both be better off. At the same time I felt lonely without Ted; I worried about him and wondered what was happening in his life."

"Are you similar today?"

Fred Kleisner laughed. "Well," he said, "we certainly look alike! We are similar in other ways, though, too. We chose the same field. Ted's the general manager of the Southampton Princess in Bermuda—"

"And you're in the Waldorf-Astoria," I added.

"Yes, that's an example of how we're similar and different," he said, "because Ted wouldn't like the vibrancy of big-city activity. He likes the resorts, the five-star resort life. We seem to have progressed equally, but in different atmospheres."

"Fred," I asked, "when you're worried, what do you do?"

"I pick up the phone," he replied, "and call Ted. We talk frequently. We are very close, closer than most anyone can possibly understand. It's hard to explain, but often I will call him on impulse and he'll say, 'Thank God you called.' "

"Did you ever have a big fight?"

"One day when we were seventeen," he said, "we each had a date that night and we were dressing in the men's locker room of a restaurant where we both worked. Ted decided I had his slacks. It began as an argument and ended in a sprawling fistfight. In the midst of it, my brother's nose got bloody. A waiter came in and was stunned to see two brothers fighting. He thought I won because of Ted's bloody nose. Actually, Ted had won."

"Fred," I said, "can I meet Ted? I'd like to see him alone."

"Sure," he promised, "he'll be here next month."

Is it our genes or our chromosomes or some other chemical factor that determines who we are? Only partly. With heredity our uniqueness merely begins. Heredity—all those genetic combinations that tell our cells to produce brown or blue eyes, curly or straight hair, predispose us to and sometimes immunize us against certain ailments or diseases —is like the car we drive.

Road conditions and weather are the environment. The car may be capable of speeding one hundred miles per hour on a bright, sunny day along a freshly blacktopped highway, but change the environment to a muddy logging trail at night during a hurricane and the car may not move at all.

Heredity dictates how high we can jump under perfect conditions. It determines how much information we can possibly absorb and retain, how tall we can possibly be, how fast we can possibly run. Heredity is our potential; environment is our opportunity. If you were genetically capable of being the greatest long-distance swimmer who ever lived but, unfortunately, you had been born two centuries ago to an Eskimo family in the northern reaches, it's a safe bet you would never have achieved your potential. You would have lacked opportunity, environment.

Stop now and remember the story of the pebble in Chapter One. You are about to begin to conquer the hill of understanding who you are. If heredity is the car and environment the condition of the road, *you* are the driver. It is you, more than any other factor, that decides the speed and safety of that car.

Who you are evolves from the potential you've inherited, the opportunities you receive and the choices you make. The final factor, your response to heredity and environment, is more profoundly important to you than the arithmetic of 300,000,000 multiplied by 300,000,000 multiplied by 300,000,000. It is your choices that make you uniquely you. Thus, identical twins like the Kleisners, though raised in the same environment, become different by their individual choices, just as the Mairead Corrigan Maguires and the Walter Andersons learn to overcome their environments. When one twin chooses to read rather than watch television or to wear a red shirt rather than blue, a free will—a person—has been asserted.

I was surprised by the uneasiness I felt when I met Fred Kleisner's brother for the first time, a date that was, as Fred had promised, scheduled one month later. Ted Kleisner truly was a double, even to the precision, the fit and polish of his clothes. Fred and I had been friends for years and I had shared many confidences with him. Nevertheless, I was unnerved meeting his brother. Who is this man in Fred's body? I secretly wondered. Can I really ask him personal questions?

As we sat for lunch in the Marco Polo Club of the Waldorf-Astoria, the restaurant's maître d' interrupted us to introduce a guest to the man he obviously thought was Fred Kleisner, his general manager.

Ted rose from his chair, politely listened to the introduction, shook the guest's hand, apologized to the maître d' for failing to introduce himself earlier, and, in a voice identical with his brother's, said, "This happens frequently. I'm Ted Kleisner. Fred and I are twins. I'm delighted to meet you. I'm sure my brother will be too."

The reluctance I had felt about asking intimate questions of a stranger evaporated. He really was like Fred. He listened *before* he explained; he too was gracious. Did they, I wondered, even think alike?

"There have been times I have called Fred," he told me a few minutes later, "and he has actually picked up the telephone before it has rung. I can't explain it. I just know there's a special symbiosis between us. Yesterday, for example, I woke up in one of the suites here at the Waldorf, got dressed and came downstairs to meet Fred for breakfast. We were wearing identical outfits! I suggested we change, and he said, 'Come on, Ted, forget it. Let's eat.' Well, we got so many looks, heard those old jokes again: 'There go the Bobbsey Twins . . . which twin has the Toni?' Last night I slipped on a navy blue argyle sweater to watch some sports on television with Fred. Can you guess what Fred was wearing when he met me at the door?"

"A navy blue argyle sweater?"

He nodded, and we both laughed.

"When were you and your brother first separated?"

"The school system tried to separate us in kindergarten," he said, "but I cried so hard and for so long that, for the first time in the district's history, they allowed twins to attend class together. I cried for a week before they gave in. Fred was less emotional. He coped better. Our first real separation occurred in the sophomore year of high school. Our parents suggested that either Fred or I attend high school away from home. They could see that more than sibling rivalry was brewing between us. Everything was *ours*, not really mine or his. I said, 'I'm going.' When my parents said OK, I was euphoric, exactly the reverse of what I had felt in kindergarten."

"Did you two fight?"

"Yes," he said. "Once we had a rip-roaring fistfight in the locker room of a restaurant in which we worked. I don't remember what we fought about, but I remember a man walking in on us and how absolutely appalled he was to see two brothers fighting."

"Who won?"

"Neither," he replied. "As in every case, we both ended up crying because we had fought."

"When did you and Fred become close again?"

"Only after we separated in sophomore year," he said. "We've been apart ever since—and closer because of it. I think each of us needed to be free to go his own way."

We are handed our heredity with no apologies and often our environment is beyond our control. We have the power, though, to face life, to make choices and, most important, to hope. A stroke may render a person helpless, but it is hope that moves him to stretch, test his muscles, learn to speak again. True hope dwells on the possible, even when life seems to be a plot written by someone who wants to see how much adversity we can overcome. True hope responds to the real world, real life; it is an *active* effort. False hope, on the other hand, is dangerous; it's pathological. False hope is the cancer patient denying his illness; true hope recognizes the disease and seeks to conquer it.

True hope reminds us that each of us is the driver of our own car, that we are not helpless behind the wheel.

I can speak with conviction because I feel it deeply. I remember one night when my mother asked me to walk to the telephone booth across the street from our apartment house to make a call to my older brother. I was fourteen. We had no telephone at the time.

I can't remember the message or our discussion, but I clearly recall the incident because, when I replaced the receiver, I noticed blood on my hand. I touched my face with the other hand and found more blood.

I wasn't bleeding, but whoever had used the phone before me had been hurt or wounded. Opening the glass bi-fold doors, I looked to one side, then to the other. I ran across the street, bounded up the stairs to our apartment door, nervously opened it, stepped inside and up to the kitchen sink and washed the blood from my face before my mother could see it.

About an hour later I sat alone on the front stoop and wondered about the mysterious person whose blood had covered my face.

Then I became angry.

I'm getting out of here, I promised myself and, for the first time that I can remember, I meant it.

He'd been a career serviceman, and when he retired in 1959 as the Coast Guard's first chief journalist, he plunged full tilt into a writing career. For several years he had written nearly every day and, as he'd complete each unsolicited manuscript, he'd put it into an envelope and mail it to publishers, only unfailingly to receive rejection slips in return. Despite failure upon failure, he continued. One morning he opened an envelope from a little magazine called *Liberty*. It held no rejection slip. Enclosed was a check in payment for two articles he had submitted and, when he cashed it, he requested a hundred one-dollar bills. He stuffed fifty in each of the front pockets of his trousers and strolled down Broadway in New York squeezing the money. "I've been paid for writing!" he told himself, and from that moment on nothing could sway him to pursue a different vocation. Later, a young editor asked him to interview the great jazz musician Miles Davis, which he did, and when he turned his report in to the magazine, the editor, Hugh Hefner, introduced it as the first *Playboy* Interview. His study of a charismatic black leader, *The Autobiography of Malcolm X*, became a runaway best-seller in several languages. It was, however, another achievement that led to his fame: his epic search for identity. He is the author of *Roots*. His name is Alex Haley.

We met in the fall of 1980. Earlier, as editor of *Parade*, I had sent him a letter asking what he would tell his grandsons if they were standing with him in Henning, Tennessee, on the very day my letter arrived.

He replied, "Well, I hope that I could help them understand what it meant to be especially blessed, that within a five-mile radius once there had been the early homes, churches, the schools, the farms—and now there were the graves—of their ancestors dating from their great-great-great-great-grandfather 'Chicken George' to their great-grandmother Bertha Haley, who was my mother.

"Somehow, I'd tell them, I'd grown up and become a writer, and along the way I'd tried to research and write our family's story. And that the book *Roots* which resulted had, by some miracle, motivated many millions of people of different nationalities and races throughout the world to become more conscious of their families, to search for more knowledge of their ancestors. And I'd tell my grandsons that, as members of the family whose written story had played this important role, they were blessed in a way not easy to describe."

Alex Haley, shortly after his letter to me, started to write articles for *Parade* and we grew closer—close enough so that, as a guest in his Norris, Tennessee, home in 1984, I could ask him as a friend to describe for me the agony of the twelve-year ordeal of *Roots*, particularly the moment when he considered ending it all, including himself.

"Will you share the experience?" I asked.

"Yes," he said, "I will."

Alex Haley had to learn who he was not only to write one of the most important books ever published in America, but also to choose between life and death. His struggle, as you will see later in this chapter, was with himself.

Sometimes, we can confuse who we are with what we own; we seek recognition or self-esteem in an object or a possession. I've made that mistake. I remember one afternoon when I was a teenager walking down McLean Avenue in Yonkers, New York, shopping for the one thing that would show everyone who *I* was. Having recently gotten a driver's license at the age of sixteen, I had managed to save nearly a hundred dollars from working at various part-time jobs after school, and I was hunting for *the* car. After three or four hours of examining used-car lots, my enthusiasm had diminished. What I liked was too expensive; what I could afford was a well-worn "family" car, not exactly what I had in mind.

Then, there it was! My dream car, glistening black, sparkled among the rubble behind a chain-link fence of what I had promised myself would be the last lot I would inspect. The car was a 1955 Chevrolet

with a red interior. Written across its windshield in soap was the word
HOT followed by three exclamation points.

"What do you need today?" the salesman hailed me. He was round
and red with a great nose and a booming, gravelly voice. His skin was
mottled and cratered. If ever a voice fit a body, it was his.

"Is that a good car?" I asked, pointing to *HOT!!!*

"Good?" he asked, then answered, "No, it's not good—it's great!"

"How much is it?" I asked.

"Come take a closer look," he suggested.

"How much?" I asked again.

"Come on, come on!" he insisted, his face squeezed with puzzle-
ment and pain as if I had hurt his feelings. "What difference does it
make what it costs if you don't like it?"

I tried the door. It was locked.

"Here, wait a minute," he said, "I'll get the key." He fumbled in
his jacket and withdrew a mammoth brass ring jingling with at least
thirty keys, each marked with masking tape and, I noticed, a number
written in blue on each.

"*This* is seventeen," he announced, picked a key, inserted it in the
lock and, sure enough, the door opened.

"Go ahead," he told me.

It was as if I were seated where I should be. It was home—no,
heaven! Luxury abounded. I stretched my right hand across the seat.
I breathed deeply. This, I knew, was *my* car. It was *me*. I touched the
dashboard with my fingertips.

The salesman, who had been silent, interrupted, "You've got a good
eye, my young friend. This is the best car on the lot. A classic! I'd buy
her myself. She just came in yesterday. It's a good thing you came
today. She'll never last the weekend. Here, here . . . start her up. Wait
till you hear this! A kitten, I tell you, a kitten . . ."

I turned the key and "she" instantly started, rumbling smooth and
throaty.

"Can I take her for a ride?" I asked.

"I'd like you to," he replied, "but I'm the only one here and I can't leave the lot. Let me see . . . do you really want to buy her?"

"I think so," I said, then qualified, "but I'd have to drive her first to be sure."

"Of course you would!"

"Well?" I asked.

"Well, what?" he responded.

"Can I drive her?"

"Of course!" he insisted. "Didn't I already say, 'Of course'? . . . I'm just trying to figure out how to make this easiest for you."

"What do you mean?"

"I know you want the car," he said, "and you're absolutely right about driving her first—don't let nobody try and tell you otherwise!—but I'm just worried about you losing this car."

"How?"

"If I try to keep her here," he explained, his voice patient and instructive, "it will be sold to someone else. You can see how pretty she is, and she's in perfect condition. Only thirty-one thousand original miles! If I let her sit here, she'll be sold tonight!"

My stomach ached. I had found what I so desperately wanted, and it was being taken away from me. I loved the car. It was *mine,* I could tell. I couldn't let it go.

"What do you want me to do?" I asked.

"Give me a deposit," he said, "and I can hold her."

"How much?"

"She'll go for about seven hundred—"

I winced. I had planned to spend three hundred, three-fifty tops.

"—but, wait a minute, and let me see what I can do." He walked to a small tin shack at the far corner of the lot, opened the door and stepped inside. A few minutes later he emerged, his big red face glowing.

"Five-fifty," he told me.

"What?" I said.

"Five hundred and fifty dollars—she's yours! But I need a deposit."

"How much?"

"Half," he said.

Crushed, I told the truth: "I don't have half."

"How much do you have?"

"About seventy-five dollars."

"I shouldn't," he said, "but, oh what the hell, you're a good kid. Give me the seventy-five!"

Relieved, I counted out the seventy-five dollars, handed it to him, then asked, "Can I come back with my father and test-drive the car?"

"Absolutely!" he insisted. "And remember what I told you—don't buy any car without trying her first. You tell your dad I told you that, OK?"

"OK!" I said and started to walk away, but stopped abruptly and spun around to ask, "I can't lose the seventy-five, can I?"

"No," he assured me, "we got laws . . . look at your receipt." He had handed me a piece of yellow paper on which he had written, "Received seventy-five dollars."

"This doesn't say for what," I pointed out.

He took it back, studied it, nodded, scribbled some more words with a ballpoint pen and returned the paper to me. He had added his name and my name, which I had to give him again, the date, a description of the car and a "buy" date of only four days away.

"Did I get it all there like I said I would?" he asked.

"Yes," I told him, "but what about the four days?"

"I can't hold this beauty forever, son," he said, "I'm making this deal only for you, and only because you're buying it quick . . . If you want to change your mind."

"No," I said, "no."

A few minutes later, while I was in the bus rolling to Mount Vernon, my nerves seemed to flare. I wished that the bus would go more slowly; I didn't like the questions I found myself asking. What had I done? What would I say to my father? What mood would he be in? Then I remembered that my father had been working the midnight-to-eight shift—he was an emergency lineman for Consolidated Edison, the power company—and suddenly I wanted the bus to move faster, not slower. He would just be getting up!

· · ·

Alex Haley was explaining, describing his sense of emptiness, his inability to "feel" the torment slaves must have experienced as they lay trapped in chains aboard wooden ships heading to strange new lands: "One night it came to me what I had to do, or at least try. I needed to thrust myself into some position, some circumstance that could let me feel at least something of what those Africans must have felt.

"I borrowed enough money to fly to Africa, and there I purchased a one-way passenger ticket back to the United States aboard *The African Star*, a Farrell Lines cargo ship that sailed from Monrovia, Liberia, to Jacksonville, Florida. Because I understood the physical design of vessels from my Coast Guard career, I was able to sneak at night into one of the ship's unlocked holds. I couldn't reveal my plan to the captain or the mate because passengers are understandably denied access to cargo holds.

"For two nights, after dinner, I sneaked into the cavernous, darkened hold. I stripped to my underwear and I lay on my back on some broad, thick, rough-sawed timber that had been wedged between sections of cargo to prevent shifting in heavy seas.

"I had a miserable cold by the third night and I never felt more inadequate. How ridiculous could I be? Here I was, a passenger, safe and snug on a strong steel cargo ship, eating three meals daily and trying to 'feel' the suffering of those chained so many years before in the bowels of a slave ship!

"On the fourth night I was simply unable to return to the dark, alien, empty cargo hold. I found myself, instead, at the ship's stern. I stood there with my hands holding the topmost rail and watched the ship's trail. It was a frothy, bubbling whiteness in the dark sea, and as I studied it, I felt that all my troubles were descending; they were enveloping me. I was frustrated and discouraged and disgusted. I was in debt, it seemed, to everyone. I had grown weary of hearing my publisher, my editors and even my closest friends question whether I would ever finish the seemingly interminable project that I had started, this book that I had been promising for years.

"Amid my despair at that rail, at the most painful moment, I suddenly, almost buoyantly, saw a solution to my problems. I realized all

34

I had to do was slip through the ship's railing and drop into the sea only a few feet below. My anxiety, the hurt I felt, would end within minutes. It will be over quickly, I thought. I remember feeling no alarm, no fear. I found myself, instead, drawn to this easy release. I began to feel peace, but as my hands tightened on the rail, voices began. It was as if I was listening to people speak in a dream, Walter, but they spoke distinctly, quietly and calmly. Somehow, and I can't explain this, I knew the speakers. They were the voices of my ancestors. There was Kunta Kinte and his daughter Kizzy, her son 'Chicken George,' his son Tom, who was a blacksmith, and, finally, I heard his youngest of eight daughters, my late maternal Grandma Cynthia, the woman who had first told me the family stories when I was a small boy living in her home in the tiny town of Henning, Tennessee."

"What did the voices say?

" 'No, you mustn't stop . . . you keep going . . . you finish writin' that book, hear me, boy?'

"As I said, I can't explain it, but standing alone, I was tempted to answer aloud, responding, 'Yes, sir,' and 'Yes, ma'am,' which was how Grandma Cynthia had raised me.

"I loosened my fingers from that ship's stern rail. Turning in the dark, I stumbled across a large hatch cover, then another, until I reached my small single cabin. I flopped down on my narrow bunk, and I guess I cried as hard as I had since I was a baby. To this day I'm not sure why I cried, but, finally, when I was drained of emotion, a quiet feeling came over me. I sensed in my own way that my ancestors had somehow evaluated my worthiness, whatever its worth, and had concluded that I was doing all that I was able, that I should write the book of their lives.

"During the remaining voyage I busily made notes. When I returned to San Francisco, I collected again my boxes of files, cartons that had been untouched for weeks, and I began writing. Pages became chapters. Gradually I felt myself swept up more and more in the unfolding drama of seven generations. Then one day I was finished and it was called *Roots.*"

I remembered that when it appeared on television as a miniseries,

Roots attracted a larger audience than any previous broadcast and Alex Haley overnight became a worldwide celebrity.

"How do you keep it all in perspective?" I asked.

"My memory of Grandma Cynthia," he said, "remains for me a spiritual presence. I fantasize sometimes that she sits on my shoulder, that when I get too 'big,' she settles me down, that when I need reassurance, I hear her words. I try to see the world as she would have seen it. I try to remember what she might have said, to see through her eyes."

I had been in auditoriums with Alex Haley and had watched countless times as admirers of every race shyly approached, often reaching out to touch him. No matter the intrusion, he never, *never* refused to respond. He waved to children; he returned all greetings. He was, more than anyone else I've known, accessible. Once, after I kidded him about being asked to sign so many books, he told me, "The most valuable copy of *Roots* may be the one I haven't autographed." If anyone has ever seriously asked the question "Who am I?" he is Alex Haley—his smooth brown skin unblemished, his gold-rimmed aviator glasses riding high on his nose, his smile perpetual and sincere.

My father's car, a 1955 two-tone blue Packard Clipper Custom, was still parked in front of 159 South Eleventh Avenue. So far, so good, I thought, as I ran up the flight of stairs to our apartment. I unlocked and pushed open the door. He was sitting at the table, coffee cup in hand.

"Dad, I need your help," I said.

"You in trouble?"

"No," I replied, wanting to bite back the words as I spoke them, "I bought a car."

"You told me you were going to look at cars," he said, his eyes narrowing. "Now you say you bought one?"

"No," I answered quickly, "I wouldn't do that without *you*. What I meant was that I saw one that I liked and I put a deposit on it." I braced for the explosion. None came.

"What do you need?" he asked.

"I need you to look at it, ride in it with me, tell me to buy it or not, and if you think I should, co-sign the note."

"What is it?"

"A '55 Chevy."

"How much?"

"Five-fifty."

"I don't know," he said.

I strained to say what I knew I had to say, "If you tell me not to buy it, that's that, Dad. No problem."

"When do I get to see this '55 Chevy?"

"Could we go now?" I asked, crossing my fingers under the table.

"I'm busy right now," he replied.

"OK, Dad," I said, "whenever you're ready or—"

"Or what?" he interrupted.

"Or not at all, Dad. If you don't think I should, I won't."

He looked down at his wristwatch and said, "Well, maybe we can do it now. Where did you say it was?"

"McLean Avenue in Yonkers."

"Let's go," he told me as he rose from the kitchen chair.

When we arrived at the used-car lot, the salesman bustled over to my father. "Mr. Anderson, you have a fine son there—"

"Where's the car you sold to my boy?" my father asked.

"Right there, sir." The salesman pointed to the black Chevy, the windshield of which had been cleaned of *HOT!!!*

"Here are the keys, Mr. Anderson," he said. "You take her right out. You don't even have to show me your license. I'll sit in the backseat and answer your questions."

I sat in the front seat next to my father. He turned the key and the engine started. I smiled.

"Let's go," my father said, and he put it into drive.

"What's that?" he asked.

"What's *what?*" the salesman replied.

"The transmission slipped," my father said. My stomach quivered.

"It's just tight, Mr. Anderson. It's just been adjusted. We do that before we sell them. I'm sure it's OK. Take her for a ride and you'll see."

As we drove around the block my father pumped the brakes and tested the steering and the automatic transmission. He parked the car several times.

"I don't like the way it feels," he said. "Maybe I'm used to the Packard. You try it, Walter."

He slipped over to the passenger seat. I walked around the car and entered the driver's side. To me, it felt wonderful as I drove it. Everything felt wonderful. I noticed a little hesitation but, as the salesman had said, the transmission had just been adjusted.

"You like this?" my father asked.

"I love it, Dad," I said.

The salesman, who had been noticeably silent, interrupted, "Mr. Anderson, sir, I'll tell you what. If you got any doubts, I'll give you your son's seventy-five dollars back"—he reached into his jacket pocket— "any doubts, at all, I'd say don't buy it. I want you and your boy to be satisfied. That gives me customers in the future—"

"I only buy *new* cars," my father said.

"Of course," the salesman agreed, nodding, "I can understand that! But if you're concerned—and you have every right—Mr. Anderson, you might want to read our guarantee real careful."

"Guarantee?"

"Yes *sir!*" the salesman exclaimed. "We would not sell a car without a ninety-day guarantee. It's written right here on the back of the order. Here I'll show you."

The word "guarantee" was in large type, but the rest was small and my father didn't read it. Instead, he said, as if he were assuring *me*, "It's guaranteed, Walter."

"Yes *sir!*" the salesman agreed.

"I guess you can buy the car," my father said. With his OK, I'd be able to get the loan I'd need.

"Thank you, Dad," I said, one more time witnessing and wondering how the man who could be so terrifyingly explosive could also be so kind. I realized he had agreed to the sale only because I wanted the car *that* badly.

In the main display building of the Museum of Appalachia in Norris, Tennessee, a black-and-white glossy photograph grabbed my attention. I had left Alex Haley's home, which was only a few hundred yards down the road, a few minutes earlier. The picture was of a white-haired man sitting cross-legged, his back straight with dignity, in front of a wooden cabin smaller than a suburban garage. The joy in the subject's eyes was magnetic. This was a *happy* man.

The caption read, "Fiddlin' Tom Cassidy is shown on the porch of his Beard Valley, Union County, Tennessee, home. 'It's big enough for a cot, a chair, and a little stove—and my fiddle—what more does a man need?' "

A flight up I found some of the belongings of Charles "Polka Dot Charlie" Fields, a fellow who, to conquer his loneliness, had painted his home and his possessions in polka dots—and attracted one hundred thousand visitors!

I spotted the actor Wally Taylor, who was also a guest of Alex Haley, across the museum floor and waved. A veteran of more than fifteen movies, twenty-five stage roles and more than fifty television appearances, Wally Taylor was one of those actors whose faces are more often recognized than their names. A child of the Depression, he had tried several vocations, including prizefighting, but he *found* himself on the stage. Wally is an actor to the marrow of his bones. In *Roots* he was Marcellus, the first slave to fight Chicken George.

"What did you think of Fiddlin' Tom and Polka Dot Charlie?" I asked.

"They knew who they were!" Wally replied, laughing. Like Alex Haley, I thought, like the man who found his roots in a painful moment at the stern of *The African Star*.

Earlier we had stood near a stream by the museum and I had asked Wally why he had not quit the theater, a wholly unpredictable business, during tough times.

"Because I can't," he said.

"Why not?"

"It is who I am," Wally told me. "It has taken me years to find out who I am, and, starve or die, I'm going to live it."

Wally, it was clear, had found himself in his work as surely as Alex Haley had found himself in his family. I remembered how I once sought my identity in a car—and why I failed.

During the first twenty-four hours that I owned the 1955 black Chevrolet I polished it more than I drove it. During the second twenty-four hours, I *couldn't* drive it.

"What's wrong?" I asked the mechanic, who had placed the car on a lift to inspect the transmission.

"Uh huh," he murmured.

"What?" I pleaded.

"The tranny's bad," he said, "and it's loaded with some kind of gook. That's why you can't hear it grinding. I'd say you'd be lucky to go fifty miles with this one."

I might as well have been told that *I* had been stuffed with some kind of gook, that *I* was a terrible, nightmarish person, a monster. It was as if I had died with the car. My skin was cold and clammy. I was too hurt to cry. I punched the rear tire of the car, which now looked ugly to me.

When I told my father, he grew furious. "What about the guarantee?" he asked.

"It doesn't say anything about the transmission, the brakes or the tires," I reported.

"I told you it didn't feel right!" my father bellowed, slamming his fist on the kitchen table. "Now I'll make that salesman eat it!" The veins on his neck trembled, his face and eyes glowed red. I worried, as did my mother. She said, "I don't want you to get in trouble, honey. I have an idea—"

"What?" my father demanded.

"Let's send Walter to Izzy, see if he can help."

Like a match dropped into a water glass, the anger was extinguished. "Izzy" was Isaac Rubin, a prominent Mount Vernon attorney who had grown up with my mother on the other side of town. My father respected him.

"See Izzy!" my father ordered.

Only a few years before in the same state where Wally Taylor and I had been enjoying the Appalachian Museum there occurred one of the most extraordinary examples of public courage to be found anywhere.

A young woman raising three children on her own had worked her way through Vanderbilt University and had been appointed to one of the highest positions ever held by a woman in Tennessee, the chairmanship of the Board of Pardons and Paroles. Finally, after years of waitressing, typing term papers, doing odd jobs, scraping to hold her small family together, she had financial security.

But she discovered corruption, and she refused to look the other way. Instead this woman, who was not much larger than Mairead Corrigan Maguire, stood alone to fight a political machine. She was fired in disgrace and then vindicated when the details of the state's worst scandal became public.

Peter Maas, the acclaimed author who also wrote *Serpico* and *The Valachi Papers*, brought this young woman's dramatic ordeal to national prominence with his book *Marie: A True Story*, which was the basis of a major motion picture with Sissy Spacek playing the heroine.

During the morning of January 22, 1984, the real Marie Ragghianti, the subject of the book and the movie, sat across from me in the living room of my home. A couple of hours later she was scheduled to be the commencement speaker at the Mercy College winter graduation ceremonies in Westchester County, New York, and I had been asked to introduce her. With her permission, I knew exactly what I wanted to say.

"Marie," I asked, "can I read aloud the diary entry you wrote the night you decided to risk it all and fight?"

"You have *that?*" she asked.

I showed it to her; it had been excerpted from Peter Maas's book.

"If you think it's important," she said, "it's fine with me."

More than most of the millions of words I have read during my life, this brief journal entry reveals someone who has answered the question "Who am I?"

Let me share it with you:

> I thought back to all the hard times that the kids and I had known, and all the meals of macaroni and cheese, and the cups of milk I'd borrowed, and the postdated checks that we lived on, and the juggling of bills and the jobs and the tears and the Ivory soap smells of my babies interspersed with the telephone calls of bill collectors—and I thought, too, of all the dates I was asked for, and the marriage proposals, and the other proposals, and how easy it would have been, at any time, how *easy* it would have been to "sell out," to let some poor fool spend all his money on me and the kids, if I would lead him on, or sleep with him—but for me, in my simplistic fashion, it all boils down to a question of love and integrity; I couldn't let anyone spend money on me or my children unless I *loved* him, otherwise, it would have been a lie, a prostitution of myself and my little ones. And so it is today. Even to "look the other way" when all this dirt is flying through the air would be to prostitute myself and my integrity.

Marie Ragghianti received a thunderous ovation.

Who am I?

Who we are, I wrote earlier, evolves from the potential we've inherited, the opportunities we receive and the choices we make. Marie Ragghianti found herself in a struggle to hold her family together; her integrity was not for sale. Mairead Corrigan Maguire made it her business to overcome her tragic environment, not only for her own sake but for the sake of others. Alex Haley found in his past the voice of moral authority, a discovery that not only saved his life but also inspired a people. Wally Taylor *had* to be an actor. We learn from the Kleisner twins that even when heredity and environment are identical, we must find ways to be ourselves. Although I didn't know it at the time, when I made my pledge, "I'm getting out of here," I had taken my first step to live with hope. My father was always unpredictable and sometimes violent. He terrified me. Yet, when I tried to find self-esteem in a car, I found my father's affection instead. *Who am I?* This book is the story of some of the choices that I have made. And it's about others who have also learned to say *yes.* Yes, I can.

It was a quarter of a century ago, but I remember the meeting so clearly it could have been yesterday. Isaac Rubin's receptionist called me *Mr. Anderson* and received me enthusiastically.

"So you're Ethel's son?" Mr. Rubin said as he greeted me.

"Yes."

"Well, come on in," he said, placing his arm around my shoulder and leading me to his inner office, "and tell me what the trouble is."

I explained what had happened. The year was 1960, a decade before the consumer movement would be in full swing. Lemon laws didn't exist. I handed him the "guarantee." He studied it. "Well," he announced, "that's no guarantee."

"I guess I'm stuck then, Mr. Rubin?"

"Maybe not. Let me speak to this fellow."

Mr. Rubin dialed the number himself, leaned back in his chair and suddenly, but cheerfully, said, "Hello!" into the mouthpiece.

He said he "represented the Andersons," that obviously a misunderstanding had occurred and that he was calling "to try to be of some help."

I could hear only his end of the conversation and he said, "I understand" and "Of course" several times. Finally, he said, "Neither of us wants to litigate . . . more trouble than it's worth."

Then he added, "Only what's fair."

He placed his hand over the mouthpiece and asked me softly, "Is it worth twenty-five dollars to you to get five hundred and twenty-five dollars back?"

I nodded as hard as I could.

"He'll bring the car back tonight," Mr. Rubin said into the telephone and added, "Thank you," before placing it back in its cradle.

"The salesman will give you a check for five hundred and twenty-five dollars, Walter," he said. "Don't argue with him or be rude. Take the check and say thank you. Do you understand?"

Speechless, I nodded again.

Isaac Rubin would in succeeding years distinguish himself first as a city judge in Rye, New York, then as a county judge, a State Supreme Court justice and, finally, as an associate justice of the Appellate Division of the State of New York. But on that afternoon more than twenty-five years ago he was a local lawyer with a frightened boy before him.

"How much do I pay you, sir?" I asked.

"Nothing, son," he said, placing his arm around my shoulder again. "The look on your face is payment enough. I think you've learned something."

Chapter 3

DO I BELONG?

His Royal Highness Prince Michael of Greece—the son of Prince Christopher of Greece and Princess Françoise of France, the grandson of King George I of Greece and Grand Duchess Olga of Russia, the first cousin of the Duke of Edinburgh, the second cousin of the King of Spain and the Queen of Denmark, the man whose blood relates him to every European royal family—kneaded the Greek worry beads in his fists, his face unusually solemn, and weighed my question.

I had asked Prince Michael to describe his loneliness as a child following the death of his father when he was one and the death of his mother when he was thirteen. Prince Michael, an only child, had been cared for after his mother's death, in 1953, by the family of his uncle, the Count of Paris.

We were sitting at his exquisite Louis XVI desk, cluttered with bric-a-brac, in Prince Michael's private study, two flights up from the door to his Park Avenue penthouse in Manhattan's East Seventies. He is a slender man, with salt-and-pepper hair crowning a delicate and fine-featured face with large, expressive brown eyes. If he were an actor, he would be cast as a prince.

A normally ebullient and gregarious personality, his body and hands are always in motion—you could imagine a grandmother scolding him,

"Sit *still*, Michael!" But now he sat across from me silently and, except for rubbing the black beads in his hands, he was motionless.

"My childhood was happy," Prince Michael said, his words breaking the silence in the room. "I had all the comforts I could want, a good education, no financial problems. After my parents died, I went, as you know, to live with my cousins, who were like brothers and sisters to me. I shared great love."

He paused, then said, "I had a very peculiar experience. I imagine I was one of the very few children who have experienced life as an only child and as a member of a large family, a family of eleven children. Of course, when you lose your parents and you are an orphan, even when you are surrounded by affection, you are lonely. You are lonely because, although people make every effort to help you forget the differences, *you* feel the differences. You are one of them, but you are not. My personal problems, my situation, my nationality, my character, my financial situation, everything made me different. I didn't have the same name. I didn't have the same nationality. I didn't feel lonely. I *was* lonely."

"What did you learn from it?" I asked.

"The loneliness matures you more quickly than when you are surrounded by your real family. You have to make decisions and you learn to observe others more, even if you are surrounded by comfort and affection. My cousins, my aunt and uncle made me feel totally one of them. They were extremely kind, and for that I will always be grateful, but somehow as a child I still felt unprotected."

Prince Michael dropped the worry beads in a dish and folded his hands in front of him.

I started to ask, "Prince Michael—"

"Walter," he interrupted, "please call me Michael."

"*Michael*," I emphasized, and we both laughed, "do you remember the first time that you felt like an orphan?"

"Quite clearly," he responded, reflective and serious again. "A month or two after I arrived in Paris to live with my uncle's family a photographer came from a magazine, *Paris Match*, to photograph the family. I was not included. What troubled me was not that I didn't appear in the photo; it was that the photographer did not invite me to be in the picture. I was not a member of that family. It was a silly detail, and no one else in the family knew what I felt because I kept it to myself. I *never* showed what I felt."

Everyone craves to belong—even princes. Like most other living things, we were not meant to live alone. Remember the simple amoeba, the one-celled creature every high school student studies. Separated from its group, it struggles to return. Or close your eyes and picture white-tailed deer huddling in their great herds in winter. Rather than leave the herd to forage for food, many a buck and doe will die of starvation.

How we identify ourselves to one another is more often than not merely a recognition of our membership in certain groups, whether a family, a nationality or whatever. Our clothes reflect the group we belong to. What message would be conveyed if the President of the United States showed up at a summit meeting wearing purple leotards, white patent leather boots, a wide gold-leaf belt and hair dyed pink? On the other hand, not too many rock stars dress like the President. In the last chapter we saw that we defined ourselves by our heredity, environment and our response to both. Now let's talk about the universal desire to be accepted by others, the desire that makes us behave in certain ways.

I still remember clearly an incident during my teens when I was playing pool in a Mount Vernon youth center called Teen Town. Another fifteen-year-old, named George, insisted that it was *his* turn to play.

"No, it's mine," I said.

"It's mine!" he repeated.

Seven or eight other teenagers were drawn to the noise and started to form a steadily closing circle. They coaxed George, egged him on, left him no choice but to assert himself or be humiliated. No sooner would he respond than the catcalls and the prodding would turn on me: "You gonna take *that*, Anderson? I wouldn't take *that!*" Neither George nor I wanted what was happening, but looking back over a quarter of a century, I realize now that we were trapped in an age-old ritual of adolescence. We were too scared to admit we were scared, so the plot unfolded in a familiar manner. Rather than be ostracized, we behaved as the group demanded.

"Give me the stick," George ordered, reaching for the pool cue I held in my hand.

"You want this?" I said and glanced toward the cue. "I'll give it to you—" and I brought it up as you would a baseball bat. "Still want it, George?"

Before he could answer, the cue was snatched from my hands by a counselor, an older teenager, who ordered both of us, "Cool off! Now neither one of you can play."

The circle that had formed broke apart and disappeared, its members disappointed. Relieved, though I tried not to let it show, I walked through a hallway to another room to get a soda. George, at the counselor's order, walked in the opposite direction.

I sat at a table with a tall, blond boy named Donald and his friend, a thickset, brown-haired youth named Roy. We played gin rummy for about a half hour, then decided to leave. As we rounded the corner at Second Avenue, heading for Third Street, we heard a shout, "Hey, Anderson!"

It was George and four friends, each a couple of years older than George and I. They laughed and seemed to be whispering instructions to him.

"Hey, punk, wait up!" George shouted, he and his friends drawing closer. With each of their steps, my heart pounded harder, my throat dried, my stomach tightened.

We take our groups seriously. Millions of lives, *millions* of lives, have been forfeited to wars as humans have historically defended the ideals of the groups to which they have belonged. That craving, that need to belong—that urge to act as the group expects us to act—is a powerful instinct. Sometimes it helps us and sometimes it hurts.

"You staying?" I asked Donald and Roy.
"Yeah."

48

"Thanks," I said, and meant it, respecting their courage in backing up someone they hardly knew.

"You with him?" one of George's friends asked.

"That's right," Donald replied, his voice even. Roy nodded, then said, "Why are you askin'?"

The teenager looked hard into Roy's eyes, which stared back unblinking. George's friend hesitated, looked toward one of his companions, then suggested, "Let *them* have it out."

Donald said, "That's a good idea."

Everyone but George and me took a couple of steps back, leaving us a few feet apart and facing each other. One of his friends stepped forward and whispered in George's ear. It was a dark, cool November evening, the streetlights yellow on the pavement. George and I were about the same size. If he wasn't "carrying," I thought—no knives or belts or other weapons—it would be a fair fight.

"You better take off your glasses, Four-Eyes," George said.

"It don't matter," I said, "you won't touch 'em."

"Take 'em off!" George ordered.

George wanted to talk, not fight. I had seen this before. Two teenagers who are about to fight argue instead. Neither really wants to scrap, but neither knows how to back out without losing face. George's "friends" were going to have none of it. They came to see a fight.

"Nail him, George!" someone shouted.

"Cut 'im up, cut 'im up!"

"Break his glasses . . ." the teenager who had whispered to George began. Donald and Roy watched like silent sentries. George stepped toward me.

"That's it! Go get 'im, George!"

He came at me, both arms wide and flailing. Rather than step back, as George had probably expected I would, I stepped forward and threw a straight right hand, which was a move my older brother, who was a boxer, had taught me. It caught George in the neck. He was off-balance and we came together so suddenly the force flipped him back. His head sounded like a sack of flour dropped on a linoleum floor when it slapped the pavement. He didn't stir, his eyes glazed and only half open.

"George, you all right?" I asked and leaned down. He made no sound. "You all right?" I asked again.

"Is he breathin'?" Donald asked.

I looked up. George's "friends," sensing real trouble, had already begun walking away.

George stirred, mumbling.

"What did you say?" Donald asked.

"My head hurts . . . my head really hurts," George said.

The three of us gingerly helped him up. After a few steps he was able to walk unaided, though a large knot had swelled at the base of his skull.

"Thanks," George said.

"Hey, I'm sorry," I said, my relief genuine.

"Me too," he replied.

"We knew *you* were sorry," Roy said, prompting all of us, even George, to laugh.

The first group we belong to is especially important and we usually don't recognize this at the time. Composed of two persons, it has been the source of endless legend and speculation. It is you and the person who cares for you as an infant.

At first you can't differentiate yourself from the world around you. Your body and the crib are not separate; the smiling face and warm breath you sometimes see and feel are not yours, but you don't know that yet. Then changes occur. You notice that when you move your head, the view is, well, different. Touching your foot and touching your face are not quite the same, but either is considerably different from touching someone else's hand. You learn that you can't by yourself make that smiling face and warm breath appear. And, as every parent can attest, you learn to communicate. You are no longer the sole inhabitant of your world. You have begun to perceive, to feel your need for others. Pleasure and discomfort are sensations that can depend on someone else. The first separation in our lives is our discovery somewhere in infancy that "I" and "they" are not the same. Our dependency on others grows; our sense of vulnerability grows equally, because we have learned we cannot control everything around us.

Considering that all of us began as howling and helpless infants completely dependent on other people, it's no wonder that throughout our lives we share a sense of vulnerability, a fear of being separated from those we depend on.

"Walter," the vice principal of Mount Vernon's A. B. Davis High School, a gentle white-haired man named Maurice Childs, asked me, "why do you want to drop out of high school? You're only sixteen. What will you do?"

I wanted to escape my home, my neighborhood, all that I had seen. The tension between my father and me never had been more volatile. Quitting school was my way out. My older brother, Bill, realizing wisely that one way or another I was going to leave home, had encouraged me to volunteer for military service. He helped my mother persuade my father to sign my enlistment papers so that I could join soon after my seventeenth birthday.

"I'm failing every subject except English," I told Mr. Childs. "I have enough 'cut slips' to serve detentions for twenty years and I'm tired of people messing with me."

Mr. Childs reminded me that two years earlier I had been an honors student who had been skipped—that is, passed directly from the eighth to the tenth grade.

"Walter," he said, "I cannot stop you, but I want to know why you're doing so poorly."

"There's nothing to know," I replied, aware that he had guessed I was intentionally failing my courses. "I don't want to stay in school. That's all." Would you like to know, I thought silently, why I sometimes feel safer on a street corner than in my own bed?

"What do you plan to do?" he asked.

"I am going to be a Marine."

"Don't you think," he asked, "that the Marines might 'mess' with you even more than your teachers?"

"You don't understand, Mr. Childs," I said.

He reached across the desk and squeezed my hand.

"Good luck," he said.

"Michael," I told the prince, "you and I were in the military service of our countries about the same time—1960 to 1964 for you and 1961 to 1966 for me."

"Yes, that's true."

"What was it like?" I asked.

"It was another peculiar change in my life. First, I went from being an only child to belonging to a large family. Then one day I left Paris, my French family, the university, my house, to find myself in a Greek barracks with another family nearby, my father's family, another language, another surrounding, another country. In the beginning it was miserable. I was shut up in the barracks for six months before I could leave in the evenings. Yet it was a huge success for me. I never enjoyed myself more."

"Why?"

"Because it was the best way to learn about my country and my compatriots. I had not lived before in Greece. Because of our position, we would know the people but we would never know the *real* people. Because the position dictates it. You can visit people, you can talk to them, but you will *never* know them because they will always have that reserve in front of people they consider important or royal. But in the barracks I was among people from every class, from every corner of Greece, so I learned to know them, I learned to know my country— we went on maneuvers all over Greece—and I learned to know myself better."

"Michael," I asked, "do you remember your first day?"

"Very well," he said. "It was one of the contrasts of my life. The barracks were outside Athens at the foot of Mount Hymetus. The grounds were huge, rocky and dusty. All of Athens could be seen from the cliffs of Hymetus. The buildings were built in the 1920s, in two rows, one after the other. The outside was pale yellow. Inside were green metal beds lined up side by side in rows. I arrived at the barracks in a court car with a crown on the plates. I was twenty-one. The monarchy was in Greece at the time. I left the car and I walked alone through the gate of the barracks—and then there were shouts, more and more shouting. I was put in a barracks with fifty other soldiers. I started as a soldier. We suffered *together.* There was no difference among us. I was nervous the first day; the first week was terrible. I worried every day that I was not going to make it."

It was five-thirty in the morning of September 6, 1961, and as I stepped out of the doorway of 159 South Eleventh Avenue I took a deep breath. The block was quiet. I walked slowly across the street, paused, turned back and looked up toward the second floor. My mother, who was holding the blinds to one side, smiled and waved to me.

I waved, turned and started to walk up Third Street toward the Bronx. After a few steps I stopped again to look back. The window was empty. Years later I would learn that my mother had stayed at the window, that she had not wanted me to remember seeing her cry. She hid behind the blinds and watched me until I was out of sight. My seventeenth birthday had been August 31, only six days before. It had been almost three years since I washed someone else's blood from my face, the night I sat alone on a stoop and promised myself in the darkness, I'm getting out of here. I strode past the telephone booth and, almost involuntarily, raised my hand to my cheek. I laughed. Not anymore, I thought. I was on my way and, though I hadn't slept well and it was early in the day, I was exhilarated.

As I walked toward the subway at 241st and White Plains Road to start the hour ride to 39 Whitehall Street in lower Manhattan, my excitement dimmed and the butterflies started in my stomach. I thought about a movie called *Marines, Let's Go,* which I had watched a few nights earlier. I had noticed, painfully, that everyone in it seemed to be old enough to be my father.

I wondered if anyone at Parris Island, South Carolina, would be near my age. "What if I don't make it?" I worried. The next few hours I remember only through the haze of too many years.

About a half-dozen Marine recruits from the New York area, all about my age, were formed into a group to take a train to Yemassee, South Carolina, which would be the last stop before we reached Parris Island. Because we lined up alphabetically, I was given everyone's orders by a corporal at 39 Whitehall Street and told to present them to a Marine who would be waiting for us at Yemassee.

"Don't lose 'em, boy!" the corporal warned me. "Your drill instructor won't like that." He chuckled.

Why me? I thought.

Our nervous half-dozen changed trains in Washington, D.C., after a considerable delay. A much larger group, composed of recruits from throughout Pennsylvania, joined us. Although day had become night, no one really slept, though everyone pretended to.

Shortly after dawn the train arrived at Yemassee. I saw a Marine on the platform. He was tall and thin and, I noticed, he was a sergeant.

Wanting to be helpful and to be rid of the orders I carried, I hailed him, "Hey, Mac, these for you?"

Thus began my first lesson as a Marine: A recruit does not call a sergeant "Mac." A recruit does not call a sergeant at all. *This* the sergeant was able to explain to me and the other recruits very quickly.

"Boy!" he began, his mouth only an inch from my face but his voice loud enough to be clearly heard fifty yards away. "I am a sergeant. You are a turd. Understand me, boy?"

"Yes," I said, my voice ready to crack.

"Yes, what?" he demanded.

"Yes, *sir!*" I shouted.

"How come I hear only one boy?"

Every recruit bellowed, "Yes, *sir!*"

"I can't hear you *girls!*" he taunted.

"Yes, sir!" we shouted in unison.

The next few hours were a blur of angry voices, uncertainty, running, falling and rushing. We passed through Recruit Receiving, packaged and mailed our civilian clothes home, were issued a green "utility" outfit and black boots, had our heads shaved and were assigned to a platoon. Then we met our drill instructors, two lanky and unsmiling men who were wearing Smokey the Bear hats pinned with the marine emblem.

"When you were home, your momma took care of you," Staff Sergeant Sawchik told us. "Now you're mine. I'm not your momma. I'm not your friend. But I'm all you got. Welcome to Parris Island, girls!"

"Yes, sir!" Platoon 166, First Battalion, shouted.

"I can't hear you girls," he said softly.

"Yes, sir!" we tried, voices cracking.

"Down for pushups!" he ordered, and down we went.

After lights out that night our barracks sounded like a pneumonia ward. Everybody seemed to have the sniffles, including me.

What have I done? I asked myself, convinced I'd never survive Staff Sergeant Sawchik and his assistant, Sergeant McCall.

"Did you ever cry in basic training, Michael?"

"I cried once," the prince replied, smiling broadly, and he lifted his worry beads from their dish and started to work them. "But not in the first week. It was at the end of the first month.

"I was summoned by my family and allowed to leave the barracks. I left as a soldier, and five minutes later I was dressed with decoration at an official function and treated as royalty. The contrast was too hard. I remember coming back from the official function and then crying. If I could be left in the barracks—*bon!*—no problem. But jumping from one situation to the other was too much. I remember crying, and my neighbor in a bed nearby talked to me, consoled me, made me feel better."

He lowered his worry beads and continued, his words spoken more softly.

"I learned an important lesson, Walter," he said, "never to complain. The Greeks I met had many problems. Some came from very poor families. They had hard lives. They expected to have hard lives. They *never* complained. Instead they were filled with gaiety, generosity, always ready to help someone else. Greeks invented tragedy in antiquity, but they reject depression. They enjoy every minute of a day.

They make every instant a feast, every moment count. To be depressed among Greeks is to be totally alienated, because you will be the only one depressed. Among Greeks, you can be worried, you can be afraid, but you cannot be depressed. Life is a magnificent theater with Greeks. You are never bored, because they are never bored. That was a great lesson for me, to find something of value in every circumstance."

It was 2200—10:00 P.M.—on November 22, 1961, a cool evening, and I looked into the darkness smiling. I made it. I made it! The joy was palpable in the silence. We all felt it. The next morning we were scheduled to board buses to leave Parris Island for Camp Lejeune in North Carolina for advanced infantry training. *We* made it! Of the original seventy-five, eight had dropped out and four were added along the way. Platoon 166 numbered seventy-one Marines.

"I know you're awake," Staff Sergeant Sawchik's voice rasped and echoed through the barracks, "so listen up."

"What now?" I worried.

"I'd be proud to lead this platoon anywhere. Never conduct yourselves less than the best, because you are the best. You are United States Marines."

He paused, then said, "Good night, *men.*"

The barracks exploded into a uniform shout: "Good night, *sir!*"

For the second time in boot camp, my eyes filled.

I first met Prince Michael on December 16, 1983, to discuss a writing assignment for him. (His credits were impressive. He had already published a novel called *Sultana;* an illustrated book, *The Crown Jewels of Europe;* a book of memoirs entitled *History, My Sister;* a study linking the island of Crete to the lost continent of Atlantis, *Crete, Wreck of Atlantis;* a biography of the Byzantine emperor *Andronic I;* and a study of Europe under Napoleon, *When Europe Feared Napoleon.*) And I was late.

Catching a cab in Manhattan during the Christmas season is like trying to seize a trout swimming upstream by the tail. *Somebody* managed to flag a taxi that day, but it wasn't me. I started to walk the thirty blocks from my office to Prince Michael's apartment, dodging and skirting as best I could the crowds thick with holiday shoppers. As I struggled against the tide of bodies, my nerves went raw. My stomach tightened, and I felt increasingly tense and angry. I grumbled when a package-laden shopper didn't move fast enough. Like a fullback carrying the ball in a broken play, I plunged forward. My old companion, anxiety, was back and in Technicolor. I wanted someone to blame, anyone to whom I could direct the tension I felt. And then I found him! He was stretched tight as a child's balloon about to pop, and he was bulling his way forward across Sixtieth Street at Park Avenue. He was *me*.

I slowed my pace as I threaded through the bustling noonday crowd and, for the first time since I had left my office, I began to think clearly. What was I afraid of? Surely it wasn't merely being late. At most, that would only be ten to fifteen minutes. No, I grudgingly realized, it's an old specter for me. It's the little boy inside remembering that rich people live in houses and that poor people live in flats. It's cold voices from my past reminding me to stay in my place, that I'm not good enough, that I'm from the wrong class, that I'll say or do the wrong thing, that I won't be accepted.

Am I worried, I wondered, that a prince might discover that Walter Anderson is not a prince, that I am inferior, vulnerable, that I should be rejected? I knew what I had to do.

I stopped walking. There was joy in the brisk air and only then did I appreciate it. The voices were light, the walkers and their Christmas packages colorful. The press of shoppers moved as one. I was the only one who had been out of step. I started walking again, this time *with* the flow. My anxiety lessened, my breathing came easier. I finally took hold of the person who was on his way to see Prince Michael.

For years I suffered some of my most miserable moments for fear of being humiliated, for fear that people I thought were "better" would reject me because I wasn't good enough. How about you? Have you ever walked away from a person thinking that you'd really like to know him but, for fear you weren't good enough, for fear you'd reveal your inadequacy, you said nothing?

But what really happens when someone does reveal himself? How do we actually react when someone we've met reveals his anxiety to us, shows us his fears and what he thinks are his weaknesses? Almost always, we feel close to him. We want to help. We want to share with him our anxieties, include him—if only for the moment—in our group. Isn't that what we felt when we read about Alex Haley's struggle to live? Didn't we all stand with him on the stern of that ship and ask whether life was worth the effort? Did you think less of me when I told you about the mistake I made by buying that 1955 Chevrolet or how I allowed myself to be drawn into a fistfight not because I was brave but because I was frightened? When someone discloses to us his hopes and aspirations, his fears and his mistakes, the revelation often challenges our own preconceptions of that person. That's the result we seek when we advise someone to spend more time with a friend: "You'll like him when you get to know him!"

"But if I say too much," the fear haunts us, "the other person will know how stupid I am, how *unworthy* I am." The prince will discover I'm not a prince. The scientist will realize my ignorance of science. The psychologist will perceive my innermost thoughts, the educated person my ignorance, and all in twenty minutes of conversation, or so we think.

Can anyone be known that quickly? How many years, how many thousands of intense hours, has it taken psychiatrists to "know" their patients—sometimes, after all that, only to be wrong. When we're really honest with ourselves, we realize that in our early contacts with another human being only two things become clear: how similar our attitudes and beliefs are to those of the other person and how his needs relate to our own. But that information, however interesting, is small potatoes compared with the truth. *What we really respond to when meeting someone else is the degree of interest the other person shows in us.* Aren't we most complimented when someone asks us about ourselves or asks us for advice? When someone tells us our opinion matters?

The approach to take, if we're to make anxiety our ally when we join small groups or when we meet people for the first time, is not to fret about what other people might learn about us, but to focus on what we'd like to learn from them. This gets anxiety working *for* us. It sharpens our questions and underlines the sincerity of our interest. What I had forgotten for a few minutes as I barged through the crowd of Christmas shoppers was that Prince Michael was really not that different from me. Is a prince or a president or a famous star or the guest across the room less a person than you or I? Aren't they also complimented by a genuine curiosity about their views?

To communicate your sincere interest in another person, you might find useful some don'ts and one do that I've learned and practiced, and that have worked for me:

• *Don't monopolize.* Even the best speakers grow tedious after a while. Keep in mind how many times you've yearned for a speaker to finish. Also, remember that if you're talking, you're not learning about the other person. And if you talk too long, he or she is yearning.

• *Don't declare!* People who too frequently speak with exclamation points rather than question marks are boring. If you disagree, for example, frame it in a question. If that won't work, soften your approach: "I'm not sure I feel the same way, but I'm really interested in how you arrived at your conclusion." Absolutes—"I'm sorry, but I can't agree!"—stop a conversation cold.

• *Don't correct.* How do *you* like to be corrected? Or, for that matter, interrupted? Do neither.

• *Don't change the subject.* It's rude to ask someone a question, wait for the answer, then respond by bringing up another topic.

• *Do show a real interest.* Do more than listen. Nod, smile or frown when it's appropriate. It's not just the speaker who needs to demonstrate, to be active; a good audience responds. I've been told that I look like one of those plastic dogs with the moving head when I listen. Once, during a job interview, the executive who was evaluating me talked incessantly. Truly I did not contribute five words. I later saw his report, which described me as "bright." Why? Because I listened to *him.*

Good listeners, like precious gems, are to be treasured. Be an active, *enthusiastic* listener.

The most sincere compliment we can pay is attention. If we remember to spend the first minute or two putting the other fellow at ease, we'll put ourselves at ease too.

I was eleven minutes late when I arrived at Prince Michael's building. The uniformed doorman courteously directed me to a private elevator, and I stepped out confidently. But there were two doors! The fable of the lady and the tiger came to mind and I chuckled. What would happen if I knocked on the wrong door? Would a tiger emerge? I chose the first door on the left, pressed the buzzer, and a serious, erect fellow with a crew cut appeared. He asked, "Mr. Anderson?"

I was led into a study in which a tall, thin man with salt-and-pepper hair and bright brown eyes was speaking French on a telephone. This was the prince. His hands and body were in motion. His back was to me, but as he turned he spotted me, interrupted his conversation immediately and apologized, then, after speaking some more French into the phone, hung up and said, "I'm so happy to meet you."

"Thank you very much, Prince Michael," I said. "I'm so happy to meet you, and I only hope we have enough time. There's so much I want to learn—"

"*Bon!*" he said. "Wonderful! What would you like to know?"

We are raised in America to be particularly sensitive to notions of class, largely because our nation was created by people escaping from the oppressive monarchies of Europe. We're often uncomfortable with showy displays of class difference. Our heritage began with George Washington, who refused to be a king, and our government to this day dubs no man a knight.

Yet for all our democratic resistance to class barriers, it is considered high praise in any of our fifty states to be told, "You have class." But what does class really mean? To find out, I took advantage of an opportunity to ask the man who wrote the book *Class—What It Is and How to Acquire It.* His name is Mortimer Levitt, and he is a self-made millionaire, the founder and sole owner of Custom Shop, Shirtmakers, which has sixty-two stores across the country, more than five hundred employees, and has served during four decades more than two million customers.

Mortimer was seventy-seven when we met one night in the fall of 1984 in a New York penthouse. We had both come to hear a reading of a novel-in-progress by the author Barbara Goldsmith before a professional group called Poets and Writers.

Actually, I met Mortimer in the elevator. He had apparently heard me ask directions to the right floor. Realizing we were heading for the same event, he asked, "What do you do?" The question was not rude; it was friendly and it was curious. I told him I was an editor. "What do you edit?" he asked. The doors opened.

I learned later that this dapper man who dressed pin-perfect with a self tied bowtie was also the chairman of Young Concert Artists, a board member of Lincoln Center's Film Society, a former chairman of Daytop Village for the Rehabilitation of Drug Addicts, a founder of the Manhattan Theater Club, where he produced twenty showcase productions, the founder and main support of the Levitt Pavilion for the Performing Arts in Westport, Connecticut. In addition to *Class*, he wrote *The Executive Look* and had been a frequent lecturer on self-image. Interestingly, he had started Custom Shop, Shirtmakers, when he was only thirty and had retired from the day-to-day operation of the firm four years later in 1941.

A few days after we met I asked Mortimer, a gentleman of high style and great dignity, to answer for me the fundamental question: Can a person acquire class?

"Yes, that's easy to answer," he told me as I entered the second-floor library of his elegantly appointed home on Manhattan's Upper East Side. The room in which we would sit had been decorated country-style with lush green carpeting, green-and-white patterned drapery and upholstery of heavy linen. A seventeenth-century Dutch painting filled a small recess along a wall of floor-to-ceiling bookshelves. Over the fireplace hung a Gasparro portrait of a black woman. "Remember," he said, "that I was born on the wrong side of the railroad tracks and I am a high school dropout. I was born without any appurtenances of class whatsoever. My father was a Russian Jew; my mother came from Berlin. We were poor and I was raised in an ordinary Brooklyn neighborhood—yet I wrote the book on class.

"Wealth is not synonymous with class, although people frequently confuse the appurtenances with the substance of class. The substance of class is a recognition that the price one pays for the gift of life is an unending series of disappointments and problems, which can range from the ridiculous—being upset because your tailor did not deliver your dinner jacket on time—to the tragic—the untimely death of relatives and friends. I remember taking off my stocking and discovering what I thought was melanoma, the most deadly form of skin cancer. It's deadly because it acts so fast. I looked at my leg, and I knew what melanoma looks like because I had had skin cancer, and this was clearly melanoma. I could see it, absolutely black, raised and shiny. In that moment I knew I wouldn't change anything. I would go right on doing what I was doing. That was ten years ago. It turned out that it was not melanoma, but what I discovered in that instant was revealing to me: I wouldn't change *anything*. Real life is not a question of if an ax will fall, but when an ax will fall. Life has problems, and some are tragic. When we understand there's no end to our disappointments, when we don't selfishly ask, 'Oh God, why me?' when we learn to live with and face our losses, however major or minor, only then do we begin to have *the ability to think of others instead of being consumed by ourselves* and our problems—and that is the substance of class. When Fernando opens the door to let me into my Rolls-Royce, that is merely an appurtenance of class. The substance of class is how I treat Fernando. It is the difference between what you see and what you are."

As Mortimer Levitt spoke—"the ability to think of others instead of being consumed by ourselves"—I recalled how, during our first meeting, Prince Michael had demonstrated what Mortimer called the substance of class. At lunch in the dining room he himself served me as we talked. There were more utensils, each subtly different, surrounding my plate than I was familiar with. I did not know which to choose; the prince, courteously, would not begin until I started. Sure enough,

I chose correctly because whichever utensil I selected was the one he also chose. It would be months before I recognized his gracious gesture. Only after I had come to know the prince better did it occur to me that he had selected the utensils I chose so that I would feel comfortable.

Few people I have known have been as skillful as Prince Michael of Greece at putting guests at ease, making them feel at home. As he sat across the antique desk from me, I decided to ask him how he had learned this art.

"I think there are two explanations, if it is true that I put people at ease," he replied. "First, there is education, because for centuries we have been trained to do just that. We assume rightly or wrongly that people who meet us are not at ease because they do not know precisely how to act. From childhood we are told we have to be extremely polite and put people at ease so as to break the barrier, the ice.

"I remember that when I was fourteen I was forced to appear twice a week at official dinners. And each time I was seated between two people, with no idea who they were. Each of the children experienced this. The people we were seated between we inevitably had never met before, and we were forced to make polite conversation in order to make *them* feel at ease, to be sure that they enjoyed the house or the meal or the family. If we didn't do it, our parents always watched and there was a court-martial after: 'I saw that you did not talk with your right neighbor, I saw that you behaved very badly with your left neighbor.' Thus we were trained.

"Second, I think I feel at ease with myself. I have met in my life so-called important people. Yet, the biggest stars I have met put *you* at ease at once.

"People can learn to put others at ease and to put themselves at ease. When people fail to do that, it has nothing to do with social class. Psychological problems, complexes, appear in every class of society. And people with no complexes appear in every class. If I put people at ease, it is because I am interested in *them*. I am curious and I have little time. It is essential for me to put people at ease because then I don't lose time learning about them. I ask questions because I really am interested."

"Michael," I asked, "with all your background and training, are you ever nervous about meeting people?"

"Socially, because of the experiences I have lived," he began, "I'm not nervous when meeting people, but very often I feel intimidated before I have professional meetings because I want to achieve something. I want to succeed in a meeting, get something I want—"

"*You* feel intimidated?"

"Yes, then I feel intimidated!"

It had been a year since I had first met Prince Michael, and as he spoke I reflected on a question I had not asked at that time. In 1965 he married a painter and sculptor named Marina Karella, the daughter of a Greek industrialist. Two children and twenty years later their marriage was strong, and he would describe his family as "the creation I am most proud of."

"Michael," I asked, "why did you marry someone who was not of royal blood?"

"It's quite natural that I did not marry someone from a royal family, Walter," he said. "It's a psychological process starting with the fact that I was an orphan and I was practically alone. To say the word 'orphan' is very melodramatic, and I recall an anecdote about that. In Greece people always beg for a favor. Once when my uncle, King Constantine, was on a tour in the provinces, an older man came to greet him and said, 'Please, Your Majesty, help me.'

"My uncle asked, 'Yes, but why?'

" 'Because I am an orphan,' the man, who was sixty, replied.

" 'Me too,' my uncle, who was fifty-five, said." Michael broke into laughter.

"So using the word 'orphan' is melodramatic, but being an orphan helped me to realize what the social class is to which I belong and to take my distance from it.

"Why do I say so? Because my social class and the education it provides is overwhelming. It surrounds you totally. It affects much of your thinking, your feeling, your choosing. Most of the people who belong to the small group of royalties, which only number about three hundred, have a trademark in their way of talking, of thinking, of feeling. Usually they never get out of that.

"Being alone helped me to realize two things. First, that I was in a very minor position in that group. If you have the chance to be the queen of England and you take an active role in your country, then you can consider working toward that goal. If you are a minor character in a very remote position, then I think the job is not very interesting.

"Second, I think very early I had the ambition not to be recognized for my title but to be recognized for myself."

He paused, considering his words. "Most of my cousins content themselves to be recognized for their titles, behind which they can hide their weaknesses. They put forward the title, always in front, like a protection, like a screen. They expect everyone to be influenced by that title and have an attitude dictated by that title."

He paused again. "I did not want to be treated on the basis of a name I didn't earn but was given. I wanted to be treated for myself—for *my* value, high or low. That's why my marriage is not extraordinary. It is in line with what I believe and what I live. I don't consider people in terms of their position or their title, but for themselves. When I found the woman I fell in love with, I knew I would marry her, title or no title. Why not? It's my whole attitude toward life."

Clearly Prince Michael of Greece had gained more than he had surrendered. I thought about his work, the long manuscripts he wrote by hand, then had typed by a secretary. It was a demanding process. "Michael," I asked, "why do you work so hard?"

"I work so hard because I choose to work. I do not have to financially, but emotionally I need to work. I can do nothing else. Writing is always with me. I either write or think about writing. I cannot go a week without writing."

I asked, "But don't critics expect a prince to do better?"

He shook his head. "It's not that many people believe a prince can do better work; it is that so many people do not believe a prince can do work at all. We are considered first to be terrible amateurs: 'You work? Why?' This is mainly in Europe. There, if you work, you're considered idiotic. In America it is not quite the same.

"My name was a terrible handicap in Europe. I was judged by my name and not my writing. Some critics even in America reflected on my title. *That* surprised me, because this is America. One critic in particular dismissed my writing by the fact that I had been raised in a palace. I was refused television appearances because of my title. Nevertheless, the books sold—and then I was acceptable even with my title!"

Michael's need to belong, I realized, was as great as my own. Each of us had learned that we can live with others only through interest and compassion, as Mortimer Levitt suggested. I didn't understand this important principle when I was drawn into a street fight as a teenager, and I forgot it as I pushed my way up Park Avenue. In boot camp I learned I had to share my life with others—*We* made it!—which was what the prince learned as a boy when he was instructed to speak with strangers at the dinner table.

As we walked down the stairs of his apartment a few minutes later, I stopped, having made a very personal discovery, and said, "Michael, I have a curious question for you. Do you think we are similar?"

"Totally," he replied, then added, "The only difference is one more reason that you have my respect. I suspect that you did not have financial help behind you. I respect anyone who has the courage to start his life without help and to succeed."

As Michael and I faced each other I considered how remarkably different our lives had been to that moment. There we stood, though, a community, a group of two. I could only wonder how our relationship would have developed had I allowed my anxiety to run amok the first time we met, had I continued to forget what I had spent a lifetime learning. I knew then that the anxieties the prince had experienced could have been no less painful to him than mine had been to me, and I also understood his achievement.

"What I respect about you most, Michael," I said, shaking his hand, "is how you've made your life a success by working hard and honestly. You didn't have to. And"— I paused —"something else, my friend.

Your candor reminds me that all of us need to be accepted. We all want to belong."

"Walter," he said, *"everyone* wants to be proud, and we need to find the things that make us proud."

"Even a prince?" I asked.

"Even a prince," he replied.

Chapter 4

MUST I WORRY?

Senator John Glenn sat erect, his body lean and his posture perfect, as we spoke in his brightly lighted office, Room 503 of the Hart Building on Constitution Avenue in the nation's capital. It had been almost twenty-three years since his historic spaceflight when, as a Marine lieutenant colonel, he became the first American astronaut to orbit the earth. As we faced each other across his tidy desk on an unusually warm December afternoon in 1984, he didn't fidget, didn't move much. His light, almost white, powder-blue eyes were riveted on mine. His voice was clear and distinct. If he had not been John Glenn, he might have been Walter Cronkite or Peter Jennings and anchored a television news broadcast for millions. His tan tie had the center dimple that all Marines are trained to wear, and it complemented his neatly pressed dark brown suit. The carpet was tan and the walls were high and white, one adorned with a large eight-pointed star tapestry. Directly behind him was a photograph of an American flag—and as I looked at it more closely I saw the image of John Glenn rising in the corner opposite the stars.

In this age of moon walks and space shuttles I had to remind myself of the significance of his achievement—what it meant to the morale, the very fiber, of our nation, how it catapulted this former combat fighter pilot who had flown one hundred forty-nine missions in World War II and Korea to a legendary prominence rarely equaled in our history. I remembered as I listened to John Glenn answer my questions that for four years and four months after the Soviet Union successfully launched Sputnik I, two successive presidents, Eisenhower and Kennedy, had to send congratulatory telegrams to the Russians. In April 1961 Soviet cosmonaut Yuri Gargarin became the first human space traveler, capping American frustration.

Then, John Glenn. What a hero we had! He had grown up in a small town—New Concord, Ohio. It even had a Main Street and a Crooked Creek. As a boy, John Glenn had a newspaper route; later he married Annie Castor, his high school sweetheart. On every Memorial Day his father, who was a plumber, played taps at the town's cemetery while the boy who would someday be an astronaut played the echo from the woods.

On February 20, 1962, he was, like Private First Class Walter Anderson, a marine. My barracks at Camp Lejeune, North Carolina, was alive with the excitement of his flight, marines huddling shoulder to shoulder to study every word of every newscast.

"All right!" someone would exclaim at good news.

"All *right!*" the rest of us would cheer.

It was good to remember those moments because the enormous height of his victory would help underline the depth of his failures, the human failures I had come to ask John Glenn about.

"Probably the low point of my life was the direct result of a physical injury," he told me as we faced each other. "I slipped on a bathroom throw rug, fell and hit my head. The impact caused a little crack down through the labyrinth, the cartilage and the bone area of the left ear. Because blood and fluid had collected, whenever I moved my head a little too fast, the whole world would spin. The doctors told me that whatever recovery I could expect would take at least eight to twelve months. It was a bad time. It would take me ten minutes just to work my way from the bedroom downstairs to the couch. I didn't know if that was how I'd have to live the rest of my days."

I knew that the accident had occurred in 1964, two years after his triumphant spaceflight, and that it had forced him to withdraw from his first race for the United States Senate. What I didn't know was the full measure of the uncertainty John Glenn had faced.

"That was a gloomy period," he recalled, his voice steady. "It was difficult to be optimistic. I would go along for several weeks and then there would be noticeable improvement three or four days in a row. Then I would plateau again. It went that way for nine months, and finally I had a complete recovery."

Six years after his fall he ran again for the United States Senate and lost. I asked him about it.

"It was a big disappointment," he told me. "There was a letdown and I had a few bad days. I had to remind myself that the rest of my life was ahead. Was I going to sit around moping about my loss? I knew it was going to take a while for some of the psychic scars to heal, but I decided that if I were not to serve in the Senate at that time, then I would consider other opportunities—and try to provide in the next few years a little more financial security for my family by working in the business world.

"I became president of Royal Crown International. I also helped start several Holiday Inns. This left me in better financial shape, and gave me invaluable experience. Sometimes, I have learned, a failure may be a blessing in disguise. I'm not saying I got beat the first time because there was some divine plan to give me better experience, but I think those were times that were very important in helping prepare me to go ahead with what I was able to accomplish later."

In his third try, in 1974, he was elected to the United States Senate, and in 1980, when the successful Republican presidential candidate, Ronald Reagan, swept Ohio, Democrat John Glenn regained his seat by the largest plurality in the state's history, one and a half *million* votes. In 1984, at the age of sixty-two, he had tried for the presidential nomination, but the Democrats nominated former Vice President Walter Mondale instead. Now the campaign was several weeks behind him and he seemed, as we spoke, to be at ease. The personal questions I raised he answered confidently, having, I was sure, come to grips with them earlier and alone. John Glenn, it was clear to me, had much more to share.

Many Americans early in their lives acquire a contagious, crippling disease of inestimable pain, an illness of such potential severity that literally thousands upon thousands take their lives rather than try to find its cure. This dread disease is *worry*. It touches everyone.

How has it affected you?

It has made *me* miserable. Nothing that I've experienced in my life, no matter how tragic or dangerous, has been as downright destructive as my worrying about things that might happen: *What will I do when they find out I'm me?* Heroes like John Glenn, I thought, somehow escaped anxiety, and because I was foolish enough to believe that the strong and the successful didn't worry, I pretended not to. I *acted* unconcerned. I might just as well have tried to cap a volcano.

What I did not understand was that worry, prompted by fear or anxiety, was an expression of nervous energy; it was potentially helpful, healthy and good. *Successful people worry.* Prince Michael, Mairead Corrigan Maguire, Alex Haley, Mortimer Levitt and Marie Ragghianti certainly had fears. John Glenn had much to worry about. In succeeding chapters you'll see how other people have learned to live with their mistakes, curb their anger, start new lives, face death and welcome criticism. What these people have learned, and what you'll learn as you continue reading this book, is how to act *with* fear, how to say *yes*. Yes, I will. Worry is, after all, an indication that we care about something we consider important. It's only when our imagination fires blanks, when we exaggerate our fears, that worrying is unhealthy: I start school Monday; *no one will like me.* Thank you for the opportunity; *I know I'll fail.* I have imagined such outrageous consequences of everyday concerns—well, they *could* occur!—that I can blush. Not satisfied with merely sneaking into my son's bedroom when he was an infant to check to be sure he was breathing, sometimes I'd pinch him, then tell my wife, "Honey, Eric's awake!"

To keep our worrying healthy and to make anxiety an ally, we must learn to direct into productive channels the energy that fear and anxiety provide.

That's accomplished in two steps. First, by understanding what we fear. Second, by taking action.

Worry often disappears when we analyze it, because it's hard to go on worrying when we begin to examine what troubles us. Anxiety, as I have described in Chapter One, is a response to *anticipated* danger. Well, what is it we anticipate? If our imagination is in full bloom, the consequences we foresee can be so mountainous as to humble the mightiest among us—which is especially sad because those consequences rarely come to pass.

Try this experiment for the next month, an exercise that has worked wonders for me. Write down what worries you. Whatever it is, however small or large, log it. At the end of thirty days, evaluate your findings. When I taught a class a few years ago in abnormal psychology at Westchester Community College in New York, I asked the students to keep such records of their worries. What we found was that most of what we worried about never happened, and much of what we worried about happened for the good, not the bad, and less than five percent of what we feared actually occurred. We also learned that we eliminated a large number of worries simply by writing them down. It became apparent that many were vague and, well, silly. Another important lesson was that when we tried to measure the possible consequences of what we were concerned about—when we asked, "What's the worst thing that can happen?"—often our anxieties diminished, because we discovered in many cases that the worst wasn't that bad, after all.

Action is the best medicine for worry. Think of John Glenn, who could have let his worry paralyze him, but didn't. Although an accident caused him to withdraw from his first Senate race, he tried again. When that failed, he campaigned *again*—and was elected! As we've all experienced, worry doesn't stop the future from unfolding; it only ruins today if we let it. Once we've thoroughly examined our concerns, more often than not we find out what we can do. Sometimes it takes a practical effort, like studying for, rather than worrying about, an exam. Other times we may have to condition ourselves for the worst: What can we do *now* to prepare for the future to happen? Remember that doing nothing, waiting, wringing your hands, only increases the torment.

Once I believed that worrying was negative, unique to losers and a sure sign of failure. What I know now is that we all worry and that worrying is a sign of strength, of caring. The greatest of heroes, the most successful and triumphant people, even astronauts, worry. The difference is that they do something about it.

"You can't help but worry," John Glenn told me. "When you're worrying, you're concerned about the future. What is the greatest unknown for all of us? It's the future. And the greatest antidote to worry, whether you're getting ready for a spaceflight or facing a prob lem of daily life, is preparation. The more you prepare, the more you think, the more you try to envision what might happen and what your best response and options are, the more, I've found, you are able to allay your fears about the future."

As he spoke I remembered a situation John Glenn had not foreseen, a dramatic moment from the movie *The Right Stuff*. He had been informed as he circled the earth in 1962 that a problem had occurred, that his capsule would be reentering the earth's atmosphere at risk. What intrigued me most was the four-and-a-half-minute period when he could not communicate with earth.

"John," I asked, "what were you thinking?"

"That's called a 'blackout period,' " he replied. "The craft is moving so fast against the air, about eighteen thousand miles per hour, that it creates an ionized layer which makes it impossible to get the radio signals through. Communication isn't that important at that time, however, because there's nothing anyone can do. Anyone except you, right there.

"I was very busy and did not want to be talking to anyone at that time anyway. If there had been a loose heat shield, as one of the signals had indicated, the craft would probably burn up, me included. But it wouldn't do any good to panic. We had trained for every emergency we could think of, and we were to use that training and work on through. To act otherwise would have increased any hazardous condition I might have been in.

"I think, as I've said, the best antidote to anxiety and fear—fear that would overcome you and disrupt your proper actions—is to try to prepare yourself in advance as thoroughly as possible. Obviously, there's a limit to how well we can prepare for everything, because our lives are continually made up of unforeseen events. That's why I stress so much to my own children the value of education. It enables them to have as much preparation as possible for the unknowns that are in the future for all of us. The same thing was true in that spacecraft. I had spent hundreds of hours in simulators trying to foresee every emergency. But there happened to be one we didn't foresee. We did not expect to make a reentry with the retropack still on in front of the heat shield, but some of the engineers, unknown to me, had run some wind tunnel tests to determine if the spacecraft would still be aerodynamically stable with the retropack in place. As you know, we made it back."

"Did you think you'd die?"

"I thought that might be possible. In fact, the first of us in the space program had come out of a military test-piloting background, where people being lost was not uncommon. We would wonder sometimes how many of us would be around at the end of Project Mercury. I thought we would be lucky if we didn't lose at least one or two because of the new speeds, complexities and heat."

"Why?" I asked. "Why did you do it?"

"It was important to my country," the former astronaut replied, his voice even, his words clear. "I have never lived with my own longevity as my prime concern. Through World War II and Korea as a combat pilot, and then as a test pilot, I was proud to serve this country. Project Mercury was again a way to serve. I have always felt it was more important how you live your life than how long you live."

"I've saved the best question," I said.

"Go ahead, Walter," he said.

"Throughout your life, considering all you have experienced, who is the most courageous person you've ever known, the person you most admire?"

For the first time during our talk, the senator grew animated. He sat forward, placed his hands palms down on the desk and told me, "That's easy." He smiled broadly.

"I've known," he said, "some very courageous people—in World War II, Korea, the space program, and others—but what I believe you are asking about is not courage in the face of physical danger, but about courage in facing up to adversity in personal affairs that cause difficulty beyond one's own control. In that sense, *Annie Glenn is one of the* most courageous persons I have known. It isn't that I happen to be married to her either. I can say some things she might not say about herself. We've known each other all our lives. We grew up together and our parents knew each other."

His voice rose higher as he spoke. He lifted his hands, leaned back in his chair, then shifted forward again. "Annie was an eighty-five percent stutterer, which means she stuttered on eighty-five percent of the words she would try to say. Her father had been a stutterer also. Annie spent her whole life not being able to communicate as well as she would have liked. Imagine someone who could never use the telephone—in this day and age!—never had taken a taxicab on her own because she didn't want to be embarrassed, a person who would walk out of a department store rather than ask a clerk where something was, had never given a speech or a recitation.

"And there she was when I ran for the Senate again in 1980 giving an actual speech before a group of two hundred and fifty to three hundred women!" He tapped the desk for more emphasis and his voice rose. "It was the first time she had ever given a speech in public in her life. Talk about raw courage? *That* was it!"

His words made it easy for me to recall my first meeting with Annie Glenn on a chilly October afternoon in 1982. The senator had spoken at a small Boy Scout banquet near Huntington, New York, and I was to escort him and his wife to the Rye Hilton in Westchester County, where he was to be the principal speaker that night at a scholarship fund-raising dinner for Mercy College. I was chairman of the board of trustees. The ride lasted about an hour.

"You speak beautifully," I told Annie Glenn as our car made its way over the Whitestone Bridge.

"Thank you," she said, "you do too!"

To those who've never suffered a speech impediment, such conversation is ordinary and unexceptional. To anyone who has climbed the hill, it's poetry. A stutter might be defined as an involuntary repetition of words and sounds, while a stammer might be called an involuntary pause. If you suffer from either or both—if you cannot talk in a world of talkers—the embarrassment can flare to rare intensity. I understand its sting, because for a time—mercifully brief—I stammered.

My ears redden even now as I recall what should have been an uneventful rifle inspection during a spring afternoon in 1962 on the pavement outside my barracks at Camp Lejeune.

"Private Anderson," the staff sergeant asked, "what is your rifle number?"

No words came.

"Anderson," he repeated, "your rifle number?"

No words.

"What is it?" he asked again, raising my M1 to his eyes to read the numbers stamped behind the rear sight. A giggle erupted in the row immediately behind me, followed by another. My face burned, my stomach ached, but no words came.

"Anybody see something *funny* here?" he asked, his voice hard. The giggling stopped cold.

"Anderson," he said firmly as he handed me back my rifle, "see me after inspection."

After the staff sergeant had inspected the ranks, he dismissed the platoon. As a group of us began to walk back to the barracks, one Marine burst into laughter. When I couldn't respond fast enough, he laughed harder and grabbed his side. Enraged—and silent—I leaped at him. Before we were separated, I had hit him.

Twenty minutes later I stood nervously before the same staff sergeant who had conducted the inspection. Aware of the fight I had been in, he demanded, "Should I court-martial you, Anderson?"

Few times in my life have I wanted to answer a question as desperately as I did that afternoon. And, fortunately, I did.

"No," I said.

"How long have you had trouble talking?" he asked.

I stammered. My words came haltingly, but they came. I told him I didn't remember having much of a problem in high school or at home. At least no one in my family ever seemed to notice pauses when I spoke. On Parris Island I had some trouble for the first time, but my buddies covered for me.

"How?"

"Made a noise or did something to draw attention so that I'd have the time to talk. It only happened bad once. At the rifle range, with an instructor."

"Get away with it?"

"Yes," I said, stammering only slightly, "and when I went home on boot camp leave, I think I spoke OK. Anyway, no one noticed."

"Can you sing?" he asked.

"Lousy," I replied.

"That's not what I meant," he said, chuckling. "Do you have a problem when you sing?"

"I don't know."

"Call cadence," he ordered.

Marines usually march to a singsong cadence. What may sound like "luf-iddle-luf-rye-luf-iddle-luf" is clearly heard by the marching troops as "left—left—right—left—left." The rest of the command, "wuh-hoo-hee-iddle-luf-rye-luf," is received as "one—two—three—left—right—left."

I called cadence.

"You didn't have a problem," the staff sergeant said.

I wasn't court-martialed, but I did get "extra police duty," which translated into cleaning and sweeping for several days. In the weeks that followed, some of the noncommissioned officers frequently ordered me to march other privates, which meant I had to call cadence. I also began to read assiduously about speech and vigorously practiced finding more than one way to complete sentences as I spoke them. When I was transferred four months later to the West Coast, my stammer was less perceptible. Today I still speak with pauses—and sometimes my predicates don't precisely fit my subjects—but it's only a skilled ear that can detect the stammer.

Comparing my own mild stammer with Annie Glenn's stutter was poignant for me, because I knew it represented the difference between burning your finger and being consumed by fire. Annie Glenn's impediment was a thousand times more agonizing than mine, and her triumph that much more spectacular.

This understanding was still clear to me two years after her visit to Westchester County when I walked over to hug the woman who had entered Senator Glenn's office.

"Hello, Annie," I said. "I'm really happy to see you again!"

Her posture, like her husband's, was erect. Large clear glasses framed her brown eyes and a cranberry scarf seemed to light up her white dress. She might have been your favorite schoolteacher or your best friend. There's no mistaking Annie Glenn.

As I watched her and her husband I recalled a dramatic scene in *The Right Stuff* when the actress who played Annie seemed to ignore a friendly gesture from the wife of another astronaut. Only in a later scene did the audience learn that the problem had been Annie's crippling stutter. In an even more dramatic scene—one that really happened—Annie refused to allow Lyndon Johnson into her home to be followed by a phalanx of reporters. Annie called her husband, who, without hesitation, supported her—effectively rebuffing the Vice President of the United States! It's good theater and it rouses a cheer, but the movie ends without showing how she finally overcame her stutter.

"Annie," I asked, "when did you first become aware that you spoke differently?"

"When I was in the sixth grade, we were asked to get up in front of the class to recite a poem. I picked my favorite, 'The Highwayman.' I ran into a block and I heard someone in the class snicker. That was the very first time I realized that I was not like everyone else. And, after that, I was never again asked to stand up to read before others.

"When John and I were growing up—we went to high school *and* college in the same town—no one ever talked about my speech. I was quite active in school. I held office, although I never made a speech. I always wanted to try out for plays, but that was a dream I knew would never happen. I was never depressed during those years, though, because I knew that my parents accepted me and I felt that I was included in everything.

"It was not until after I had graduated from college that I had a hard time, that I discovered what could be meant by the expression 'cruel world.' My parents wanted me to stay in the vicinity of New Concord, but I wanted to go off on my own. I just wanted to try.

"One of my college professors was sure that I could be a good secretary, but she knew that I couldn't handle an interview. She asked to write my résumé. I said yes and, résumé in hand, I took off for Dayton, which was one hundred miles away from New Concord.

"I rented a room in a private home, found an office needing help and presented my résumé. I was immediately hired. I was working there several months when one morning my boss asked me to take dictation over the telephone. I couldn't do it. I was never asked to answer the telephone again.

"I still recall the very first time I had to go to the bus station to ask for a round-trip ticket home to New Concord and back to Dayton. I knew I couldn't ask the ticket agent. I wrote out where I wanted to go and what I wanted. He thought I was deaf, and he answered me in writing.

"Whenever I'd go shopping, I could never ask a clerk for help. I would hunt and hunt and hunt for my size. Often I would walk out without buying what I was after, rather than ask."

"You married John," I said, "and he became one of the most famous men in the world. How did you handle that?"

"Throughout my adult life, as we moved from one station to another, I chose my friends slowly. When John was selected to be an astronaut, to me it was just like another assignment. I didn't expect it to draw that much attention. I knew it was an opportunity for John, and I was very proud of him. When the press began paying more attention, I began to realize I was going to have trouble."

"Did you worry when John went up in the rocket?"

"Yes, but John had prepared us well. Right from the very beginning, he would tell our children, Dave and Lynn, and me about the program and what he was learning. John would take us to the various places where he would be training so that we would know even more about the program. If something happened, he wanted us to be able to understand what was going on. The unknown about anything is what frightens you. John really prepared us. I remember I never asked for John's life to be spared when I said my prayers, because that's not up to me. What I would ask for was strength to take care of our two children."

"Annie," I asked, "when was enough enough?"

"One morning," she said, her voice confident, "when John and I were eating breakfast, we heard Dr. Ron Webster interviewed on a news show. He explained why he thought a person stuttered, and he talked about his particular program. It was different from anything that I had heard. I had also reached a point in my life where I needed help more than ever before. I didn't know where to go or what to do; I had tried three other times and had not been successful. I was almost fifty-three.

"John asked me, 'Would you like to go to Dr. Webster?'

"I said, 'It sounds very exciting. I would like to.'

"But I couldn't call. I just could not call. John made the phone call for me, and I was accepted into the program just before Christmas. During the holidays we went skiing, as we always do, and my stutter was never so bad; I couldn't talk at all.

"If people could only have seen the lot of us who entered Dr. Webster's class at Hollins College in Roanoke . . . so scared and so quiet. One stutterer in one class got off the airplane and couldn't take a cab. He didn't write out the directions as I had. So, rather than ask, he walked from the airport to the school. It was several miles. He was bound and determined to get some help. He told me he was at the end of his rope. I understood that. And he *was* helped."

Not once had Annie Glenn stuttered as she spoke. I had no doubt that today she could read aloud her favorite poem, and I could visualize her, as Senator Glenn had described, speaking before a large group of women during his election campaign, but I could only imagine the grinding, discouraging days she had struggled through with her classmates for only the most minute improvement. This victory, I knew from my own experience, had been earned painfully by straining with syllables and sentences, practicing one word at a time, day by excruciating day. Her triumph is a lesson for all of us that anxiety *can* be an ally, that worry need not paralyze us. Annie Glenn examined her fear, found it real, then took action. She said *yes*.

"When," I asked, "did you finally feel, did you finally know that you had improved?"

"I called John," Annie replied and she smiled. "I actually called him myself on the telephone—long distance!"

And the distinguished former combat pilot, the unshakable astronaut who had circled the globe, the man who had been a Marine in war and a corporate chief executive officer in peace, the seasoned United States senator—how did *he* respond?

"I cried," John Glenn told me.

Chapter 5

WHAT IF I MAKE A MISTAKE?

"I had an explosive father and an imperturbable mother," one of the country's most widely read columnists confided to me as we sat in his office at 1401 Sixteenth Street, North West, in Washington, D.C. "Dad was a human Vesuvius who erupted over the slightest tremor. Mother was a glacier, cold and immovable. When she spoke, there was steel in her voice. The volume was always low, but the message was always clear. If she said 'Sit,' I wouldn't even check to see if there was a chair to sit on. Mother hid her feelings behind a Scandinavian reserve. For the same reason she would not display her emotions. She didn't show affection. But I never doubted that she loved me. She would slip me forbidden things. My father would give me twenty-five cents for a date when I was in high school. And he would calculate how it should be spent down to the last penny. Ten cents apiece for a malt, five cents for cookies. He had it figured out. But my mother would slip me an extra *dollar*."

The speaker had smooth, almost translucent baby-soft skin, and his voice was large and deep like that of a revivalist preacher. His snow-white hair rose gently, then fell back into place neatly when he laughed aloud, a hearty baritone, as he remembered his mother's kindness. He had circled the globe many times since the days he was reared in a strict

Mormon family, but he had never left his faith, even when it might have threatened his livelihood. As a teenager he had been a missionary for two years in the Deep South, an experience followed by a trek halfway across the earth where, behind enemy lines, he served as a correspondent in the Pacific theater during World War II. He had since been awarded the most prestigious honors in his field and, having been cited by at least one national survey as America's most trusted reporter, had achieved fame and won the confidence of many of his countrymen. He was, as we spoke, the Washington bureau chief of *Parade,* and I was his editor. His name is Jack Anderson.

"Both my parents had tremendous integrity," he continued. "One year my father was lugging a Christmas tree down a festive Salt Lake City street. It was a cold, wintry night, and he was breathing icicles. He paused to rest when a close friend of mine came upon him. Dad was fuming and muttering. He was angry! He was indignant! He had not bothered to count his change after purchasing the tree, but later, to his consternation, he had discovered that he had been overpaid by twenty-five cents. He was furious! He had to go all the way back to return that quarter; he grumbled about the inconvenience this had caused him. 'Why can't these people at the cash register count their money more carefully?' he complained. It didn't occur to him to dismiss the small overpayment as the merchant's fault and, therefore, *his* tough luck. It didn't occur to Dad. I was not surprised to hear this story from my friend. *This* was the father I knew."

As I listened to Jack Anderson share the anecdote about his father, I weighed how to raise a sensitive topic that would surely be painful to him. Maybe, I thought, I can back into it. I asked, "Have you ever tried to act like anyone else?"

"I have never tried to imitate anyone," he began, his voice sure. "I have certainly tried to learn from them, but I've never tried to be like them.

"The man who had the most influence on my career was the late Drew Pearson. He was a journalistic and moral giant, with the toughness and courage to act on his better impulses in the worst weather. Drew had more courage than I will ever have. He was a role model for me. But at no time did I ever want to be exactly like him. I objected frequently to some of his ideas and some of his tactics. I remember my first confrontation with him. It happened immediately after he hired me. I was a twenty-four-year-old reporter, the youngest he had on his staff. I had no Washington experience, no social sophistication, no Ivy League education. He hired me only because he knew I had been a war correspondent; fortunately, he didn't know how undistinguished a war correspondent I had been.

"The first thing he said was, 'Jack, I do a broadcast Sunday evening. Sunday is our big day around here. I'll be needing you all day.'

" 'I go to church on Sunday,' I replied. I had a moment of anxiety; I thought he might fire me before I could start with him. But I had certain ideals. I don't smoke. I don't drink. I attend church.

"No subordinate had spoken to Drew Pearson like that. He was at the pinnacle of his influence, more widely known than many of the celebrities he wrote about. He let out an abrupt, impatient snort. Then he smiled and said, 'OK, we'll excuse you.'

"A later confrontation occurred over a mistake I had made in a column. I had written about a juvenile who had been thrown into a prison with an adult. The story condemned the practice of sheriffs across the country dumping juveniles in cells with adults. I wrote about one incident as it was described to me by a social worker who had been there. His recollection, it turned out, was wrong. I said it was a cement jail. It was a *brick* jail. I said it was a one-cell jail. It was a *two-*cell jail. I shouldn't have relied on memory. It was an intolerable mistake.

"The local newspaper wrote a blistering piece about Drew Pearson's casualness with the facts. *Time* magazine picked it up, and it caused Drew great embarrassment. He was furious with me.

"He ripped off a response, arguing that the important thing was not what the jail looked like, but what practices were going on inside. He declared that the essential facts were accurate but that his assistant, Jack Anderson, should have been more careful about the trivial details.

"I said, 'Drew, you are entirely justified in sending this out. I should have done what you say I should have done. You are blaming me for the mistake. I should be blamed for the mistake. But if you're going to blame me for the mistake, then I want you to put out an additional news release giving me credit for all of the accurate stories I have given you for your byline.' Then I started naming them.

" 'As long as I get credit for the good stories I do,' I said, 'then I don't mind taking blame for the bad.'

"So he deleted my name.

"Drew was a man of great compassion, of high ideals. It shows something that a big man would back down even when he was angry —and he was fuming at the last case."

I had not interrupted Jack Anderson as he spoke. He leaned back in his chair and folded his arms across his chest, waiting. *Waiting.* We had known each other professionally and personally for seven years, and I was sure he sensed I was going to ask him about his biggest blunder, which I understood remained a sore and sensitive memory. I was equally convinced that the final story he told about Drew Pearson was meant to make it easier for me to raise the hard question.

"Jack," I said flatly, "let's talk about Eagleton."

He nodded and unfolded his arms.

During the presidential campaign of 1972 Jack Anderson reported that the Democratic vice-presidential candidate, Thomas Eagleton, had a record of arrests for drunken driving—a sensational accusation, but one, it turned out, the reporter could not verify.

"How has the mistake stayed with you?" I asked.

"My mishandling of the Thomas Eagleton story has caused me more grief, more anguish, more soul-searching than anything else I have ever written," Jack Anderson replied; his expression and his tone unusually subdued, he was no longer the charismatic preacher. "At the time," he said, "I had hoped that the reader was a child of the moment, that he would soon forget my Eagleton misadventure or, if he remembered the contretemps at all, would mistakenly attribute it to Robert Novak or perhaps William Buckley—"

The allusion to others was the result of frustration, I realized, not an attempt at humor. I sat quietly, only nodding.

"But this unhappy incident has been a recurring nightmare for me. It happened more than a dozen years ago. Yet I seldom deliver a lecture or appear on a TV talk show that someone doesn't ask about Eagleton. I have never been able to shake my big goof."

"Jack," I prompted, "why did it happen?"

"I moved too fast with the story," he recalled. "I heard that the St. Louis *Post-Dispatch* was doing a story—in fact, they did do one—about Eagleton's alleged drunken driving. The *Post-Dispatch* quoted a former state highway official as saying he had stopped Eagleton three times and other troopers had stopped him on other occasions. But no arrests were made, the *Post-Dispatch* reported, because of Eagleton's high position.

"At the time, Eagleton was in the headlines. I didn't want to be beaten on a story that I had worked on for several days. I was filled with competitive zeal. So I rushed out with the story prematurely on my radio broadcast. The *Post-Dispatch* and I hit Eagleton on the same afternoon. The *Post-Dispatch* handled the story more cautiously, more professionally. My story was more bold, more brash and, unfortunately, more widely heard. So I caught the backlash.

"It was a story I thought I had checked adequately. I had heard that Eagleton had a drinking problem. I phoned a veteran Missouri correspondent, who offered some help if I would keep his name out of it. He said he had heard about some drunken-arrest incidents and gave me the names of three state policemen who might provide details. I kept checking until I got the names of some patrolmen and a local magistrate who were supposed to have personal knowledge of the incidents.

"I spoke to one who started to tell me about stopping Eagleton on the highway. But, halfway into his account, he backed off and refused to discuss it. Another name I had been given turned out to be that of a retired trooper. He was willing to talk but had little of value to say. He could offer no personal account but claimed to know several who could. He gave me names and offered to send documentation. I never heard from him again.

"The most damning report came from a trooper who seemed to be credible. He said he had worked under a captain who had become upset over Eagleton's alleged traffic record. According to his account, troopers who stopped Eagleton usually would not ticket him because of his position. But a few tough troopers wrote out tickets.

"My informant said that one copy would go to the local magistrate, another to the capitol at Jefferson City. But a third copy would be retained by the arresting officer. According to the trooper, Eagleton's friends usually managed to kill the first two copies but overlooked the copies held by the individual troopers.

"As the trooper explained what happened, he was asked by the captain to mosey around and collect as many of these copies as he could pick up. The trooper said he collected about a dozen arrest citations. Some alleged drunken driving, some careless driving, some speeding.

"My source said he photostated the traffic citations and delivered separate sets to Eagleton's political opponents.

"Two of them, True Davis and Senator Edward Long, were running against Eagleton in the Democratic primary. The third, Congressman Thomas Curtis, was the Republican candidate.

"I reached True Davis first. He said he had personally received the photostats at a campaign appearance in central Missouri during the primary race. He said the photostats were handed to him in a plain brown envelope by a man in civilian clothes who identified himself as a state trooper. He said he did not keep them.

"Senator Long said yes, an envelope containing photostats of arrest citations involving Eagleton had been presented to one of his aides. The aide had reported the delivery to Long, who said he was not interested in the photostats and did not examine them himself. He said he didn't know what had become of the photostats.

"One of my reporters reached Curtis, who had a vague recollection of some traffic records but did not see them and could give no precise information.

"The trooper promised to send me a set of the photostats. I had full confidence in the story and expected the final proof in the mail. I tried several times to reach Eagleton, who was on the campaign trail and didn't return my calls. So I jumped the gun and reported a story that had not been pinned down solidly.

"Eagleton struck back with angry denials. The controversy hit the headlines. I telephoned the trooper, who said he would rush the photostats to me. So I stuck to my story. I waited for the photostats, which I planned to produce triumphantly. I waited and waited. But the photostats never arrived. The trooper finally told me, 'I'm not sending them.'

"In the news business, you have to assume that any documentation you can't get doesn't exist. So I assumed the traffic tickets never existed. I trudged up to Eagleton's office. I wanted him to know that I hadn't made up the story, that I had believed it at the time I reported it. I told him I would make a full retraction. He agreed to step into the hall with me and accept my apology in front of a battery of television cameras. I took a deep breath and apologized. He accepted it graciously."

"What happened next?" I asked.

Jack paused for what seemed a few seconds, and when he spoke again his voice was somber: "I was unprepared for the backlash. I had broken several major stories. I had come up with proofs of stories that Richard Nixon, Henry Kissinger and Richard Kleindienst had denied. I had proved my credibility against all the resources of the Nixon administration. I had received journalism's top award, the Pulitzer Prize. Then overnight I was devastated by a wave of scorching, scathing editorials. I really didn't think I had done anything as heinous as my colleagues seemed to think. I guess I have always viewed myself as more noble than I am. Yes, I had gone off half-cocked with a story I believed. Yes, it was *bad* journalism. Yes, I made a mistake. Sure, I shouldn't have done it. But once I realized that my documentation was not on its way, I apologized. The apology was unconditional. I stood in front of the nation and said I was wrong. I even appeared the next morning on the *Today* show and repeated my apology. I couldn't go back and relive the incident. I didn't know what more I could do."

"How did you respond privately?"

"I had never before in my life cried—that is, not since I was a small child. But one night I lost control. I sobbed uncontrollably. I was filled with anguish. My stomach was tied in knots. Yes, I cried."

Jack Anderson's words were soft as he stopped speaking. He wiped his forehead with the back of his right hand. When he spoke again, it was apparent he had been considering another, deeper question.

"Was I sorry for Eagleton?" he asked aloud.

"No, I was sorry for myself," answered the son of a man who had trudged through snow to return a quarter to an errant cashier. "I'm not proud of the incident. I'm not proud of my emotions. But you asked for the truth. My whole life has been devoted to the truth, as nearly as I can determine what the truth is. So I must tell you the truth. It was the worst experience of my career, but it taught me my most important lesson."

What is a mistake?

It can be a wrong choice or a misunderstanding. I have rewritten this paragraph, for example, five times. It has shrunk from more than eighty words to fewer than thirty. Oops, fewer than *forty*.

From my own countless foul-ups, I've learned to recognize at least four kinds of mistakes, which I remember by using the acronym SLIP:

• Mistakes of *Similarity*. These are probably the majority of our errors. We often repeat behavior when signals seem similar. We might rise one Monday morning, dress for work, hoist a briefcase, open a car door, sit behind a familiar steering wheel and drive to the place where we used to work rather than where we work now. A stranger reminds us of someone we have known and we respond as if the stranger were the other person; or we complete an important report and toss it by mistake into the wastepaper basket. *Familiarity* prompts these mistakes, but it's important to recognize that the same behavior could easily have been correct. We erred because we responded to familiar signals that existed under different conditons.

• Mistakes of *Lapse*. Our memory takes a hike. You plan a route to complete some errands and forget several anyway. You're interrupted by a telephone call as you clean your room, and after the call you leave the house with your room unkempt. You can't recall where you've put your coat; you walk into the kitchen and you can't remember why you entered the room. Or, more seriously, we forget to take medicine, have the brakes checked, complete an important work or school assignment.

• Mistakes of *Ignorance*. We *know* we don't know, but we act anyway, as I did when I ignored my father's concern and bought the 1955 Chevrolet with a bad transmission. Self-explanatory, these mistakes run from the humorous—ordering from a foreign menu and finding something unfamiliar staring back at you from the plate—to something that can have tragic consequences: "What's there to handling a boat?"

• Mistakes of *Perception*. We *think* we know. We mistakenly assume on a chilly day that the water in a swimming pool has been heated, so we blissfully plunge in. Often we insist on making these mistakes, as I did when I started to elbow my way rudely through holiday shoppers along Park Avenue to visit Prince Michael; I saw obstacles, not people. When we vehemently argue a point based on information we're sure exists, as Jack Anderson did in the Eagleton affair, only to discover later that the information does not exist, we commit a mistake of perception. Our desire overwhelms reality, and we blunder because we refuse to see.

Now, there is a fifth mistake, which would be to think that I've covered everything in four. No doubt we could squeeze errors into more types, but SLIP covers a large number that we can agree to.

I've stumbled in every category, but particularly troubling, even after more than twenty years, is a mistake of perception that I made in the fall of 1963 when I was a Marine lance corporal stationed at Kaneohe Bay on the island of Oahu, Hawaii.

I had been assigned Duty NCO for the night, which meant that I was responsible until the following morning for the marines in my unit, their equipment, their safety and the condition of their barracks.

At 2130—9:30 P.M.—I toured the barracks and found only a handful of Marines scattered among more than a hundred empty bunks that had been evenly distributed into two large rooms, or "squadbays."

The first squadbay had only one occupant, a private who was reading a letter as he sat on a footlocker alone in a corner. "Sweep down," I ordered. "I'll inspect in fifteen minutes."

I gave another private, who had been playing cards with two others at a table in the center of the barracks, the same directive in the next squadbay.

When I checked the "head" adjoining the second squadbay, I found the showers and stalls empty. Thus alone, I studied myself in a large mirror bolted to a wall over a long row of sinks. The chevrons I had earned, a stripe with crossed rifles, had only recently been sewn to my sleeves. Although I had griped about getting Duty NCO watch on a weekend, I relished the responsibility. I was "stuck" with Saturday night because I was new and my unit was temporarily short of the next higher rank, which was a full corporal. The lance corporal I saw in the mirror looked very important with his official "duty" belt and clipboard. He was me, but bigger, it seemed. Few times in my life have I been so totally aware of my own existence. My concentration was interrupted only when a Marine wrapped in a towel stepped through the doorway. My watch indicated 2150. I cleared my throat, straightened myself to full height and walked through the doorway and entered the second squadbay again, which had been neatly swept.

"Good job," I told the private, my voice at least two octaves lower.

"Right," he replied.

As I strode past he seemed to murmur something, so I asked, "Did you say something?"

"Nope," he answered.

Two Marines a few feet away chuckled. My ears and neck grew heated. They were laughing at me!

"Are you laughing at *me?*" I demanded.

"Oh no," one replied, his tone too sincere.

I *felt* their laughter as much as I heard it. When I stepped out of their squadbay and into the first one, my anger was flaring white-hot. I marched nearly halfway through the room before I noticed that it had *not* been swept.

My neck and ears still blistering, I hunted for the private who had defied me. He was easy to find, sitting alone on the same footlocker reading the same letter.

"You!" I shouted.

He didn't even look up.

"You!" I shouted, "you've got five minutes to clean this pigpen up. Now get on it! I'll be back!"

He raised his hand with the letter. I spun away and ordered, "Now!"

Outside, in the night air, I could feel my heart beat in my temples. I had been laughed at, humiliated. I turned to glance through the window to check the private's progress—and he was *still* seated. It was as if a rubber band at the base of my brain had snapped. He was *still* seated!

"You!" I screamed, throwing open the door. I bellowed a stream of curses and threats as I tore through the squadbay. I couldn't get to his footlocker fast enough. The private, the letter still clenched in his hand, raised his arm again when I got to him. With the back of my fist, I slapped it away. It floated down toward his boots. He did not rise from his footlocker. He leaned forward, squeezed the paper with two fingers, lifted it to his lap and, as I cursed loudly above him, started to turn his head toward me. The sense of responsibility I should have felt as Duty NCO evaporated in the heat of my anger. I clenched my fists.

When he turned his head completely, I saw his face, which was moist and blotchy. His eyes were red and running with tears. Confused, I reached down and picked up the letter he had been offering me.

I read the message. The private's mother had died.

Jack Anderson, who has invested his entire adult life examining and exposing the abuse of power, told me, "Walter, I have learned from agonizing experience that an exposé can be a cruel thing. Every success of the investigative reporter means ruin for some human being who is typically weak rather than evil. Most of the time I am convinced that the trade-off is necessary to maintain a free society. But there are times when it seems a close call. Abuse should be exposed, but as I tell my staff, 'If you enjoy doing it, I wouldn't like you.' "

As he spoke I recalled a small but revealing incident a few years ago.

After dinner with our wives, we were riding along a Washington street with Jack at the wheel when his wife, Olivia, pointed out a young woman who seemed to be under attack by a man. With no hesitation Jack pulled the car to the curb, stepped out and briskly walked to the couple—a fray studiously ignored by other pedestrians.

"What are you doing?" he demanded of the man, who was about the same size but much younger than himself. The man seemed to be trying to lift the woman off the pavement.

"I'm trying to help her!" the man replied.

Jack leaned over to speak to the woman, who was mumbling incoherently. "Leave her alone," Jack said, his voice firm.

A police car, its lights not flashing, rolled to the curb before the man could respond.

"What's going on?" an officer asked.

"I'm trying to help her," the man replied.

"We can leave now," Jack told us, "she'll be all right with the police here. They'll find out what's what, whether he was helping her or trying to hurt her."

As we sat in his office months later and he told me about the lessons of his largest mistake, my memory of the incident was a reminder that Jack Anderson was a person who got involved, who, despite his reputation as the toughest investigative reporter of them all, was sensitive.

"I had always felt compassion for the people that I had to write unfavorably about," he told me, "but I also think Eagleton helped to impress this upon me. I told myself that I had kicked him in the stomach, that I had done some serious damage to his reputation at the high point of his life. Just as he had a shot at becoming vice president of the United States, I came along with a derogatory story that I could not back up. Believe me, I've been more careful ever since. Today I have five people review every column. Then a lawyer checks it for libel. And I lecture my staff on fairness. This all began after the Eagleton affair."

Jack Anderson, the acclaimed American reporter who had probably uncovered more mistakes of important and powerful people than any other living journalist, walked to the fireplace in the center of his office,

93

then turned back to me and said, "It is painful for me to write derogatory stories about people. I know something about the terrible anguish they feel."

No one had notified the Marine Corps that a death in the young man's family had occurred. The private hadn't even received a telegram, which could have arrived in time for him, if he hurried, to attend his mother's funeral. In fact, the letter itself was not intended to inform him; it was an expression of sympathy from a neighbor who assumed he knew. It was irrelevant at that point how the tragic mistake had occurred. What mattered was the Marine.

I locked the private's wall locker and encouraged him to walk with me to the Duty NCO office, where I called the Officer of the Day, a first lieutenant who joined us within minutes. He located by telephone a chaplain who suggested that, to save time, we bring the young Marine to him. So I walked with the private to the chaplain's office a couple of buildings away.

"I'm really sorry," I apologized as we made our way between two barracks, "about how I talked to you."

"It doesn't matter," he replied. "I wasn't paying attention anyway."

A few feet from the chaplain's office the Marine stopped, grasped my hand, shook it firmly and said, "Thank you for helping me. I really appreciate it. Thank the lieutenant for me, will you?"

"Yes," I promised.

It was nearly 2300—11:00 P.M.—when I arrived back at the barracks. The lights, which should have been turned off at 2200, were on in the first squadbay. The room was still empty. In a corner the private's footlocker was askew. I aligned it in front of his rack, straightened his bed, then removed a broom from the closet. After I swept down the barracks, I turned off the lights.

Back in the Duty NCO office, I called the lieutenant and gave him the private's message.

"Is everything else squared away?" he asked.

"Yes, sir," I replied, "everything is squared away."

. . .

If we are to make anxiety an ally in our lives, we must first accept this fundamental rule: *To succeed, we must be prepared to fail.* Life is, after all, trial and error. Isn't success almost always the last of a string of failed attempts to get it right? If we did not test, did not experiment, did not try, did not flub, we would not grow. Look outside. Nature has been correcting itself, successfully adapting to new circumstances, since the first cell split and didn't look quite like the original. A rattlesnake is not a cobra, and neither is a worm. Have you ever seen two identical maple trees? Is a crocodile a chameleon? Is a rat a hamster? Is either a mouse? If our cave-dwelling ancestors had not tried—and failed—so many times, you and I, if we existed at all, might be throwing stones at the moon tonight to chase away the clouds. Not only would life be unproductive without error, it would be boring; the opportunity to learn would be lost. It's not whether we make mistakes that matters, it's understanding the opportunity they afford us.

She had helped produce, among many other movies, *Kramer versus Kramer, The China Syndrome, Taps, Nine to Five, Quest for Fire, Modern Problems, The King of Comedy, Without a Trace* and *The Verdict.* In an earlier career as a model, her unusually large blue eyes, fair skin and black hair got her a job acting in commercials for Max Factor and Alberto-Culver. As a mathematics teacher, she had taught in Watts only a year after the riot of 1965. As an actress, she had appeared in the television series *Ironside* and *Dan August* and with John Wayne in the Civil War movie *Rio Lobo.* As a student of primitive culture, she had lived alone for weeks at a time among tribes in South America, Africa and Australia. Despite all she has accomplished, though, it was a single opportunity that thrust her into the glare of unquestioned celebrity, a signal achievement that catapulted her name and her picture to the top of the news columns from coast to coast. In January 1980, when Sherry Lansing at thirty-five was appointed president of production at Twentieth Century-Fox, she became the first woman in the history of Hollywood to run a major movie studio.

Sherry Lansing and I first met three years later. We were introduced by Lisa Birnbach, the editor of the popular *Official Preppy Handbook*, whom I'd had assigned to conduct several interviews of famous people, including one of Sherry. Lisa's profile of the first female promoted to the post of studio president appeared on January 23, 1983, one month after Sherry Lansing had resigned from Twentieth Century-Fox to become an independent producer. When asked to comment by Lisa on her three-year record as president—which included box-office successes like *Taps* and *Modern Problems* and box-office flops like *King of Comedy* and *Author! Author!*—Sherry replied, "I never put a film into development that I really didn't believe in. Some of those pictures worked, some didn't. But I thought every one of them was going to go through the roof, or I wouldn't have made them."

During the winter of 1985, as I waited one morning for Sherry to join me for breakfast in Los Angeles, I remembered how impressed I had been by her honesty in accepting her mistakes, the box-office flops. No blaming others. No excuses: *"I thought every one of them was going to go through the roof, or I wouldn't have made them."* If, I thought, I can just ask the right questions, there is much to be learned from Sherry Lansing.

She arrived on time wearing a dark purple wool sweater, charcoal-gray slacks, black flats and no jewelry. She is only two inches short of six feet. Her jet-black hair was brushed shiny and straight; those familiar blue eyes were clear and alert. We exchanged greetings and hugs, and I realized I had forgotten her laughter. Sherry Lansing is one of those rare people with an infectious laugh, a deep-throated, fun-filled, contagious laugh—a rich, hearty sound others enjoy and inevitably respond to.

"Let's discuss your book," she suggested.

"What do you think of the idea?" I asked.

"It's a good subject," she replied, "because I don't think that most people really understand the anxiety and doubts that very successful people have. The myth is that the successful are never insecure. The truth is that most of them are highly insecure, but they use their insecurity as a motivating factor. Because they want to overcome their anxieties, they push themselves twice as hard."

"Hey, Lansing," I said, "*you* want to write the book?"

"No," she answered, laughing, "I'm doing a movie."

Her life had been rich with varied experiences of joy and pain, and I wondered where to begin. Her father, David Duhl, died when she was nine; three years later her mother married Norton Lansing, a business-man. Sherry married after her sophomore year at Northwestern University and divorced when she was twenty-six. In 1970 she began reading scripts at $5 an hour; ten years later she was earning more than $300,000 a year as the head of Twentieth Century-Fox. Only four months prior to this breakfast interview, her mother—with whom she had stayed very close—died after an agonizing struggle with cancer.

"Sherry," I asked, "how do you handle a mistake?"

"First," she replied, "I try to analyze what has gone wrong. If it's a movie that doesn't work—and I've certainly made those—I try to learn so that the next one will be better. If it's a mistake in my private life, I also try to learn from it. And I try to remember how lucky I am to have another chance. I try not to indulge in self-flagellation. I'll allow myself to be depressed for no more than one or two days."

She paused, seeming to search within herself for something else—and when she found it, she continued: "I never felt that I was my work. In other words, if I made a mistake in my work, I was not a hopeless mess as a person. If I produced a movie that failed, it did not mean that I was a failure as a human being, or that I couldn't handle a personal relationship, or that I couldn't have a life, or that I couldn't be successful in other work. The biggest mistake that any of us might make may be to think that when something we do fails, *we* have failed. It's not the same thing. I have seen really good people make really big mistakes, but they're the same people who create giant successes. If you stay in the game long enough, you're going to have your share of successes and you're going to have your share of failures. As I said in the beginning, though, you must analyze your mistakes and learn from them so that you can grow and be wiser for the next opportunity."

"What about your personal life, Sherry?" I asked.

"The same applies," she said. "I was married when I was young to a very nice man, and we both grew up—but I don't view either the marriage or the divorce as a mistake. The truth is that I honestly don't regret any business or personal experience that I've had. That does not mean that I have not been disappointed, that I have not trusted people who have let me down, friends included. It means that everything I've experienced has helped me to grow as a person . . . and do you want to know something else?"

"Yes," I said.

"I realize just as we're talking that I rarely, if ever, use the word 'mistake.' I might say that a business decision was 'disappointing' or that a personal relationship was 'not very happy,' but I do not call them mistakes. It's not that I don't recognize a failure. I do, but I don't dwell on what went wrong. I analyze it, understand it, then move on from there. In the same way, I tend not to think about movies that I've made in the past that were hits or disappointments, or about personal relationships that did or didn't work."

Her reply led me to the question I most wanted to ask, the question that would dramatically reveal the rewarding perspective in which she viewed both the suffering and the promise of life.

"Sherry," I asked, "would you discuss with me your greatest disappointment?"

"Yes," she said, "I will."

Life is the sound of a baby crying, of autumn leaves rustling; it's the scent of talcum, pine, frying bacon and freshly turned earth; it's the feel of velvet and moist skin and sand; it's the taste of salt, chocolate and lemon; it's blues, reds, greens, yellows in a billion shapes and textures; it's a smile, a frown and, sometimes, a tear.

And it's the cake that falls: *if you do nothing, you don't make mistakes; if you don't make mistakes, you do nothing.* To get anxiety working for you, expect mistakes to occur and practice what I call RIP, an acronym for Responsibility, Insight and Perspective. It also means, as you know, *Rest In Peace,* which in itself may not be a bad way to look at many mistakes.

- *Responsibility.* Accept responsibility for your errors. A mistake does not mean you're a bad person; it only means you're one of us. If failure meant incompetence, we'd still be throwing rocks at the moon and sleeping in caves. Never ignore mistakes—if you do, you condemn yourself to repeat them. If you own up to a blunder, you can learn from it, which is the next step.

- *Insight.* As Sherry Lansing suggested, separate yourself from your error: "If I produced a movie that failed, it did not mean that I was a failure." You are not your mistake. Remember to study your error only for what you can gain from it. What went wrong? Why? Ask, "What have I learned so that I can do better next time?" Do not waste time and effort agonizing over your guilt.

- *Perspective.* The vast majority of mistakes are merely problems you have the opportunity to solve. They are rarely personal tragedies. Try not to confuse the possible consequences of a mistake with the mistake itself. As I suggested in Chapter Four, simply ask, "What's the worst thing that can happen?" The answer will often diminish your fear, because the worst may not be that bad, and once you've found it, you can focus on the solution, not the mistake, and let anxiety work *for* you. Don't resist its force. Instead, use the precious energy anxiety provides to keep you alert as you explore your possibilities. You've never been more sharp.

I have known few people who have understood and practiced the RIP principles as well as my friend Sherry Lansing:

"My greatest disappointments," she told me as she began to describe her personal sense of perspective, "were losses more tragic than disappointing. My father died when he was forty-two, only two years older than I am now. I was nine at the time. He was born with a bad heart and could never do the things other fathers could do, but he stayed cheerful and he was up and he had a good life, though he died so young. My mother, who died . . ." Her voice lost its timbre, her eyes misted and she paused.

"We don't have to discuss this," I offered.

"I want to," she said.

When she started speaking again, her voice had regained its tone: "I watched my mother for the last year and a half die of cancer . . . It's hard for me to talk about it . . . it has only been four months."

"How old was your mother?" I asked.

"She was only sixty-three," Sherry replied, "and for the six months prior to her death she lived with excruciating suffering. Death was a blessing in that sense, though I miss her. In the cancer ward were women who were only twenty, and they, too, were dying . . ." She paused again.

"That's the difference between disappointment and tragedy, as well as I can describe it. I'm sure that one of the reasons that I don't get destroyed when a picture doesn't work or a business setback occurs or a boyfriend doesn't call anymore is that I try very hard not to lose perspective. Weigh the suffering of a quadriplegic against the failure of a film and the difference between tragedy and disappointment is evident. If I were in pain and dying of cancer, I'd have the right to be depressed. If a new movie that I love doesn't do forty million dollars, that may be disappointing, but it's *not* tragic.

"Most people have been exposed to tragedy. Because my father died when I was so young and he was sick, I've always had a sense of perspective. So even when I had my accident, I thought: Well, it's not such a bad accident . . ."

"Sherry," I interrupted, "when was that?"

"About eight years ago," she replied, "I was thirty-two and had only recently become an executive at Columbia Pictures. A car traveling forty miles an hour struck me as I crossed the street. Everything was right, the light was right, I was right, but the accident happened. I had no control over it.

"I was thrown twenty feet and my head was split . . ." She traced a path from between her eyes to the top of her skull with her finger. "And they expected me to die. When I woke up in intensive care I was told that they might have to amputate my leg. I remember thinking that at least I was alive. A wonderful surgeon was able to save my leg, but I wore a nineteen-pound cast for eighteen months. I didn't die. I healed. I got better. I was lucky. I was *able* to heal, to get better. Those who suffer and cannot heal are the ones who can complain. I think a sense of perspective also allows you to become successful because it doesn't permit your defeats to seem so terrible."

"Sherry," I asked, "what would you advise someone seeking success?"

"One, enjoy the day," she replied. "And, two, stay in the game. Let me explain. I began as a reader earning five dollars an hour. I tried to be the best reader I could be. Then I was made head of all the readers. I liked both jobs and I tried hard. I didn't say, 'This is a crummy job, and what I really want is to run a studio or to produce movies.' If you enjoy what you're doing, your days will be enjoyable and the experience will inevitably lead to success.

" 'Stay in the game' means just that. The major difference I've found between the highly successful and the least successful is that the highly successful stick to it. They have staying power. *Everybody* fails. Everybody takes his knocks, but the highly successful keep coming back. Last week I had lunch with a girlfriend who is a successful star of a television series. We had been commercial models together. She asked me, 'Did you ever think we'd be able to have lunch like this twenty years later?' We just kept plugging along."

I reported in the last chapter how Annie Glenn had examined her fear, found it real, then took action. Earlier, Alex Haley told us how he considered ending his life at the stern of a ship but, instead, accepted the moral authority of his ancestors' words, then took action. After my mother suggested to my father and me that we talk to an attorney about the used car I bought, *we* took action. In each case someone accepted responsibility, someone examined the situation and someone found a solution. *You* are someone. If you accept responsibility, examine your experience and *focus on solutions,* not only will you apply the principles of Responsibility-Insight-Perspective successfully and thus profit from your errors, but you'll also find that anxiety can be your ally. RIP isn't just for mistakes; it's for life. Only when Jack Anderson finally owned up to his biggest blunder was he able to set stricter rules for himself so that he would be a better journalist. "I have seen really good people make really big mistakes," Sherry Lansing said, "but they're the same people who create giant successes."

As I watched Sherry Lansing's car pass out of sight as she returned to a movie on location somewhere in Los Angeles, I considered her reply to the last question I had asked her: "Are you afraid to fail?"

"No," she had answered without hesitating, "I'm not afraid to fail. I think that if you're afraid to fail, you won't take risks—and *if you always play it safe, you'll fail for sure.* I don't want to fail, but I *have* failed—and I've survived it to succeed again."

I thought about an early afternoon twenty years earlier when, at a place only a couple of hours' drive away, *I* had to decide whether to play it safe. I could almost feel the moisture beading on the back of my neck as it had the day I stood at attention under the warm midday sun with more than a hundred other Marines a few yards from our barracks at Camp Pendleton, in California.

I remembered wondering why we had so unexpectedly been ordered to formation. Our executive officer, a tall, lean captain, emerged from one of the offices, walked briskly toward the assembled men, stopped, turned stiffly and faced us. We'll find out now, I thought.

"I need volunteers—" he began, and I silently groaned to myself. Not this time, I vowed. It was 1965 and I was a twenty-year-old corporal, an NCO with only a few months left to serve on active duty. Not me, sir.

"—for duty in Southeast Asia," he continued. "Not all of you will be assigned," he said. "Some will stay back at Pendleton. Volunteers take one step forward . . ."

It must be chilly in New York this time of year, I told myself, but it will be steaming hot in Vietnam. No reason to volunteer, none of that gung-ho stuff for me. I should play it safe. I'm a short-timer. Let someone else step forward this time. Why do they have to ask me *now?* Most of these guys won't volunteer anyway, not the Marines I serve with, not these, the world's greatest gripers. Well, some of them might, but I'll bet half don't. Knock it off, Anderson. Are you going with them,

I asked myself, or not? If I volunteer, those who don't will tease me unmercifully. I took a deep breath. I don't believe what I'm about to do. I know I'm going to make a mistake. My jaw tightened. I stepped forward.

"At ease!" the captain ordered, and for at least half a minute he was silent.

I looked to my left, to my right. A single laugh erupted, followed by another, then another, until everyone, even the captain, was laughing. Each man had assessed the risk and had drawn his own conclusion.

Every Marine, officer and enlisted man alike, had volunteered.

Chapter 6

WHY AM I SO ANGRY?

I placed the letter in a manila envelope on my desk at *Parade* magazine. Awaiting the arrival of author and social historian Barbara Goldsmith, I thumbed through some clippings to review her background. She had been a senior editor of *Harper's Bazaar,* a founding writer and editor of *New York* magazine, a contributor to the *New York Times,* the *New Yorker, Esquire* and, with my encouragement, *Parade,* for which she'd interviewed Betty Ford and Robert De Niro and profiled, among others, the couple who helped to capture the infamous Nazi Klaus Barbie. She wrote the prize-winning best-seller *Little Gloria: Happy at Last,* the story about the ordeal of heiress Gloria Vanderbilt that inspired a popular television miniseries, as well as one of the most interesting novels I've ever read, *The Straw Man,* which explores an intense relationship between a father and his son.

I withdrew the letter from the manila envelope and studied two paragraphs in particular:

> My father's rage to live spilled over into every area. He was a dynamo and I adored him. I think it was this rage that propelled him through life and let him leave poverty and privation behind. But this was a twin-edged sword. I think he also resented that his own children had it

so easy and he felt that they could never appreciate the struggle he had gone through.

Finally, I think that there can only be one bull in the herd, which is a theme that I amplified in *The Straw Man.* The father in my novel felt that if he were not dominant he would lose power, and he thought of his son as a possession. I took that directly from my relationship with my own father.

I again replaced the letter in the folder.

This would be an extraordinary interview, I suspected. Although Barbara Goldsmith was a daughter, not a son, and her father had been a brilliant business leader, a millionaire many times over, her relationship with him was, I knew, remarkably similar to what I had experienced in my own family. In this chapter you'll see how Barbara and I, under decidedly different circumstances, resolved the tension between ourselves and our fathers. More, you'll learn about anger itself, its value as well as its costs. *Why am I so angry?* My story begins shortly after I arrived in Vietnam.

"Here's some papers for you!" the Marine PFC shouted as he lifted across his lap a tightly wrapped bundle of *Stars and Stripes* and tossed it out the window of his truck, a green camouflaged personnel carrier. The package landed softly in the sand a few feet away.

"How bad was it last night?" he asked. His voice was excited, too excited to suit me.

"Move it," rasped an unshaven staff sergeant seated near me, his voice and patience worn reed-thin after the sleepless night we had shared.

Disappointed, the PFC raised his eyebrows, shook his head and said, "Well, anyway, there's your papers." He thrust the truck noisily into gear, and it rolled toward another group of Marines who were also seated in the sand about thirty yards away near a large green canvas tent.

"How bad was it last night?" shouted the PFC to the new group, his voice carrying clearly back to us through the silent, steamy air.

It was hot. I was moist and sticky and my undershirt and trousers felt heavy and wet. It was 0900, October 26, 1965, at a helicopter landing strip in East Da Nang, in the Republic of Vietnam. I was a corporal. The China Sea was only a few feet away, and nearby Marble Mountain seemed to rise like a foreboding hill of charcoal out of the sand. A few hours earlier, four minutes after midnight by my watch, this camp and its few hundred servicemen had come under a surprise attack by the Viet Cong—a thunderous assault that instantly awoke everyone, including me. Several helicopters were lost in brilliant, searing explosions. Some Marines died.

"Hey, Andy," a lance corporal called to me, "look at this crap!"

He handed me a copy of *Stars and Stripes,* which he had taken from the bundle. I read the story that had angered him, a report of an anti-Vietnam protest demonstration.

I stood.

"Where are you going?" the staff sergeant asked.

"I'm going to see if I can find a typewriter," I replied.

"In that mess?"

A few yards away another unit's "headquarters" tent, a small office complex, had become a casualty of the night, its overturned chairs, cardboard file boxes, volumes of reports, orders and paper folders in disarray. I lifted and probed and finally found a sticky, stained, but serviceable manual typewriter.

I set firmly in the sand a cardboard carton holding C-rations, placed the typewriter on top of it, inserted a sheet of paper I had found, sat on a small stool, and with the sun burning into my neck and back, I started to write a letter that, though I didn't know it at the time, would help decide the course of my life. I typed:

> Just what is Vietnam?
>
> It is a most beautiful 16-year-old girl, who fluently speaks three languages . . . an elderly man who can barely speak his own village dialect. It is a Montagnard chieftain sawing out a girl's teeth as she reaches the "age of wisdom" . . . she sheds not a tear. It is a cocktail party in Saigon . . . a raiding party in Plei Me.
>
> It is an orphanage in Da Nang with a Marine "adopting" a small child

for the day . . . that Marine in a foxhole at night. It is fear . . . and humor as only servicemen accomplish. It is receiving a letter from home . . . and no mail. It is our paper . . . the *Stars and Stripes.*

It is heat, dust, sand . . . and it is monsoon. It is jungle . . . and mountain range. It is insects . . . and malaria pills. It is never-ending shots from the "Doc" . . . it is shots from V.C. It is a people fighting for their freedom . . . and those against it.

It is Charlie who believes he is "liberating" the Vietnamese peasants . . . It is Charlie defecting when he learns he was duped. It is the sorrowful experience of reading about an anti-U.S. Vietnam demonstration.

It is pride when reading of congressmen and college students giving blood. It is hate . . . and it is love. It is boys becoming men . . . and it is men dying. It is a sense of knowledge . . . and doing what is really right by God and country. It is cleaning a rifle . . . and firing a rifle. It is a rich American . . . and a poor child.

It is rice paddies . . . and it is Xichlo (cyclo) cabs. It is sampans . . . and it is the U.S.S. Coral Sea. It is Military Pay Currency, "funny money" . . . and it is piasters. It is an ARVN friend . . . and a Viet Cong prisoner. It is an order obeyed . . . and a mission accomplished. It is aiding a villager . . . and curing the sick . . . helping the needy help themselves. It is a chaplain at Chu Lai . . . It is the .45 on his hip.

Above and beyond all else . . . it is Americans helping a people remain free . . . not by blood alone, but by the more important concern, realization of human compassion. It is, by the alertness and courage of our country, accomplishment! As God will judge, we are right!"

Only when I had finished typing did I become aware that the staff sergeant and the lance corporal stood side by side behind me.

"That's *something,*" the staff sergeant said.

"What are you going to do with it?" the lance corporal asked.

"I don't know," I said, "maybe send it home."

The obituary I had withdrawn from the manila envelope appeared in the *New York Times* on April 6, 1983:

Joseph I. Lubin, co-founder of the Eisner & Lubin nationwide accounting firm, who gave more than $10 million to universities, died of a heart ailment Monday at New Rochelle (N.Y.) Hospital. He was 83 years old and lived in New Rochelle. Mr. Lubin, who was born in Brooklyn, made large donations to Pace University, New York University, Syracuse University, the Albert Einstein College of Medicine of Yeshiva University, and Hebrew University in Jerusalem, among others . . . In August, 1981, he gave $7.5 million to Pace University—the largest single private donation ever given that institution . . . Many of Mr. Lubin's philanthropies were made jointly with his wife, the former Evelyn Cronson, who died in October, 1981. In 1966, the Lubins donated $1.3 million to found the Evelyn and Joseph I. Lubin Rehabilitation Center on the Bronx campus of the Albert Einstein College of Medicine . . . Mr. Lubin graduated from Pace Institute in 1921, before it became Pace University. Attending night classes, he received a law degree from New York University in 1928. In addition to Eisner & Lubin, Mr. Lubin was active in real-estate investment and development. In the late 1950's, he headed a syndicate that bought the Astor Hotel on Times Square, a hotel at which he had worked as a pageboy when he was in grade school.

I was studying the report when Joseph I. Lubin's younger daughter, the author Barbara Goldsmith, entered my office. She was in her early fifties, but she looked at least a decade younger. Her black hair was long and full, her wide-set brown eyes alert behind amber glasses. She was thin, her gray flannel pants and gray wool sweater neatly matching. She gestured gracefully and spoke in a vibrant, compelling voice.

"Let the questions begin," she announced.

"First, the feast," I suggested, pointing to a tuna salad delivered from a delicatessen only a few minutes earlier.

She smiled. "This is better than going out," she declared. "We'll really get some work done!"

A half hour later we sat together in an adjoining office where no phone calls could reach us, and I asked Barbara Goldsmith to describe her father.

"He was absolutely brilliant," she began. "He came from the poorest of the poor families. As a child he had to stuff newspaper in his shoes to cover the holes in his soles. He went to school thirteen years at night to become a lawyer and an accountant and a tax expert. He was fiercely determined to move ahead."

"Were you afraid of your father?" I asked.

"I realized very young," she answered, "that the way to get his attention was not to give in to him. Members of our family would say that I was the only person not afraid of my father. They were wrong. His anger was terrifying to me, but somehow I sensed that if I let him break my spirit, he would not like me. The truth is that any small child is scared of a volatile parent. I appeared to be unafraid, but I was, of course, afraid."

"Barbara," I asked, "was your father violent?"

"Yes," she said, "he was, and the eruptions could not necessarily be anticipated. Once, on a train, my mother was about to sit down when a man quickly slipped into the seat, which left her standing. My father grabbed the man by his collar, jerked him out of the seat and tossed him down the length of the car."

"Did he ever hurt *you*?"

"Yes," she replied, "for example, when I was eleven he thought I was acting fresh; he'd ordered me to be quiet, but I insisted, 'I'm going to tell you what I think!' and he wrenched my arm hard enough to dislocate my shoulder. My mother pretended that nothing had happened. She told the doctor that I had slipped in the street and injured myself. Then, when she brought me home with my arm in a sling, my father *cried*. I had never seen him cry. It was terrible! I felt guilty. The fact that he had violently dislocated my shoulder was lost in this enormous guilt that I suffered. *I* had caused my father to cry.

"A child at home is defenseless, not really knowing how to cope. When I was researching *Little Gloria: Happy at Last*, I came to understand that there are no class distinctions as far as violence is concerned. No one knows what shame occurs behind closed doors, even those that open to the most lavish of mansions. Whitney Tower told me that as a child he had climbed a tree to watch his grandfather, Harry Payne Whitney, play tennis when he fell from the branches and snapped his collarbone. Harry Payne Whitney, he said, stormed off the court, fuming, 'Get that kid out of here—he's ruining my service!'

"When Frank made *Mommie Dearest*," Barbara Goldsmith continued, referring to her husband, Frank Perry, the director of several major films, including *David and Lisa* and *Diary of a Mad Housewife,* "he researched Joan Crawford independently of the book that Christina Crawford wrote. He discovered alcohol-induced rages contrasting with moments of cloying sweetness. The children had no anchor in reality at all. For example, one story that's not in the book occurred when Joan Crawford arrived home with friends, produced a box of chocolates to offer to her guests but, when she opened it, found one piece missing. It was the middle of the night, but nevertheless she woke up her adopted children, confronted them, and when the boy named Chris admitted that it was he who had eaten the missing chocolate, Joan Crawford forced him to eat the whole box in front of her guests. When he finally vomited, he was sent to bed. No one protested, because their hostess, the star, was too powerful.

"In self-made people there's often a deep residual anger because they recognize that their children have it much easier than they did. I know of no self-made man who can perceive his own children to be as resilient, as tough, as persistent as he is. My father felt that my older sister and I were ungrateful, that we took what we had for granted— and he was right! How could we be grateful for what we always had?

"My father insisted when my sister and I were very young that we experience what he called 'the real world,' which to him meant the rough-and-tumble life he had lived. Thus, he ordered that we be enrolled in public school.

"My mother, on the other hand, was the daughter of a distinguished surgeon, and she was gentle in every way with her perfect needlepoint, her perfect sewing and Chopin on the piano. Because the daily care of the children was left to her, my sister and I became a battleground on which our parents played out their unresolved conflicts about child rearing and social class. When I was sent to P.S. 93 at Ninety-third Street and Amsterdam Avenue, I would unstrap the leggings my mother made me wear as soon as I got outside, because I knew that if the other kids saw me with my English coat with the velvet collar and leggings, I'd be laughed out of the school. When I contracted head lice at P.S. 93, every night my English nanny would comb my hair with a fine-tooth steel comb dipped in kerosene as I read French fairy tales.

In the afternoons a nurse would drop me off at ballet class, and in the evenings I'd have foreign language lessons. On weekends my father would take me to play the pinball machines at the Blackstone Hotel and warn me with the words I heard frequently as a child, 'Don't tell your mother.' "

She paused, reflecting. "It was most painful in my childhood," she began again, "to recognize from the earliest age that my father really wanted a son. He called me 'Bobby' and encouraged everyone else to do the same, and they generally did, except for my mother, who called me 'Babs.' They didn't even call me by the same name. I was the only girl on the baseball team; I was the catcher. My father from time to time took me to the fights at Madison Square Garden. He'd be delighted when, at seven years old, I could recount who knocked out whom in what round.

"There was never a 'Good enough!' in my childhood. An A was not an A-plus. A silver medal in swimming was not a gold. My father was never able to separate his children from himself. If they failed, he failed, which I could not understand as a child. Instead, I tried to be everything, to succeed with diametrically opposed goals. For example, as a senior at New Rochelle High School—we moved from Manhattan to New Rochelle in Westchester County when I was about ten—I was a cheerleader, and I was editor of the school newspaper.

"There were, of course, many sides to my father. He literally burst with life, and sometimes his achievements became apparent in surprising ways. One day when I was caught in the rain in downtown Manhattan, I raced into a large building at Pace University to escape the downpour. Inside there was an enormous medallion of my father. It was the Lubin School of Business Administration. I was aware of his gift, but I had never seen the building. I felt small, powerless, facing this pervasive presence. This experience would become the basis of a scene in *The Straw Man*."

Anger is the child of frustration. We are not born angry. We learn it —almost immediately. Moreover, as Barbara Goldsmith discovered, anger and violence make no class distinctions. At every level of society unchecked anger has provoked violent outbursts, assaults and biting insults, murder and suicide. It has caused or aggravated physical problems like headaches, high blood pressure, heart attacks and ulcers. It's often concealed in complaining and whining. It's even possible, as many psychiatrists think, that a crippling emotional condition like depression is *suppressed* anger.

When we were infants, our desires were quickly satisfied, but it wasn't long before we were encouraged to adjust to the will of others and to live with the frustration of not having our own way. We learned to eat and sleep on a schedule assigned by others. We were forced to use strange utensils to eat with, although our fingers worked just fine. Even our bladders were disciplined. In succeeding years we had to learn to adapt more and more to school, to work, to the demands of someone else. Countless times we have been assured that controlling our temper is a measure of our maturity. Is it any wonder, then, that we frequently conceal, even deny, our anger?

As important as exercising restraint is, however, it's only half the story. The destructive potential of anger was apparent when my father tried to beat me in the middle of the night, when I raised a pool cue to threaten another teenager, when I clenched my fists over the young marine whose mother had died. On the other hand, the constructive potential of anger was evident in the pledge I made when I was fourteen: "I'm getting out of here." While we diligently study anger's ugliness, we often neglect to recognize its positive side. Anger is an affirmation that we exist, that we care. *Why am I so angry?* Asking the question begins the process of making anger, like anxiety, an ally in our lives. Anger can help us improve, motivate us to achieve noble goals and—most important—be an invaluable alarm system in our day-to-day lives. Anger is, after all, a form of *energy*. Properly directed, this energy can alert us to legitimate concerns; it can give us the needed push to face some of life's most difficult challenges. It can help us say *yes*. Yes, I care.

When the citizen pounds his fist at a town board meeting and raises his voice to decry injustice, he's really shouting that he's concerned, that he's willing to say it aloud, that he's willing to overcome his own fear of expressing his anger, that he believes strongly that good can result.

Anger gets things done. It's the energy that inspires creative acts. Anger prompted my letter from Vietnam, and it undoubtedly influenced Barbara Goldsmith to write *The Straw Man.* Anger is the push that moves you to demand a raise, the burst that sends the depleted athlete sprinting across the finish line, the nudge that moves you to find a better job or a better life.

I've learned three A's to make anger an ally: *Admit it, Analyze it, Answer it.*

First, admit you're angry. Sound easy? Often we deny it even to ourselves, especially when it seems coldly selfish or irrational, as when I pushed myself up Park Avenue to meet Prince Michael for the first time. The unfettered anger a small boy may exhibit at his mother's death—"She left me alone and I hate her!"—is easier to comprehend than the frustration we feel when a boss doesn't treat us like one of the family or we must wait in line. More than simply saying the words, feel them: *I am angry!*

Second, analyze the anger. What *is* the frustration? When you're stuck in a traffic jam, the problem's out of your control; it's out there on the road and there's nothing you can do about it. When your feelings are hurt because your teacher doesn't treat you as if she were your mother, ask yourself, "Is my anger appropriate?" Be honest; this is a toughie. The answer could end your anger. On the other hand, if you're denied a promotion because of race, sex, age or nationality, your anger *is* appropriate—and useful.

Third, deal with the anger. If you're in a traffic jam, you're stuck. Acceptance *is* your answer, because that's all you can do about it. That's when all those lessons about controlling your temper have value. Relax. No one else is moving, either. If, however, you've been unfairly denied a promotion, anger is ready to work *for* you. The adrenaline's flowing, the blood's rushing—you've never been more alert. Don't squander that precious energy agitating about the unfairness of your plight: "Oh, poor me, how I suffer." Instead, while your anger has you sharp, explore the possibilities, the opportunities. Should you quit or should you fight? If you choose the former, actively start your search. If you decide to fight, research how others in similar situations have succeeded—then proceed. *Focus on a solution,* and anger will be your ally, which I was doing, without having thought it through, when I sat down in Vietnam to write my letter.

After it lay folded in my pocket for a couple of days, I finally decided to mail what I had typed, "Just what is Vietnam?" to my hometown newspaper, the *Daily Argus* in Mount Vernon, New York, as a letter to the editor. Then I forgot about it.

A few weeks later our platoon commander, Lieutenant Brian Gillian, called me from Da Nang and told me that I had been promoted to sergeant.

"Hop a ride to mainside," he suggested, "so the company commander can make this official and the rest of us can congratulate you."

"Yes sir," I said, acutely aware that it had to be the lieutenant himself who had recommended the promotion. It was unusual. I was twenty-one, and although I had already served almost three months longer than my original four-year enlistment because of various extensions, I had made it clear that I was not going to be a career Marine. In four months I would be released from active duty, a civilian again, and, as anyone within earshot of me would have confirmed, I was counting the days.

"Why did you promote me?" I asked the lieutenant.

"Because," he said, "in case you haven't noticed, you're in the Marine Corps. No one here cares whether you're a short-timer or a lifer. Anyway, there might not be a 'four months from now' for anyone. We want the best people in charge day to day. We'll worry about 'four months' in four months. Congratulations!"

He put out his hand. I shook it and said, "Thank you, sir."

"Are you going right back to the airstrip?" he asked.

"I'm going to pick up the mail for our guys," I said, "then hitch a ride. I'll celebrate this promotion when we get back to California."

"I'll bet you will," he said, laughing.

When I signed for the mail, I was handed a canvas pouch with about forty letters and, to my astonishment, discovered that more than thirty were addressed to me. The editor of the *Daily Argus* had published what I had written that October morning in East Da Nang not on the letters page but on the front page, November 20, 1965—copies of which were enclosed with several of the letters. A boot-camp picture of me in dress blue uniform appeared with the article and, I noticed immediately, I was identified as a corporal. The page was packed with Vietnam stories: "South Viets Join Battle," "U.S. Cavalrymen Given Help in Ia Drang Area," "California Police Ready for Viet Peace Marchers," "North Viet Troops Seen Matching U.S. Buildup," "A Suggestion: Draft Cards of Aluminum," "Communist Party Plans to Appeal Conviction for Not Registering," and—flush in the middle— my picture with this headline, "Just What Is Vietnam? City Marine Tells Us."

A letter from my mother began, "Daddy and I are very proud of you."

I pause here to emphasize the choices that anger affords us. We may, as I have said, sublimate that energy into positive activities like problem-solving, jogging, rearranging furniture or working harder. We can create a sculpture or write a poem—or we can give vent to the anger by kicking a chair, unfairly punishing a child, grumbling at co-workers or picking on our spouse. But whatever we do, something happens to that energy, something we determine.

If the causes of that energy are as deeply hidden as the anger arising from lingering, unresolved conflicts with our parents, the energy's potential can be especially volatile. We can allow ourselves to repeat the very behavior we detest. That was the choice that faced me when I arrived home from Vietnam.

673 Locust Street was an apartment house in the Fleetwood section of Mount Vernon, only a few blocks from Immanuel Lutheran School. It was the address to which my parents moved after my father retired in his mid-fifties from Consolidated Edison while I was in Vietnam.

"It even has an elevator," my father told me when I arrived on leave shortly before Christmas, 1965. "But," he added, "that don't mean nothing to me." Such comments, I knew, were storm warnings. Trouble was brewing in my father's mind.

I was weary, and the last thing I wanted was an argument. This stay, I thought to myself, is going to be short. A group of us had been flown from Vietnam to Okinawa, where we stayed one raucous night, then we flew directly to El Toro, California, where we received our orders. I was assigned to the San Diego Marine Corps Recruit Depot, but was given a fifteen-day leave before reporting. I wondered whether I had wasted the few dollars I had by flying to New York.

"Vietnam ain't nothing!" my father started from the kitchen. "The Marines neither—just like your brother with his police action, Korea was no war!"

In the living room with my mother, I told her, "Mom, I love you, but I can't stay."

"I don't want you to leave," she said, her eyes filling, "but I understand. Sometimes I think it gets better, then . . ."

My father shouted, "I know you're talking in there!" I heard a chair scrape the linoleum floor of the kitchen, and looking up as I was repacking my seabag, I saw my father standing in the hallway between the two rooms. His neck and face had reddened and his eyes were narrowed. "You're going nowhere!" he challenged, his voice hard and angry.

I closed the seabag and laid it aside as I slipped on my marine jacket, then stepped toward my father.

"Where do you think *you're* going?" he demanded.

"I'm leaving."

"No, you're not!"

"Take a good look at me," I said, my voice harsh. "I'm not the kid you used to beat up . . ."

"What do you think *you're* going to do?" he taunted.

My mother pleaded, "Please . . . stop it . . . let him go . . ."

At six feet, I was two inches taller than my father, thirty-five years younger, and though I had only a 32-inch waist, I was at least twenty-five pounds heavier than he was.

"*Look* at me!" I ordered.

He looked directly into my eyes.

"What do you see?" I asked.

"Nothing much," he said, "nothing I can't handle."

It was as if a clock had stopped ticking in my brain; time dissolved. I had been driven beyond reason, even beyond anger. Inside me a little boy who had been brutalized screamed for revenge. A lifetime of provocation, of guilt, had come down to a single instant. There were only two people in the world and I was one of them. If there were sounds, I didn't hear them.

"You have beaten me for the last time," I told my father, my voice deep and even, "and if you stand in my way, I'll walk right through you. I'm no boy anymore. You have no power over me. You can't stop me. If you hit me now, I'm going to drop you where you stand. For the rest of my life I'll regret it, but father or not, I'll punch you out. Now, what are *you* going to do?"

I waited, unblinking.

My father, to my astonishment, looked away and lowered his head. I didn't understand. Was he going to try to sucker-punch me? My ears throbbed.

He raised his head, faced me again and said very softly, "Please stay."

"What?" I blurted, confused.

"Please stay, Walter," he said, his shoulders falling. My father seemed to shrink before my eyes. He tried to speak, but no words came. He squeezed my forearm, turned and silently walked into the kitchen.

I looked toward my mother.

"Go talk to him," she whispered, nodding.

I did.

"Barbara, how did you resolve the relationship with your father?" I asked.

"Gradually," she said, "I began to emerge. The irony is that the more I became my own person, the more he respected me. My husband, Frank, was wonderful in helping me to begin to form a rapprochement with my father. One afternoon my father and I were having a furious argument. In the middle of it, my father, in obvious frustration, asked Frank, 'Why is she like this?'

"Frank replied, 'Because there is a lot of her that is just like you.'

"From that moment my father began to ease up on me, and I began to admit that I was harder on him than on anyone else, because, as Frank saw so clearly, I was a lot like my father. During the next years, as my father and I grew closer, I learned to handle potentially volatile situations in different ways. When my mother was ill with cancer, my parents came to live with us because our home was close to Memorial Hospital. One morning my father, who was then eighty-one, stormed into my bedroom. 'Where's my *New York Times?*' he screamed at the top of his lungs, accusing me of taking *his* newspaper. Of course, it was *my* home and *my* newspaper, but I didn't argue. The next morning and every morning thereafter I had two newspapers delivered. When my father died, he was my friend. I loved his brilliance, his clarity and generosity, and, finally, I learned to listen to him without my own fears distorting the message.

"While my father's emotions were large and seemed unfocused, my mother, on the other hand, appeared unemotional. I don't ever remember her saying, 'I love you,' but before she died I began to understand her. She told me, 'I have one tremendous regret in life, that my father would not allow me to go to medical school. He said I was a girl and my health was too fragile.' She became human to me. Imagine harboring that regret at eighty-one. She was a woman, a person, and we learned to communicate. I can think of nothing more important for me to know than that each of my parents died with no unfinished business between us."

"Sergeant Anderson?" the freshly pressed and polished Duty NCO, who couldn't have been more than nineteen, called into my quarters at San Diego Marine Corps Recruit Depot. I glanced at the clock next to my rack. It was 0535, a Saturday morning in February 1966. One of the men in my outfit must be in trouble, I thought. I was platoon sergeant of a unit of Marines, all of whom were Vietnam veterans and, like me, were short-timers.

"What is it, Lance Corporal?" I asked.

"The chaplain needs to see you, Sarge," he said.

"Anything else?"

"That's all. Just find you."

Such a summons was not welcome news. Somebody was in trouble or sick or had a problem at home. I dressed quickly, not showering. The lance corporal stayed in the doorway.

"You can take off," I told him. "I know where the chaplain is."

"That's OK, Sarge," he replied. "I'll walk you over."

Then I knew it was I, not one of my troops, who had the problem. The lance corporal fidgeted, averting his eyes. I suspected by his uneasiness that he had been ordered not to volunteer any information.

"My father?" I asked.

"I don't have any details," he answered. "The chaplain will talk to you about it."

"Is it my father?"

"Yes."

"How bad?" I asked.

"I really don't know."

When we arrived at the chaplain's office, the lance corporal wished me luck. I thanked him and stepped inside. My father was very sick, the chaplain explained. Transportation was being provided for me to the San Diego airport, which adjoined the Marine Recruit Depot, for a flight to the Los Angeles airport, where I would board a commercial plane to New York.

Two hours later, while awaiting my flight at the Los Angeles airport, I called home.

"Daddy didn't make it," my sister-in-law told me. "Bill took him to the veterans hospital. He passed away there."

After I hung up the phone, I walked stiffly into a men's room on the same level, entered a stall where I could not be seen, and cried. I touched my tears, well aware that if I had not gotten to know my father better before he died, I would have felt nothing—because on that leave only a few weeks earlier, I had, after twenty years of tension, finally talked to him. He was an alcoholic, unstable and unpredictable, whose own parents both died in institutions, his father a suicide. He was also a World War II veteran, a former Army sergeant who had been captured, tortured and held in German concentration camps. For years he was an active volunteer fireman, a captain, and saved lives in Mount Vernon. He was an emergency lineman who toiled amid high-tension, high-voltage wires. In 1954, when I was ten years old, he was electrocuted during Hurricane Hazel and thrown thirty feet to the ground, but, after months in a wheelchair, he returned to work, although he had been told by doctors he'd never climb again.

"Walter," he told me the morning I left New York to report to San Diego, "I'm proud of you. Everything you've done, Vietnam, being a sergeant, writing that story in the paper. Everything . . ."

Our eyes filled. We both knew my childhood was irretrievable. Neither he nor I could live those years differently or take away the pain, but I could—and did—learn from him, if only for a few days. I came to understand his fears, and this released me. He was not an awesome force I would have to spend the rest of my life failing to please. He was frightened, like the rest of us.

"And," he added in the last words I would hear him speak, "I love you."

"Barbara," I said, "I once heard it argued that a boy cannot be a man until his father dies either literally or symbolically. Do you think that's true?"

"When my mother died," she answered, "we were good friends. When my father died, we were good friends. Resolving the struggle between parent and child—looking at each other honestly—may be the most important mountain we can climb. We cannot truly be ourselves until we make that resolution. I have a friend who, twenty years after his father's death, wrote his father a letter telling him all that was on his mind. It freed him. It was never necessary for his father to read the letter, only that the son write it."

I turned the tape recorder off, reached over and hugged Barbara Goldsmith.

.   .   .

I sat board-straight in a chair facing the desk of the man who was editor of the *Reporter Dispatch,* a local daily newspaper in White Plains, New York.

William I. Bookman was a slender man no taller than five feet four inches with a smooth face, more pink than white, and brown eyes that fell into laugh lines behind clear glasses. His hair was gray and neatly combed. His voice was as gentle as his manner, confident, sincere and friendly. I waited, trying to conceal my nervousness as he quietly studied my résumé, two typewritten pages I had handed to him.

It was March 1967. Upon release from active duty the year before, I had tried working for Nevis Laboratories, a division of Columbia University, but the transition from Marine sergeant to helper was too difficult for me. When one of the scientists referred to me twice as "boy," I resigned. It was an uneasy time for Vietnam veterans, I learned quickly. Personnel interviewers seemed inevitably to focus on the tour I had served in Southeast Asia, never failing to ask why I had been there, as if I had chosen an odd way to spend a summer vacation. One interviewer suggested that I undergo a battery of tests, a psychological exam. I considered concealing my service record, felt shame at the thought, reconsidered and vowed to myself that I would not deny my time in the Marine Corps. After Nevis, I was hired as a sales trainee by Metropolitan Life Insurance Company in Manhattan about ten months before the interview with the *Reporter Dispatch.* Although the people at Metropolitan were supportive—even encouraging me to speak before groups about Vietnam—I was an erratic salesman. I knew that selling policies, however valuable the service, was not for me. I wanted to write. I *desperately* wanted to write.

The editor looked up from the typed pages. He asked, "Why do you want to be a reporter?"

"Because," I answered, "I've wanted to write for as long as I can remember. It is *all* I want to do. If you give me a chance, Mr. Bookman, I won't disappoint you. I earn nearly two hundred dollars a week at Metropolitan, but I'd be willing to work at your newspaper for bus fare. Give me the opportunity to prove myself or to fail. Two weeks. If, after two weeks, you feel I can't be a good reporter, I'll quietly leave."

"Most of the people who work here are college graduates," he said. "Have you ever taken a journalism course?"

"No, sir," I replied, "I have not."

"But you still think you can be a reporter?"

"Yes, I do."

"Why?"

"Mr. Bookman," I asked, "what are the differences between someone you promote and someone you fire?"

He mentioned integrity, curiosity, sensitivity, clarity, desire, drive and persistence, enthusiasm and self-confidence.

"Never once," I pointed out, "have you mentioned a college degree. None of what you've told me can be printed as courses in a university catalogue."

He smiled. "Where would you expect to find stories?" he asked. "And what are people interested in?"

"Mr. Bookman," I said, "there are stories in every structure on every block in this or any other city. People are interested in people. Families, lives, struggles, joy, sadness, triumph and tragedy, trying and tripping —it's all there, if we only open our eyes to it . . ."

Aware that my voice was rising and that I was gesticulating, I felt my face redden and I stopped.

"No, keep going," he suggested.

"It's just that I see these stories around me every day," I said, my voice calm again, "and I'd like to write about them."

"Have you ever been published?" he asked.

"Just a letter I wrote when I was in Vietnam."

"Can I read it?"

I reached into my pocket, withdrew the newspaper clipping and handed it to him across the desk. I waited in silence, the anxiety rising. Had I made a mistake? Why did I mention it? What if he doesn't like it?

Finally, he nodded.

"That's *very* good," he said.

Three days later William I. Bookman, who had been an Army sergeant during World War II, called to offer me a job as a reporter with his newspaper at ninety dollars per week. I would have accepted much less. My flesh tingled, my eyes filled, my smile was involuntary.

"Think about it for a couple of days," he suggested.

"I don't have to," I exclaimed. "Yes!"

"Well then," he replied, his chuckle rumbling over the telephone lines, "welcome aboard."

"Mr. Bookman," I said, "thank you."

Chapter 7

CAN I BEGIN AGAIN?

Allen H. Neuharth lifted the sterling silver pitcher and asked, "How do you take your coffee, Walt?"

"Black, please," I said, "and thank you."

It was 8:00 A.M., November 21, 1984, in suite 31A of the Waldorf Towers in mid-Manhattan. Al Neuharth was the chairman and chief executive officer of Gannett Company, a billion-dollar corporation that owned more newspapers than any other chain in America, more than eighty—including the newspaper on which I had received my start, the *Reporter Dispatch*—and several television and radio stations. It was, as well, a leader in related industries and a pioneer in satellite communications. Only a few years earlier Gannett had been a small Northeastern newspaper group, but it had become, under Al Neuharth's leadership, one of America's most important and financially successful companies.

Probably more than anyone else I've known, Al Neuharth radiated energy. He even listened with intensity, shifting forward perceptibly, *watching* as well as hearing a speaker's words. His hair, in shades of gray and as wavy as a matinee idol's, seemed to match his gray shirt, black tie and black trousers. If he were cast in a cowboy movie, he'd be the silent gunfighter who did not boast, did not blink, did not miss. He was sixty, slim, and walked with the heel-to-toe roll and bounce of a young athlete. Some said he was one of the toughest executives in publishing. Others said no, he *was* the toughest. No one who knew Al Neuharth, a man willing to create as well as buy newspapers, would question his willingness to take a risk. I hoped to learn why.

"Al," I asked, "what was your childhood like in South Dakota before World War II?"

"I grew up in a world that was absolutely filled with anxiety, fear and dangers," he told me as we settled, coffee in hand, into adjoining green velvet couches. "My father died when I was two. I don't remember him. My mother, who had to care for my older brother and me, never married again. She was a tough Midwestern woman, not well educated —she only went through the fourth grade—but she made her way."

As he paused I asked, "How did she support you and your brother?"

"She did it," he replied, "by taking in sewing and washing and ironing and working in restaurants in a small South Dakota town. She could have married a farmer and lived comfortably. She had offers to do so. She decided, bless her heart, that it was better—after a few romances—for us to hold this little family of three people together."

"What did you learn?"

"I saw *every* day how many things can go wrong, but I also saw that somehow my mother prevailed. And she had her two sons to help her do that. When my brother was in eighth grade, he worked in a grocery store making a dollar or a dollar and a half a week. My first real job was a dollar a week in a butcher shop. Every dime or every dollar that the three of us brought in helped my mother hold this group of three people together, because her income was absolutely unpredictable. All she had when my father died was a small house that was paid for. I got to the point in grade school where I felt that I had to try anything— or everything—to succeed, and I learned to expect a lot of knocks, because"—his eyes moistened—"I had seen my mother take them. I really think, Walt, *that* was my real education, what I learned at home in my early years."

As Al Neuharth stood up to pour more coffee, I remembered how my own mother more than once when I was a child placed herself between me and my father, faced danger to protect me, how she'd encourage me to learn, to read, *always* to read. I don't remember my mother ever telling me there was something I could not achieve, only that I could.

"When did you first leave home?" I asked.

"I volunteered for the Army at age eighteen in 1942," he told me, "because I was afraid if I waited for the draft the war would be over and I'd miss out on it. My mom was scared, but she sent me off proudly. After infantry tours in Europe and in the Pacific with the Eighty-second Infantry Division, I came back four years later a lot wiser. I considered myself much too old at twenty-two to pursue a law career —I had started to study pre-law prior to my enlistment—so I opted for journalism. My college education was paid for partially by the GI Bill, partially by my working, partially by my first wife teaching school and helping to pay the bills. I believe the veterans' allowance for marrieds was about ninety dollars monthly. I earned fifteen dollars a week alternately in a butcher shop and as editor of the *Volante*, the University of South Dakota newspaper."

"Anything else?" I asked.

"That's it," he said.

"Anything interesting?"

"That's it."

I nodded, more aware than ever that Al Neuharth was not a man who lived in yesterday's glory; he had not mentioned two details I had picked up in earlier research, that he had received the Bronze Star in World War II and had graduated with honors from the University of South Dakota. I knew then, as he sat across from me, that if I could discover whether he handled his failures as well as he seemed to handle his triumphs, I'd be better able to understand not only a man I respected but the phenomenon of success itself.

"Have you ever said to yourself," I asked the executive who had founded the national newspaper *USA Today*, " 'What will I do when they find out I'm me?' "

"Maybe not in those exact words," he answered, "but yes . . . yes, every time that we try something different, we're not the sure, confident people that others picture."

"Have you ever failed, Al?"

"Of course I have," he said.

Can I begin again? Can I try something different or am I imprisoned by my past, by my failures, by others, by the world around me? Must I always be what I am? Can I really be more? *Can I begin again?* It may be the most difficult question we have to answer. We choose different hairstyles, paint rooms, buy new clothes, reorganize closets, straighten out personal finances, even lose old friends and make new ones. Far less often, though, do we encourage the kind of new beginnings that can make our lives more meaningful or personally satisfying. Taking those first steps means risk, means the possibility of failure. At no time do we need our allies—anxiety and anger—more.

I can still clearly recall taking a step toward a new beginning myself one spring evening in 1967 and how the anxiety rose within me as I stood alone facing the five-story *Reporter Dispatch* building in White Plains, New York.

Bill Bookman, the editor who hired me, had told me that morning to report at 7:00 P.M. to the night city editor, a fellow named Larry Smith, for training.

It was 6:15 P.M. as I looked up nervously at the second-floor windows. Should I cross the street, enter the building and take the elevator to the second floor or return to the parking lot, get in my car and drive home? Anderson, I thought, your bluff has been called; someone has given you a chance and you're scared. I looked at my watch again. It was still 6:15. I lowered my head and started to walk toward the parking lot. Then I stopped, turned and, before I could change my mind, crossed the street and pushed open the door to the *Reporter Dispatch.*

Larry Smith, whom I had expected to be a silver-haired editor wearing a green eyeshade, arrived about 6:50. To my surprise, he was only a couple of years older than I—a thin, brown-haired man with eyeglasses who wore a black vest over a neatly pressed white shirt. He gave me my first assignment, which was to attend a local beautification committee and to report back to him what had occurred. I remember that I returned three hours later with enough notes to fill a small book, enough to overwhelm and confuse me. Larry, a sincere and serious teacher, sat beside me for an hour and patiently taught me how to ferret out the few facts that I would need to write a brief report.

My first story was only a couple of paragraphs, deep inside the *Reporter Dispatch* the next day, and though it didn't contain my byline, I remember touching the newspaper, running my finger across the story as if it were alive. I *loved* the inky smell, the texture of the newsprint, the words themselves. It was as if a shade had finally been raised in a darkened room and I could see.

"I failed in a big way early in my career," Al Neuharth told me as we continued our discussion several weeks later in his corner office on the thirty-second floor of 535 Madison Avenue. Natural light entered the room through windowed walls that gave a long, wide and deep view of Manhattan's rooftops and skyline. Three television screens, each tuned to a different network, operated silently behind me and to my left as I sat facing the dark walnut desk of the chairman and chief executive officer of Gannett Company.

"Where did the failure occur?" I asked.

"In South Dakota," he said, "and it was called *SoDak Sports.*"

"What happened?"

"A pal of mine named Bill Porter," he began, "worked with me on the college newspaper, the *Volante.* I was the editor, and he was the business manager; I was a journalism major and he was in law school. We agreed that after graduation we would become rich and famous together in the publishing business. I purposely took a job with the Associated Press in Sioux Falls, which is the biggest city in the two Dakotas. Our plan was that I'd develop a name and make contacts, develop sources, become a known byline over the two years that Bill needed to finish law school.

"We met on weekends and evenings and plotted the strategy for our sportsweekly, *SoDak Sports.* We formed a small corporation, and we sold stock in our little company mainly to friends and relatives in blocks of one hundred and two hundred dollars. Our largest shareholder, as I recall, held only seven hundred dollars' worth of stock. We put together about fifty thousand dollars in cash and 'in kind'—by 'in kind' I mean that some people donated office equipment for which we'd issue stock certificates. Our appeal was their interest in sports or Bill or me. The investors, we felt, couldn't get hurt much because even *my* relatives could afford a hundred dollars.

"When Bill finished law school, I quit the Associated Press, and in 1952 we started *SoDak Sports,* which, as I said, was to be the beginning of our huge publishing empire. Our second step, planned even before we launched *SoDak Sports,* was to start a daily tabloid newspaper to compete with the Sioux Falls *Argus Leader,* the biggest newspaper around. How's that for confidence?"

"Not bad," I said, "but what happened?"

"At the end of the first year we had nearly eighteen thousand subscribers, quite a circulation success for South Dakota. But we were losing our shirts! We had readers, but almost no advertisers. The paper cost a dime and was delivered mainly by mail. Without advertising support, every new subscriber cost us more money. We had to work day and night to put the paper out with a small staff. There was no time to plan strategy or long-term financing. *SoDak Sports* was hailed publicly as a big success. It and the two kids running it were talked about everywhere. As heady as that might have been, Bill and I knew the truth. We couldn't pay the rent.

"We declared a recess toward the end of our second year—that was 1954—to assess the future. No matter how we added it up, *SoDak Sports* couldn't fly. We knew we had to quit, but we wanted to do it as gracefully and as fairly as possible. Swallowing hard, we tried to sell it to the very newspaper we had been picking on for two years, the Sioux Falls *Argus Leader.* After the publisher laughed at our proposal, we filed for bankruptcy."

As he spoke, the scene of our first meeting fifteen years earlier came to mind. He had been visiting the Westchester newspapers owned by Gannett and, as one of several items on his agenda, he wanted to meet the author of the newly created action line called *HELP!,* an idea that he had encouraged, and I had been assigned to handle it by the publisher, Thomas P. Dolan. I remember being called to the fifth floor at 8 Church Street, which was where the executive offices were located, and as I opened the door to the outer office a trim man in a black suit, white shirt and gray tie broke from a circle of executives, smiled, extended his hand and announced, "Hello, my name is Al Neuharth," to which for a few seconds, maybe longer, I said nothing. I was, well, star-struck. Al Neuharth was already well known in publishing; I recognized his face from news clippings. "I'm Walter Anderson," I said finally, releasing his hand, "I'm happy to meet you." Then, as I recall, we both laughed.

"South Dakota is a small state," he continued as we sat together years later in his New York office, "and Sioux Falls is a small town. I agonized over the decision. Closing *SoDak Sports* was the worst day of my career. I expected to be hauled off to jail. Instead, many of the people who had invested in the paper commiserated with us, told us how sorry they were that it didn't work. It was a sad time and it hurt.

"No shareholder received a penny for any stock. We weren't even able to pay off all our debts when we liquidated. We paid sixty-seven cents on each dollar we owed."

"Did you bounce back?" I asked.

"I got as far away as I could," he said. "I had some job offers in South Dakota. One, I remember, was to return to the *Rapid City Journal* as a reporter for ninety dollars a week. The editor knew I was broke and, bless him, he was trying to help. Rapid City was too close, though. I wanted to find a job in a state far enough away from South Dakota that nobody there would know that I was such a failure. I wrote letters, mailed a résumé, had friends write supporting letters—then I was offered a job over the telephone by the managing editor of the *Miami Herald,* a call that scared the hell out of me. Yes, I had prompted the offer, but I wasn't sure what to do. It was true that I wanted to get away, but Florida, after all, was really far, and the *Miami Herald* was not just another newspaper. It was a great newspaper, one of the Knight newspapers, and it was the major leagues of publishing.

"I remember asking the managing editor if I could visit Florida before I gave my answer. He told me that the newspaper couldn't pick up expenses from South Dakota. So I borrowed money from my brother-in-law, caught a train, rode a couple of nights and wound up in Miami staring big-eyed at the largest newsroom I had ever seen. I was a green country kid. The *Miami Herald* was huge! You can only imagine the doubts I had. But, despite my nervousness, I started December 31, 1954, at ninety-five dollars per week. The following day the *Miami Herald* announced a five-dollar cost-of-living increase for everyone and I thought, Wow! I've just started and I've already gotten a raise! I was twenty-nine years old."

Al Neuharth, I knew, had risen quickly through the editorial ranks of the *Miami Herald.* In less than four years he was promoted to be assistant managing editor, a post he held for two years until he was transferred to another Knight newspaper, the *Free Press* in Detroit, Michigan, where he became assistant executive editor. His career was secure and his star was clearly rising in the Knight organization, but, nevertheless, he quit to join a much smaller company, the Gannett Group, as general manager of its two Rochester, New York, newspapers on January 1, 1963.

"The choice, as I saw it, was either the satisfaction of presiding over what was rated as a pretty good *big* operation, which Knight was and is," he told me, "or the chance to help a *little* company, not highly rated, do something big."

"It's not so little anymore," I suggested.

"No, Walt," he laughed. "It's not so little."

On that day in 1963 when Al Neuharth walked into Rochester, Gannett owned seventeen daily newspapers, three radio and two television stations. The company's overall yearly revenues were not quite $60 million. Seven years later, when Al Neuharth was named president of Gannett, the company owned thirty-three daily newspapers, two television and six radio stations with total annual revenues of nearly $150 million. Now, after more than a decade with Al Neuharth at the helm, Gannett's revenues had risen twelvefold to more than a *billion* dollars a year with more newspapers and more readers than any other company, including Knight-Ridder, which was simply Knight when Al Neuharth was employed there. Fifty-five daily newspapers, including the Sioux Falls, South Dakota, *Argus Leader,* had been added since he assumed the presidency of Gannett, a corporation that also owned ten more radio and four more television stations, an international research company, Lou Harris Associates, commercial printing facilities, television production companies, North America's largest outdoor advertising firm, the national newspaper *USA Today* and *Family Weekly* magazine, which for years had been *Parade*'s chief competitor and which, in the fall of 1985, would be renamed *USA Weekend.*

"Al," I asked, "how do you begin again?"

"You have to ask yourself, What do I *really* want to do or be? Then make yourself this promise: I will not look over my shoulder; I will use whatever I have learned, but I will not dwell on the mistakes I have made. Whether you're seventeen, twenty-seven or sixty-seven, you bring experience to your new venture or adventure. If you draw from your own experience and use it as a guide, focus on today and not yesterday, your chances of success are greatly improved. Something else . . ."

"Yes?"

"The saddest people I know," he said, "are those who have spent thirty or forty years working for the same employer doing something they *almost* like."

"One more question," I said.

"Go ahead."

"How do you view the *SoDak Sports* experience now?" I asked.

"Last week," Al Neuharth said, rising from his chair to look through the windows at Manhattan's rooftops, "I was visited by an English professor who, thirty years ago, was a columnist with *SoDak Sports.* He told me, 'Had *SoDak Sports* succeeded, you'd still be in South Dakota chasing around a couple of small newspapers.' That's true, really true. Looking back, I'm pleased with the *SoDak* experience, the years with Knight and with Gannett, but . . ."

"*But?*" I asked.

"But," he said, "I'm not finished. You see, there's more to do."

The rain soaked my hair and dripped down my neck as I struggled to place a jack under the front bumper of my 1965 Pontiac. It was a steamy August night in 1967 along Pines Bridge Road, a shortcut in Mount Kisco, New York. I had attended a school board meeting in a nearby town as a reporter for the *Reporter Dispatch* and had been returning to the newspaper's northern Westchester office to write the story when a tire blew out.

The meeting had run late. I knew that my fiancée, whom I had promised to call at ten o'clock, might be worried. Her name was Loretta Gritz and we were to be married in a few weeks. She was tall and slender and beautiful, I thought, with her large round brown eyes, light brown hair and a voice that was as deep and throaty as New York itself.

We had met when we both worked at Metropolitan Life Insurance Company and had become engaged in five weeks. I smiled whenever I remembered the first afternoon she brought me home to the Bronx to meet her parents. At one point her mother turned away from me —rudely, I thought—as we spoke.

"What's wrong with your mother?" I asked Loretta. "What did I say?"

"Walter," she said gently, "you didn't say anything wrong. I forgot to tell you that both my parents are deaf. Just be sure that my mother and father can *see* you speak. They'll read your lips."

For our honeymoon in September I had bought on credit a hundred-dollar suit, a considerable investment for someone earning ninety dollars a week. That night, as I wore it for the first time, mud spattered above my cuffs and my shoes squished as I walked to the rear of the car to return the jack. As I opened the trunk lid a car passed too closely. It hit a deep puddle near the left rear tire of my car and sent a thick sheet of water over me in a muddy shower from head to toe.

"Hey, stop!" I yelled, shaking my fist at two red taillights, which grew smaller and finally disappeared into the darkness.

With the rain steadily beating the pavement about me, I dropped my hand, which was skinned and bleeding from the lug wrench, and lowered my head. What else could go wrong? My new suit, its blue wool wrinkled and soaked, clung to my skin.

I thought about some calculations Loretta and I had made the night before. Together we would earn before deductions about one hundred and eighty dollars per week, but our monthly payments for necessities would exceed what we would actually take home by seven dollars. I had three choices. I could forget writing and seek a higher-paying job in another field. I could find a second job to supplement our income. I could go to school while I worked as a reporter and apply for veterans' tuition assistance. Although Bill Bookman, the editor, and T. Eugene Duffy, the general manager of the *Reporter Dispatch*, had both enthusiastically encouraged me to further my education, they made it clear that I could expect no help. The newspaper had no tuition-reimbursement program. If I wanted a degree, I'd have to do it on my own. While the benefit for Vietnam veterans was less than what had been made available to those who served in World War II and Korea, at nearly fifty dollars a month for part-time students, it meant—if I enrolled at Westchester Community College, the area's least expensive school—we could survive as long as I passed the courses I had been assigned. Could I? I would be a twenty-three-year-old adult with nothing more than the high school equivalency diploma I had received in the Marine Corps. Although I had been an honors student during most of my elementary education, I had been failing or doing poorly in all subjects but English when I quit high school seven years earlier.

As I listened to the only sound in the air—the rain—my spirits withered. Whom did I think I was kidding? How could I work a full-time job and complete college? I wondered how I could possibly afford to marry Loretta. I shook my head and the drops flew to all sides. I could lie to myself no longer. I knew what I was *most* afraid of, and it wasn't marriage or college or hard work or a ruined suit. Once they find out who I really am, I worried, they'll send me back to a tenement, back to where I belong. This was my scorching, irrational fear, my secret agony. Who was Walter Anderson even to think that he could be a newspaper reporter? I'm going to fail, I told myself, finally allowing the dark curtain of doubt to extinguish my last fragment of will. I trembled. Minutes passed. Then, somewhere in my gloom, I remembered myself as a small boy on a stoop, a boy who had wiped blood from his face, a boy who had looked into the night and promised himself, I'm getting out of here.

I raised my head slowly in the rain and whispered, "I'm not quitting."

Do you remember your first day of school? If you're like most of us, it was scary. Beginnings *can* be terrifying. Suddenly the world is a *What if?* place: What if I stumble? What if I fail? What if they find out I'm me? For Walter Anderson, this chapter is really the beginning of the rest of his life, *my* life. It is my beginning. It's easy to forget how difficult it is to start again, particularly if we succeed at it. But if you are to begin again, try to do more, it can help to read the stories of those who have not forgotten. Was it easy for Al Neuharth to begin again? "I was a green country kid," he said, recalling the day he stared at the large newsroom of the *Miami Herald* for the first time, "and you can only imagine the doubts I had."

You're about to meet one of America's most respected actresses, a woman who, like Al Neuharth, achieved her greatest success *after* a humiliating failure. You'll also meet another friend of mine, an extraordinary man whose life was fulfilled only after he asked: Can I begin again? In their stories you'll find no formulas, but you will find truth —and something else: hope.

Her voice had a laugh in it, a crackling chuckle, a sound so distinctive it could be recognized before she was. Her brown eyes were bright, and they widened and narrowed with emphasis as she spoke. Her long, dark brown hair had the luster of a child's hair, rich, deep and shiny. She was slender, athletic, lithe, and she was animated, her hands tracing circles in the air while she spoke, as we had lunch together on a chilly February day in 1985. She was only a few months older than I, but her acting performances, her executive ability as a producer, her authentic talent had already been recognized with four Emmy Awards, a Peabody Award and other honors. Nevertheless, when I looked at her across the table, I could still see *That Girl,* an ebullient, irrepressible, compelling single woman of the sixties named Ann Marie, the television character made famous by my luncheon guest, Marlo Thomas.

She was more than Ann Marie, of course. She had since produced and starred in several television specials, including the highly respected *Free to Be . . . You and Me* and *It Happened One Christmas*. I had been introduced as the editor of *Parade* to Marlo Thomas some months earlier, and I hoped to know her better and to encourage her to contribute to the magazine as a writer. Only a week before our lunch the ABC network had broadcast *Consenting Adult* with Marlo Thomas in the lead role as a mother who struggles to hold her family together after her teenage son discloses his homosexuality.

"Is Marlo Thomas the mother or is she Ann Marie?" I asked.

"They're both parts of me," she replied, her tone even and serious, "different, but still me. That girl who wants something, who aspires, who wants to be independent, who wants to be her own person, who runs against the pack, *that* girl's alive in me. The mother in the movie who loves deeply, who is constructive, she's me too."

Her father is Danny Thomas, the popular comedian who had been the star for more than a decade of the American television series *Make Room for Daddy*, which had started in the early fifties. As the daughter of such an immensely successful entertainer, raised with wealth and privilege, she could have chosen leisure, but, like Prince Michael of Greece, she did not.

"Did it help?" I asked.

"When I told my father that I wanted to be an actress," she replied, "he was devastated. 'It's not like being a lawyer,' he argued. 'You can't go to school, then join a firm. It's something I can't do for you, and I don't know if you'll ever make it.' "

"Can you recall at the beginning of your career an early triumph and what you felt?"

She nodded.

"I remember," she told me, "performing in a little theater. There I was, a child of a pretty well-to-do family and I was absolutely thrilled to earn ninety dollars a week. What did I feel? *My* name was on those checks. Each week I'd take my check home and place it in a little metal box. After a couple of months, I'd cash them all at once. What did I feel?"—she paused and her smile widened—"Joy! I had earned money *acting*, doing what I really wanted to do."

"Marlo," I asked, "what is courage?"

"Courage is doing it anyway," she replied, "whatever *it* is. We all doubt ourselves, whether it's about performing on a stage or meeting a date or the countless number of other situations that cause us to be anxious. We all wonder whether we really have the goods. If people as attractive as Marilyn Monroe or Kim Novak could doubt their beauty —and they did!—there's hope for us all."

"What is the most courageous thing you have done?"

She paused.

"I'd really like to know," I said.

"A week or so after Martin Luther King was killed," she began, her tone softer, her words coming much more slowly, "I called Bobby Kennedy's campaign headquarters to say that I really did not want to go to Nebraska. I was frightened. The campaign leaders told me that it was an important primary and that I was really needed. 'We're counting on you,' they said. It was 1968 and *That Girl* was a very hot show. I flew to Omaha, though I was truly scared. I remember standing on a stage and thinking, I'm going to be shot. I've never been that frightened before or since."

"How do you handle failure?" I asked.

"Walter," she said, "I do the only thing we can do. I try to begin again, and that's not always easy. I had a terrible failure with the movie *Thieves* in 1977, and that really rocked me. I gave up a lot to have that movie made and it was a disaster, a public failure. I cried. I was terribly upset. I had been counting on that movie. For a while I went into a blue period. It was hard to start another project after flopping that badly. I lost some footing when I realized how wrong I had been. Finally, I said to myself, 'So you had a failure. What are you going to do, lie down and die?' I admitted to myself that one of the reasons I felt I had to do *Thieves* was that it was one of the few things I was sure I could handle. My craft wasn't honed well enough to do that many varied roles. Then I knew what I had to do. I returned to acting class to study with Lee Strasberg, an experience that I really feel has made me a stronger and more truthful actress."

"What do you think stands in the way of anyone achieving a dream?" I asked.

"Facts," she said.

"Facts?"

"Sure," she continued, "when we line up all the facts that we believe are against us, the facts can stop us before we start. Whatever we need to discourage us—'I'm too young, too old, too short, too tall, unprepared, inexperienced or not quite ready'—we can uncover. And if we miss a few details, we can always find someone to help us 'face the facts.' The facts, after all, speak for themselves—except they're not true."

"They're not?"

"No," she said. "All the facts together mean nothing. What matters more is what you really want, what you're willing to work for, to struggle for, to take risks for. The success of *That Girl* is a good example of the facts adding up. All three networks, including ABC, which finally bought it, said the American public was not ready for a single girl living alone. A maiden aunt, even a six-year-old brother, was suggested to be added to the script. I resisted. We made the pilot. Of all pilots produced at the time, mine was placed last on the list, the least likely to get on the air. Between my name and the show's premise, the chances were zilch."

"What happened?"

"A man named Marvin Koslow of Bristol-Myers reviewed the pilot. Bristol-Myers needed a way to sell Clairol products, and he thought *That Girl* could do it. Despite the network wisdom and all the facts, he was convinced the show would be a hit and so would I. Clairol sponsored the show for as long as it was on, which was five years."

"Why did it end?"

"I had grown out of it. When we started, I *was* 'That Girl.' I had graduated from college. I wanted to be an actress and my father wanted me to be married. So I wrote the outline based on my own life. Every home in America had a television and every family had a 'That Girl.' "

"Marlo," I suggested, "it was time to begin again."

"Yes," she said, "that's true."

. . .

The air smelled of rotting garbage. A brown boy, not more than four years old, struggled hand over hand up a filthy rope on a rusty fire escape as a small crowd, mainly young men and other children, cheered. Three girls, all in their early teens, chattered a few yards away in Spanish under a yellowing DICK GREGORY FOR PRESIDENT sign that had been plastered to an oily black telephone pole. Along this street of weathered storefronts, bars with broken neon signs and aged, squat brownstone buildings facing low-income projects ten stories high, near Avenue D in lower Manhattan during the New York City teachers' strike in the fall of 1968, I remember my friend Joe Kelly trying to help.

At twenty-five, Joe was a year older than I. His thick black hair, combed Beatle-style, fell over his forehead and ears. Viewed separately, like pieces of a puzzle, his nose would have been called too large, his lips too thin, his cheekbones too pronounced, his chin too sharp, his eyes too dark and too small, his skin too gravelly. Yet, viewed as a whole, his face evoked the stony, compelling image of an actor like Charles Bronson or the football star he actually resembled, the New York Jets quarterback Joe Namath. He was nearly six feet tall with the muscular body of a middleweight contender and the convincing walk, the light step, of a runner. He had grown up on Lexington Avenue in White Plains, New York, in a community of Italian, Irish, black and Spanish families, a neighborhood where poverty and pride often clashed, where tension sometimes boiled into violence—a section remarkably similar to Third Street in Mount Vernon where I had been raised. Energetic, passionate, full of confidence, Joe Kelly was *dashing*.

He had persuaded two of his Westchester Community College classmates, Tom O'Shaughnessy and me, to tutor some children shut out by the school strike. Joe and Tom, who were the same age, had both served in the Navy during Vietnam. The three of us and several other former servicemen had become friends the year before. I remember Joe taking a seat near me in the school cafeteria after one of my first classes.

"You a vet?" he asked, noticing that I was older than most of the other students.

I nodded.

"Me too," he said. "You just starting?"

I nodded again, then told him, "I hope that I can keep up. It's been a long time."

"*Everyone's* worried," he assured me. "You'll do OK!"

As the three of us stood near a broken curb in lower Manhattan a year later, Joe's assurance—"You'll do OK!"—came to mind. I remembered how badly I had wanted to believe him at the time.

Tom and I, unlike Joe, were both married and had grown up only a few blocks apart in Mount Vernon. We knew many of the same people.

As Tom, who was taller than Joe or I, slowly scanned the East Village street, he focused on a group of a half-dozen teenage boys, all wearing similar vests sewn with identical denim insignia, and asked me if I remembered two Mount Vernon gangs, the Majestic Lords, who had worn shiny black-and-white coats, and the Vernons with their powder-blue-and-white cotton jackets. I said I did.

When we stepped up to the doors, covered with graffiti, of a low-income project at 749 FDR Drive, Tom paused and warned Joe, "If I feel sorry for these people, I'm not coming back."

"OK," Joe said.

The three of us entered a soiled, darkened hallway, and walking toward the building's elevator, I smiled as I considered the irony. I was back in the world I had come from.

At the ninth floor the elevator clanked open to an empty hallway. The three of us, Joe first, stepped out and walked down the corridor to Apartment 9H.

Joe knocked.

The door moved slightly, and then, in one quick movement, it opened wide.

"Angel, Angel!" exclaimed Mrs. Santos, a woman with large brown eyes in a soft, tan face, "Millie, Millie! Joe's here. Hurry up!"

After we settled in the living room, Angel, who was twelve and a student in Junior High School 71, sat next to Millie, who was eleven and a student at Public School 64.

"Where're your assignments?" Joe asked.

Millie and Angel looked first at each other, then at Joe. "We didn't get any," Angel said.

"The teachers didn't send you any assignments?"

"No," Angel and Millie replied together.

"What's wrong with those teachers?" Joe asked, shaking his head. "They promised they'd send them!"

"OK," he told Angel and Millie gently, "forget them, then. We'll bring our own books next time and we'll make our own assignments. We don't need them. Meanwhile"—he paused—"find your coats and put them on. There's a party at the church. Let's go!"

A few minutes later, as the five of us walked along Eighth Street through a crowd of perhaps a dozen men, some of whom seemed to be arguing heatedly as others pitched quarters at the stoop of a burned-out tenement, one man, who had been leaning against the building, stepped forward and spoke in Spanish to Tom.

"What did he say?" Tom asked.

"I'll tell you later," Joe promised, discreetly frowning at Angel and Millie in a clear but silent signal not to tell Tom that he had just been cursed out.

The two children smiled at each other.

I noticed that Joe Kelly was at ease. No, it was more than that. He *belonged.* He seemed to be at home, at peace with himself in the center of dire poverty, and he was, as far as I could tell, without fear. I knew then that he was different from Tom and me, but it would be years before I would discover how different.

When we reached St. Brigid's Church, which occupied the corner of Eighth Street and Avenue B, we found that in addition to several tutors and a score of parish children like Angel and Millie, a dozen girls from Maria Regina High School had driven down to the Manhattan neighborhood from Hartsdale in suburban Westchester County. The party, which lasted two hours, was a cacophony of sound and colors and joy, and that night, as I sat in front of a typewriter at the *Reporter Dispatch,* I decided to write about it. The article appeared on November 5, 1968, and I particularly liked its ending, which reported a short discussion the two ex-sailors had during the car ride home:

Tom turned to Joe and asked, "Remember I said that if I pitied these people I wouldn't come back?"

"Yeah," Joe replied.

"Well," Tom said, "I don't. All they need is a little help."

Joe smiled.

"Guess you're right, Tom," he said.

It was an August morning in 1970 when Andrew G. Nelson, the director of admissions at Mercy College in Dobbs Ferry, New York, asked me why I had enrolled for a single course in his school.

"Because," I explained, "I can't afford more. My wife is only weeks away from having our first child. She can't work any longer, and the tuition at Mercy—though less than the other four-year schools in the area—is still more than twice what I was paying at Westchester Community College. *One* course is the best I can do."

"Have you applied for any scholarships?" he asked.

"No," I said, "I have not."

He looked down again at my transcript, a single sheet of paper that he held in his hand. It reported the courses I had completed and the grades I had received to obtain an associate of arts degree in liberal arts and social sciences the previous June from Westchester Community College.

"You graduated first among six hundred and two graduates?" he asked, not looking up.

"Actually I was one of two valedictorians," I said. "Another student and I had identical grade-point averages, one B—"

"And all the rest A's," he finished.

"Yes," I said.

I studied my watch. I hadn't expected an interview; I just wanted to register for one course and return to work. I had an appointment in White Plains within a half hour and I felt rushed.

"Mr. Nelson," I asked, "is there a problem?"

"No," he said, "there isn't, but I wish you had applied for a scholarship last spring. You might have received some assistance."

"Thank you for the encouragement," I replied. "I'm going to be twenty-six in a couple of days—I only decided to pursue a bachelor's degree in the last few weeks and I'm trying to register *before* I change my mind."

We both laughed.

"I have a few more questions," he told me.

"Can I use your phone?" I asked.

"Of course."

I called my office to delay the appointment I had scheduled and then sat back and said, "Ask away, Mr. Nelson."

He was about my height and my age and slender with sandy hair and blue eyes. He gesticulated vigorously, almost rocking in his chair. His tone reflected an exuberance, an enthusiasm that made me curious, kept me seated, in fact, when I should have been elsewhere.

"Call me Andy," he offered.

"Andy," I said, "what do you want to know?"

"Would you take more courses at Mercy College if you could afford to?"

I paused. I had worked full time when I attended Westchester Community College. Did I really want to do it again? Two *more* years of studying every weekend and nearly every night? How would my wife, the soon-to-be-mother of our child, respond?

"Probably," I replied.

"Would you continue in the social sciences?" he asked.

"Yes," I said, "I'd major in psychology."

"Not English or journalism?"

"No," I said.

"Why not?" he asked.

"Because," I explained, "I'm not enthusiastic about most courses in my field. While I was in the Marine Corps I read more novels and more nonfiction by more authors than I could ever expect to be assigned in college. I started out as a local reporter for the *Reporter Dispatch*, and a year later I was appointed its night city editor. Today, as editor of *HELP!*, the action line I started for the Gannett newspapers in Westchester County, my columns appear not only in the *Reporter Dispatch* but in seven other daily newspapers as well, and they draw nearly five hundred letters a week. Andy, I *am* a journalist. I write every day. If I concentrate my studies in English or take a lot of writing courses, I'll learn much less than I will if I major in the social sciences."

Andy Nelson wrote on a small scratch pad, then he put his pencil aside, rose from his seat, shook my hand and announced, "Welcome to Mercy College, Walter."

"Thank you," I said.

The priest was forty-one, nearly six feet tall, trim and agile, with the body of a runner. His thick black hair was streaked with gray, and he wore gold wire-rimmed glasses, which, despite his frequent attempts to keep them in place, repeatedly slipped down his nose, making made him lift his eyebrows as he spoke. He loosened his clerical collar, settled into a couch in the basement of my home and, folding his arms behind his head, asked, "Where would you like to begin?"

I wasn't sure. Seated before me was a man whose life I had found to be especially compelling. He had become a priest in his early thirties, years later than most who are ordained. He had been a singer in a group that never quite took off, Little Phil and the Mellow Lads, an enthusiastic musician who favored the bass, a tenacious competitor on the nation's top club football team, a serviceman during the Cuban missile crisis and Vietnam, a man who had loved women, who had drunk with his buddies, who had fought with his fists with rare intensity. Yet he had become as gentle now as he had been tough in the past. His life, of all those I have known, was truly a new beginning. As he sat across from me three nights after Christmas of 1984 I remembered another night a couple of years earlier when a nun intrigued a table of listeners at a charity dinner with gripping stories about an unusual South Bronx priest, a fellow so charismatic, so sincere, so modest, so believing, so humble that she could point to priests who found reasons to visit him on their days off, and I remembered her surprise when I told her that not only did I know him but I also knew he had just been made a member of the Parish Mission Team of the Archdiocese of New York. He was, I told her, my friend Joe Kelly, *Father* Joe Kelly.

"Did you have any idea when you were a teenager that you would become a priest?" I asked.

"Not once," he responded. "The thought never entered my mind."

"In the Navy?"

"Not a clue."

"How about," I tried, "when we were students at Westchester Community College?"

"No," he said, "it started a couple of years later."

"How old were you when it began?"

"Twenty-eight."

"What happened?" I asked.

"I felt for the first time," he replied, "that I was being led by the Lord."

"But," I said, "you weren't some wide-eyed high school graduate walking into a seminary. You'd done it all—and not all of it was good, Joey. Why you?"

"I've had a lot of time to think about that," he answered, "and now I think I understand why. Some people come to the Lord from the top. I came from the bottom. I was brought to the Lord broken. You know what kind of life I led, Walt, and where I was raised . . ."

I nodded.

"Well," he continued, "I entered a minor seminary in Queens, New York, without telling my parents, without telling anyone. Who would have believed me? Even *I* wasn't sure. After a year I knew. I decided to enter a major seminary, St. Joseph's in Yonkers, but the psychologist there wouldn't recommend me."

"Why not?"

"I guess I wasn't his type. I'd led too rough a life. The rector of the seminary, however, reviewed my file and interviewed me himself. When he finished his questions, he said, 'We're going to take you in.'

"I was excited. I rushed to my parents' house to tell them. How can I describe what they felt at the time? It was hard on them. I was an only child and they wanted grandchildren. They could not understand what I was experiencing. We had never been a religious family, but, nevertheless, there I was going off to be a priest. As I look back, it was probably better that it was all so sudden and we had to rush. I gave my bass to a school for the blind, sold my car to my uncle and disposed of all I owned. I bought clergy clothes, which is what I wore when my parents drove me to the seminary door.

"As the car drew closer, though, I became more anxious, more frightened, more questioning. Who am I to serve the Lord? I'm not worthy, I told myself. I'm not ready. I prayed hard for a sign.

"The seminary was awesome. It was big and brick, secure and solid, everything I was not. I shivered inside. I'll never forget the dean of students walking me to a room with my name on the door—'Joseph Kelly Room 53.' The dean told me, 'This is your room for the duration. When you hear the bells, come downstairs to the prayer hall, and we'll begin prayer with you and you'll meet your classmates.' I grew more anxious as he spoke because all I saw in that tiny room was a bed, a small desk, a Cross and a sink. It looked to me like a cell. I silently prayed, 'Please give me a sign, Lord.' I was frightened.

"When the dean left, I closed the door—and there was the sign I needed. It was a painting of the story Jesus told of the prodigal son returning to his father's love. In that painting I found my message. I knew in that moment that I was in the Lord's embrace. I kneeled and I cried. I cried happily. I was home. I've never looked back."

As he spoke of his first day in the seminary I could still picture him on his knees four years later bowed before Archbishop Terence Cardinal Cooke in Saint Patrick's Cathedral on Fifth Avenue in Manhattan. It was November 4, 1978, the day he became, finally and forever, Father Joseph Kelly. Joey knelt as a man, but he would rise a priest. When the cardinal lifted his hands from my friend's head, Father Joseph Kelly stood quickly, his dark, craggy features in a broad, boyish, uninhibited smile. Sensing, feeling his passion, a murmur arose among the congregation. He stepped across the altar, and I noticed he was again, if only for that brief moment, a proud street kid strutting to his chair. His rolling walk, his swagger, evoked tears from every person who knew him.

"Looking back over the last seven years," I asked, "have you gained more than you have given?"

"Yes," he said, "I have."

"Can you give me an example?"

"Angels," he said.

"Angels?"

"Not too long after I became a priest," he began, "I was sent to a parish in the South Bronx. It was called Holy Spirit, and it was located on University Avenue between Burnside and Tremont. It was a busy street. Taxicabs owned by a local company would double-park and sometimes even triple-park outside the school. When the children finished classes for the day and left to go home, they'd have to peek between the cars to cross the street, and sometimes they'd get hit. The parish and the cab company battled constantly over those double-parked cars. The situation was tense.

"One day, for example, I was walking to a nearby grocery store to pick up some milk when a cabdriver, who was sitting in a chair leaning back against a fence, tossed a cupcake wrapper on me as I passed him. The message was clear: *I* was garbage. He even smirked, taunting me. It was a showdown. I was angry, really angry, but I kept walking. Several people in the store tried to reassure me: 'Forget about it, Father. People like that are disrespectful. Don't worry about it, Father, it don't mean nothing.' When I left the store, I was determined to avoid any encounter, just walk directly across the street to the rectory. But as I passed the drivers the one who had tossed the wrapper glared at me and giggled. I was over him instantly, giving him no chance to rise off his chair: 'Why are you disrespectful to me?' I demanded. 'I've done nothing to you!' He couldn't move because I had him pinned against the fence. When I turned away, he jumped up and made a big scene with his hand in his pocket, as if he had a knife or something. Several people got between us. It was terrible. A few minutes later I had to say Mass with that ugliness, that hate, that anger rising in me. It hurt to pray. I was confused. What does 'Love your enemy' mean? I looked up at the Cross and I knew I had failed. I had not loved my enemy; I had wanted to fight.

"One morning, after trying and failing again to get the cabdrivers to move, I walked into the rectory right behind two little girls who stopped by the church every day for milk on their way to school. The youngest was named Jasmine. I was so wrapped up in myself I paid no attention to either girl. They left and I followed. Later, when I returned, I found a note that Jasmine had written to me:

> *I love you once,*
> *I love you twice,*
> *I love you more than beans and rice.*

"I read her poem and I smiled. These were Hispanic kids, and that's a lot of love. I understood the larger message, too. Jasmine had reminded me what's really important. To me, she was an angel. Jasmine was someone who announced that we are loved and accepted as we are. God sends us messengers like that, but sometimes we miss them."

"Have you found angels in tragedy?" I asked.

"Yes," he said, "I remember when the Sisters of Notre Dame in Manhattan called me one day to meet a young single girl named Olga who had cancer and who was five months pregnant. I was asked to counsel her and her boyfriend. They got married, but a few months after the baby was born—it was a healthy baby—the cancer really spread in Olga's body. I went to Columbia Presbyterian Hospital to visit her, but I didn't recognize the person I found. She had lost all her hair. She was very, very thin. The doctors had performed a tracheotomy; her breathing was heavy.

"As I stood over her I grew more and more angry at the sickness and the suffering of that poor child. I don't know how long I had been staring at her when she suddenly woke up as if she sensed there was someone in the room. She sprang forward, her wig slipping back off her head. She startled me. No, she scared me. Her breathing was labored and she began coughing. Phlegm oozed out of the valve in her throat. I looked into her face, into her eyes and I told her, 'God must love you very much,' which is what I felt because a young person chosen to suffer like that is beyond my understanding. Although my words may not have been what a psychology textbook would recommend, they were sincere and they brought that child peace. She calmed down and she lay back gently and she smiled. We talked for a while, the two of us, and she died shortly after. Her death, her life, strengthened me, my friend. For me, Olga was an angel."

It had been sixteen years since Joe Kelly had persuaded two Westchester Community College classmates to help a handful of students shut out by a strike in lower Manhattan. Only one question remained.

"Father Kelly," I asked, "after starting a whole new life, do you have any regrets?"

"No," he said, "I have too much left to do."

Change in our lives generates a good deal of anxiety that can, as we've seen, help to provide us with the energy we need to start over. "We all wonder," Marlo Thomas observed, "whether we really have the goods." Joe Kelly worried as he neared the seminary: "I'm not worthy." Al Neuharth said, "I wasn't sure what to do." All were anxious. Yet when they used their anxiety constructively—when they focused on *solutions*—Al Neuharth started a new job, Marlo Thomas studied to be a better actress and Father Joe Kelly found a mission. Each said *yes*. Yes, I'll try again.

The day after Andy Nelson and I met in his office at Mercy College he called me at the newspaper.

"Could you stop by the college today?" he asked.

"It was too late to register, after all, wasn't it?" I suggested, squeezing the telephone tightly.

"No," he said, chuckling, "I have some good news for you. You have a scholarship—"

"What?" I interrupted.

"—a complete academic scholarship. I showed your transcript to the president, Pat Coogan, and she awarded you the full scholarship. No strings. Just continue to get good grades. You have to stop by today, though, to register full-time. Can you do it?"

"Yes," I said.

Chapter 8

WHEN MUST I SAY GOOD-BYE?

He spoke distinctly, eloquently, and, as his voice deepened and lightened, with intensity and passion. It was not until he laughed, though —a boiling, bubbling, infectious, tone-cracking, familiar laugh—that I was reminded who he was, who he really was. Jerry Lewis, at fifty-nine, was the comic genius of our time, a talent that has endured the spotlight of fame throughout the world for nearly four decades, the clowning star in dozens of successful films, including the classic *Nutty Professor,* and he was also the recognized leader of an arduous, often frustrating campaign to conquer muscular dystrophy, a disease that cripples children. Also, he is a man, I'd discover, not without fear.

"I was raised in Newark and in Brooklyn," he told me, "shuttled like a package between some grandparents and a few aunts and uncles. Inevitably, a pair of chairs in somebody's living room would be placed together for me to sleep on. In school I was always embarrassed, having to wear hand-me-downs from my cousins. In the winter months I was dressed wrong; in the summer months I was dressed wrong. I felt out of the perimeter of my classmates. I'd imagine where they lived, have flashes of what I thought their homes must be like. I don't think I've ever told anyone this, but once I wrote a story about a tiny being that followed me down a street on a sunny day. Whenever I'd turn around, that little creature would stop. I'd see the sadness in his eyes, feel his loneliness, and my eyes would fill. After a few blocks, it came to me. That tiny being was my shadow. Even today, during those agonizing last seconds before I have to step out onto a stage to perform, when my palms are sweaty and my stomach's churning, when my anxiety's at its worst, I'll tell myself, This is what you worked for—or do you want a little shadow again? I don't want to remember a lot of what I've lived, but I don't want to let it go either.

I remember, for example, that when I was a small boy and I stayed with my grandmother Sara, I'd lie awake at night whenever I'd hear a distant train whistle. I'd close my eyes tightly and picture people resting comfortably in beautiful Pullman berths. The trains, as I imagined them, were always heading to Hollywood. How badly I wanted to be riding one of those trains! I wanted to be away. I remember one particular evening when my grandmother Sara sat down beside me, the train whistle fading away, and she told me something unusual, something that's stayed with me all these years. She told me that I wouldn't be happy until I can climb to the top of the highest mountain and shout loud enough for the whole world to hear me: 'What do you need?' At times in my life I'd remember my grandmother's words and I'd wonder if I hadn't been destined to become a priest or a minister or a rabbi or maybe a doctor, but she also told me that she thought I'd get attention in an unusual way. How could she possibly know? I was thirteen when she died, and I thought my whole world died with her."

He removed his gold-rimmed glasses, wiped his eyes, and sat down beside me again. "I look back now," he continued, "and in my own way I interpret her message to be that I'd get attention with the pratfalls, the silly, nutty professor stuff I do, and then I'd talk seriously about what's really important."

As we sat side by side on a tan couch in his suite at the Atlantis Hotel & Casino on the boardwalk in Atlantic City, New Jersey, a few hours before he was to perform on a March night in 1985, I recalled our first meeting. He had been making arrangements for a new film in New York one afternoon the previous fall, and he had called me to ask if he could stop by my office at *Parade*.

"Sure," I said.

"I'll be there within an hour," he promised.

He arrived in forty minutes. His body was as toned, as limber as an athlete's, despite the open-heart surgery that had saved his life only two years earlier. An observer would surely guess we were about the same age, although I was nineteen years younger. His black hair, combed tight and cropped short, glistened; his bright hazel eyes never left mine as we spoke. He was subdued, polite, gracious, less a volcanic screen presence than a quiet volunteer soliciting help for a charity.

"Do you remember that cover photograph that Eddie Adams took of me for your magazine?" he asked.

"Of course," I said, "it's one of our favorites."

"Do you think Eddie would sell it?"

"I'm sure it depends," I said, "on how the photograph would be used."

"The Muscular Dystrophy Association needs it for promotion. I'd be happy to pay for it out of my own pocket."

"If Eddie lets you use it for promotion," I said, "he stands to lose thousands of dollars, regardless of what you reasonably offer to pay. A picture's value is greatly diminished if it's massively promoted."

"Well, then—" he said, starting to rise.

I placed my hand on his wrist and interrupted, "But I know Eddie, and he may offer you the picture anyway. He'll never take money from you, Jerry, that I'm sure of. He's told me how he respects what you're doing for those children. Have you spoken with him yourself?"

"No."

I got Eddie on the phone and handed the receiver to Jerry Lewis, who explained what he wanted.

"Can I buy it?" he asked.

"No," Eddie told him.

Then Jerry smiled.

"He *gave* the photograph to the MDA," he told me as he put down the telephone.

A few minutes later, as we were walking through the editorial offices to the elevators, a phone at one of the desks started to ring.

"Let me answer it," he said and, without waiting for a reply, picked it up, and in the cackling, unmistakable voice of the nutty professor he announced, "This is *Parade* and I'm Jerry in reader service. How can I help you?"

It was a complaint.

For the next ten minutes Jerry Lewis brought the editors and writers in the office that afternoon to their feet in laughter. Among other helpful suggestions, he volunteered to move the magazine, erect a school building, relocate New York City; the more outrageous the ideas became, the louder the laughter grew. Astoundingly, he never lost the caller's interest and his identity went unsuspected. When he handed the telephone to a real reader-service correspondent, one with tears in her eyes, he winked at his audience and quietly left amid spontaneous applause.

Now in Atlantic City, he turned and raised his eyebrows curiously. He had noticed that I was smiling.

"I was thinking about the call you took at *Parade*," I told him.

"That was the lady," he remembered, "who wanted to move a school building, right?"

"Yes," I said, "and *you* wanted to help her."

He laughed.

"Jerry," I asked, "what was on your mind earlier?"

"Earlier?"

"You seemed preoccupied when I first arrived."

He turned the palms of his hands up and looked at them.

"Last night," he said, "I held in my arms a child who is dying."

"Would you like to talk about it?"

"Maybe," he said, "I would."

We're designed to improve until the day we die, to learn new skills, make new friends, experiment. Often, though, we resist taking a step forward, no matter how positive, if it means we have to leave behind what we've grown accustomed to in our lives. "I don't want to remember a lot of what I've lived," Jerry Lewis said, "but I don't want to let it go either." Many people feel the same way. Don't we struggle harder to hold on to what we have than to gain something new? The streets of my childhood, for example, could be discomforting, but they were familiar to me; I knew when I was safe and when I was in danger. Because I knew how to respond appropriately, I was secure in my old neighborhood. On the other hand, the responses that helped me survive my childhood are inappropriate, even dangerous, for me as an adult. I have had to reject my impulse to violence, and this hasn't been easy. As you'll see in the stories you're about to read, however, we *can* say good-bye, whether it's to a pattern of behavior, a friend, a place, a belief, a way of life or, finally, life itself. This chapter is about letting go, about saying good-bye to things we know and people we love; it's about facing loss, even death. And it is the story of how I learned to overcome my violence, a story that begins with a shooting.

"It's going to be a great day," Anthony Colombo told me.

I frowned. "Look at the clouds," I said, raising my head.

"To hell with the clouds," he replied. "The sun's coming through. It's going to be a great day."

I looked at my watch. It was 10:30. The air was warm and sticky that Monday morning, June 28, 1971, and I had arrived at Manhattan's Columbus Circle early. I was on assignment as a reporter for the Westchester Rockland Newspapers. Nearly a half-million people were expected to attend an event, a Unity Day Rally, arranged by the Italian-American Civil Rights League. The group, which had drawn considerable and increasing publicity, had been founded by Anthony's father, Joseph A. Colombo, Sr., a man who was, according to law enforcement officials, the leader of a large organized crime syndicate and the first reputed mob boss in anyone's memory to actually seek public attention. He had gone so far as to picket the FBI after another son, Joe Jr., had been arrested the previous year. He and I had met several times in the preceding weeks.

"My father said he'll spend some more time with you," Anthony Colombo told me.

"Good," I said.

A young man, who identified himself as a journalist from New Jersey, approached Anthony to ask if he could enter the press section.

"What's your name?" Anthony asked.

"Jerome Johnson," the man answered.

Anthony studied the man's credentials, which were detailed and professional, although he, like three or four other writers and photographers, had neglected to pick up a special press authorization issued only for the event.

"OK," Anthony told the man, "but get your press pass in advance next time."

"I will," Jerome Johnson promised.

Anthony turned back to me. "Look at the sky now," he said, "it's clearing up."

"You're right," I said, "and, Anthony, look at all these people"—I pointed to the swelling crowds—"and it's still early."

"I told you," he added, "it's going to be a great day and— Hey, there's my father—"

Across the press area, near a large stage erected in the shadow of the statue of Christopher Columbus, Joe Colombo emerged. Of medium build, with clear, smooth skin, a round face and thinning hair, he was not an overwhelming presence. It was only when he spoke, softly and firmly, I noticed, that his authority became clear. When the crowd, which seemed to be growing by the hundreds with every passing second, recognized him, cheers erupted, "Hi, Joe!" He waved back, drawing more cheers, then walked to the front of the stage, where he checked the floral decorations, the seating, the press section. It was a few minutes before eleven. As I watched him assure himself that all the preparations had been made as meticulously as he had planned them, I silently recalled some rumors that had surfaced in recent weeks. It was said that several mob bosses were not pleased at the attention the movement was drawing to their otherwise secret activities. One published report, which Joe Colombo had vociferously denied to me, alleged that he had been slapped by a disgruntled gangster.

As he walked toward me he chased some small boys from a row of folding chairs, admonishing, "Those are for your mothers. Stand, you're young." They did, with no protest.

I called, "Hey, Joe . . . have a minute?"

He smiled, nodding.

"How about if I follow you around some today?" I asked.

"Sure," he said.

We were joined by Tom Nestro, the director of public relations for the Italian-American Civil Rights League, who reported, "Everything's all set, Joe. Just beautiful." Joe Colombo told me he wanted to discuss an article I had encouraged him to write for the Westchester Rockland Newspapers.

"It's appearing today," I said.

"Great," he replied, "I'd like to see it . . . Wait a minute, I have to get this TV interview over with . . . I'll talk to you in a minute." He smiled widely, lifted his arm in a sign of unity and strode a few steps to the television cameras.

"This is really his day, isn't it, Tom?" I asked.

"The biggest and best," Tom Nestro replied. "He's been looking for —What the hell is *that?*"

It was four tiny bursts, popping like firecrackers, a pause, then three more.

Later, at my typewriter, I wrote:

What I had seen was Joe Colombo standing amid a group of apparent newsmen. It was 11:17 a.m., within the gray painted barricades formed on the littered street behind the statue of Christopher Columbus. I heard the gunfire, which at first I thought was fireworks, and turned toward Colombo. He had been less than fifteen feet away. But he wasn't there.

The crowd surged toward its fallen leader and, unthinking, I surged too. When the second volley of shots shattered the balmy air, the crowd did a panic retreat. Women screamed. Men screamed. A girl near me threw her hands in the air, screeched and ran. A falling photographer's tripod smashed the shins of a bystander. Folding chairs spun crazily and banged on the pavement as feet and legs kicked them. A heavy-set boy in his late teens knocked the wind out of me with his shoulder as he fought to flee.

A young policeman seemed to be grappling with someone at the center of the turmoil. Both appeared down in that second volley. Two more policemen dived on top . . . Two or three pistols were on the street, but I didn't see who had used them . . . The loudspeakers blared, "This is a false alarm. This is a false alarm. No one has been hurt."

Of course, that was not true.

The assailant, who would later be identified as Jerome Johnson, the same young man who had been allowed into the press area without complete credentials, lay face down on the pavement, dead with two holes in his back. Joe Colombo, clad in green trousers, a white short-sleeved shirt and red windbreaker, was lying face up, eyes closed, silent, his head bleeding profusely.

I remember Anthony Colombo suddenly appearing on the platform, gesturing and yelling.

"Where's my father?" he screamed.

At Roosevelt Hospital a few minutes later the hallway smelled musky and thick. Nurses and aides rolled carts back and forth across the green tile. The air conditioning was not working. Seated in metal chairs that had been lined up along the stained vanilla walls of the second floor, Joe Colombo's family waited.

Anthony Colombo, his collar undone and his tie hanging loosely, paced the corridor past me. He mumbled, "I don't believe it. I don't believe it."

Joe Colombo, Jr., who at twenty-four was two years younger than his brother Anthony, stood alone, his pants spattered with blood, his back flat against the wall, his head tilted toward the ceiling. Lucille, their mother, prayed in a small adjoining room. Loretta LaRosa, Joe Colombo's sister, sat nearby.

Anthony stopped pacing and told me, "If the Feds gave him a warrant right there, I would have believed it. But not this. Not *this.*"

He paused. "They tried to keep it from me," Anthony said, "but I found out. I don't remember how I got to the hospital."

He exhaled, shuddering.

"I don't know," he said. "I don't know."

That night, as I sat before my typewriter in White Plains, Anthony Colombo's shudder stayed with me. I thought about my childhood and

some of my experiences in the Marine Corps. Once again I had witnessed violence. Hadn't I seen enough?

"Last night," Jerry Lewis told me, "I was visited by two dystrophic
children, one twelve and the other seventeen. The older was acutely
terminal. I've seen this happen now for thirty-six years: a child won't
die until he meets me. Fifteen days ago the parents of this boy were
told that their son wouldn't make the night. A hospital nurse told the
boy that she read in the newspaper that Jerry Lewis would be appearing
at the Atlantis Hotel on the twenty-ninth and she promised him he'd
be here, that the child would make it this far. 'I will,' he told her, and
he did. I guarantee you he won't be here tomorrow, because I can tell.
I've seen the look before.

"So often I'm asked, 'How do you do it?' Strange, no one ever asks
me about the child who dies in my arms. They always ask how *I* feel.
The child's dying and people ask how Jerry Lewis is doing. I'm never
sure how to respond. Part of me wants to get angry. 'I'm well,' that's
all I can say. Is it so hard to see that it is the child who suffers? A young
boy may have lived fifteen more days because I was present. What does
that mean? To the child and his family, it's a millennium. The child
looks into my eyes and makes me important. It's humbling. It's shatter-
ing emotionally, but I cannot let the child see that. I know he's moving
on nerve ends alone, that his heart pumps out of sheer determination.

"You can't tell a dystrophic child, 'Don't hero-worship.' He won't
hear you. To him I'm 'Jerry.' The expression 'Jerry's kids' comes from
the children, not from me or the MDA. It's what the children call
themselves. So every year I make what appears to be a self-indulgent
remark, 'Please help my kids,' and I take some heat. So be it. The
children really think I'm Babe Ruth, that if I step up to home plate
at Yankee Stadium, I'll knock it out of the ballpark. I can't begin to
explain what I feel about all this, only that I'm going to keep doing it."

"Jerry," I asked, "haven't you been close to death yourself?"

"This?" he replied, opening his shirt and pointing to a long, deep
scar that ran from his neck down across his chest onto his stomach.

"Yes," I said, "*that,* my friend."

"I was lying in a bed in Desert Springs Hospital just over two years ago," he recalled, "when my heart stopped"—his voice was flat, objective, and his face was expressionless as he spoke, as if he were describing something that had happened to someone else—"and I was gone for eleven seconds before they were able to bring me back. When the paramedics came to my home that morning—I'd had chest pains earlier—I actually smoked while they gave me an electrocardiogram. Later in the hospital room, a nurse named Glenda who was monitoring me saw my T-wave invert on the screen, and acting quickly and smartly, she pounded my chest. My heart started to beat again. I only remember fragments of the experience, but I can still close my eyes and see the nurse clearly, a large black woman, her fist coming at me.

"I had been waiting for my friend Dr. Michael DeBakey, who is the greatest heart specialist in the world, but suddenly there was no time. I had five minutes to decide whether I'd allow them to operate or not.

"What went through my mind?

"Remember Michael DeBakey is my friend. I'd seen this operation, stood next to Michael as he performed it, many times. I knew where every instrument would be placed. I understood that they'd cut an incision through my skin, open my chest with a Black and Decker electric saw, crack my rib cage, insert retractors to create an opening twelve to thirteen inches wide, reach down with a scalpel, open my leg to remove arteries to be used later to replace the defective ones in my heart. I knew that it would take two to three men to close my chest cavity and that they might have to go at it more than once to be sure it was closed properly. Sometimes, information is dangerous. Normally, when patients are handed that piece of paper to sign, they have no idea what their body will experience. I *knew*. Also, I understood that Michael, though he'd try, would not be able to fly to Desert Springs fast enough to perform the operation himself. One of his students, Dr. Harold Feikus, would operate. I remember squeezing my eyes shut, opening them, then saying the only thing I could say, 'OK, let's go.'

"When I came to in the recovery room, the first person I saw was Michael DeBakey standing over me. I was confused. My friend was wearing a suit, not a surgical gown. In a haze, I wondered: Did he operate? He couldn't have, of course. My operation had lasted three and a half hours, the time it would have taken him to get from Houston to Las Vegas. What I didn't know was that he had stayed in contact with the hospital by telephone the entire time and that he stood by me in the recovery room waiting for me to become conscious."

"What happened next?"

"I had to change to live," he said, "and it was very difficult. Before the open-heart surgery, I'd reach for a cigarette when I shaved in the morning. One shave, three to four cigarettes. After smoking four packs a day for forty-seven years, I stopped. I also had to learn to eat proper foods and to exercise, which I've done. Life is worth the effort."

"Jerry," I asked, "what have you learned from the experience?"

"Now I understand," he said, "that no rockets go off. I had always suspected that people who had lost their lives but somehow miraculously recovered—in my case, through the pounding fist of a hospital nurse—saw fireworks, experienced profound insights, learned the big secret, were forever *different*. Walt, I'd love to say that I don't get annoyed any longer when room service is late, but I do. When I'm escorted as a celebrity to the head of a line, I'm uncomfortable; at the same time, I admit that I don't like standing in a line. That conflict existed before my surgery and I feel it now. The same world's still there. Maybe that's the lesson."

He rose, walked to the window, pointed to the pavement more than thirty floors below.

"Do you know what Atlantic City is?" he asked.

"What?"

"It's a crap table surrounded by a slum. You'd think these hotels, with all the millions they're making, could help some of those people."

I remembered what he had told me about his grandmother's vision when he was a boy living in a tenement like those we were looking down at.

"Have you climbed to the top of the mountain," I asked, "as your grandmother Sara said you would, and are you shouting to the world, 'What do you need?' "

He laughed. "Maybe I am," he said.

I knew that in a few hours Jerry Lewis would be standing in the wings one more time. His hands would be sweaty. He'd fumble with his bow tie, pace, suffer again what he called his "fifteen-second moment," that anxiety-ridden time before he stepped into the spotlight. Then the familiar, nutty voice would crackle into the night and he'd churn the casino audience to a roar with his humor. The world's greatest clown, the man who can still remember the sound of a distant train, would bring them to their feet.

"Do you see that?" I asked, pointing to the carpet.

"See what?"

His body blocking the sunlight, a dark shape formed at his feet.

"You cast a long shadow," I said.

I squeezed the steering wheel tightly. The editor of *New York* magazine, a legendary figure named Clay Felker, had just asked me to accept an assignment. He was a world-renowned journalist who, at forty-three, was at the top of his form, one of the most talented editors ever. Unbelievably, I was about to decline his offer.

"I don't know," I said. "To tell you the truth, as much as I'd like to write for you, Mr. Felker, I don't want to go back to the street. I've invested several months of my life exposing heroin sales and the black market in methadone and, frankly, I'm sick of it. I don't want to write about drugs again."

"I'm not asking you to start all over again, Walter," he said. "I'm interested in how you did the investigation."

"*How* I did it?"

"Yes," he said, "precisely what did you do on the street to get the information you published?"

I stopped the car but left the engine running. It was a Thursday night in the dead of winter, 1972. Clay Felker was about my height and weight with light, clear skin and light brown eyes that stayed alert and focused as he listened. He had been the featured speaker earlier that evening at a meeting of journalists in Westchester County and I had been asked to drive him back to Manhattan.

"What did I do?"

"Yes," he said. "Your editor, Jim Head, told me about the results —how you proved the country's first death by methadone, how your stories prompted mass arrests of heroin dealers and so on—but I'm willing to bet *how* you did the investigation is the most interesting story of all."

"Mr. Felker—"

"Please call me Clay."

"I received," I said, "some of the most valuable information from street people—addicts, muggers, burglars and prostitutes. The criminal records of some of my sources run on page after page. *Clay,* do you still want me to write about this?"

"Very much," he said, his tone even and sincere. "I want you to tell it as it happened."

"When do you want to receive the story?"

"Monday morning," he said.

I sat silent for a few seconds.

"OK," I said.

"Good!" He shook my hand and opened the car door; pausing, he turned back and asked, "By the way, Walt, why were you able to talk so easily to those street people?"

I laughed. "I used to live there," I said. Then I drove the car away from the curb and headed home.

Three nights later, as I stared at a blank page that I had inserted in my portable typewriter, I remembered Clay's instruction: "I want you to tell it as it happened."

Easier said than done, I thought. I had written several false starts, but each read like the newspaper articles I had already published.

Loretta and I and our son, Eric Christian, who was almost a year and a half old, lived on the third floor of a three-family house in the northeast Bronx not far from Evander Childs High School.

I stood up.

"Where are you going?" Loretta asked. She was rocking Eric on the couch behind me.

"I'm having trouble writing the *New York* piece," I said. "I don't know where or how to start it and I wish I'd never agreed to it. Clay Felker's crazy. I'm going for a walk."

I slipped into a coat, walked down two short flights and stepped into the chill air. I drew in my collar tightly and walked toward the subway.

It was as if I were traveling in someone else's body; I was oblivious to everything but my own thoughts. I must have passed storefronts, corner drugstores and bars, the subway and the housing projects, but I remember none of these things. I kept asking myself, How do I begin? How do I begin? The more I strained to think, the more difficult it became, until, finally, I told myself I'm just not good enough. I'll call Clay Felker in the morning and tell him I can't do the piece. Let it go, I thought, *let it go.*

Suddenly, as if a movie had just flashed on a screen, I was aware of where I was. I was seven blocks from home. I noticed it was cold and, for the first time since I had started out, I became aware of others— an old woman walking slowly with a cane, two teenagers moving briskly, a couple laughing as they entered a corner bar.

Close to home, it came to me: That's it! *People,* the story's about the people I know.

I took the three flights to our apartment two steps at a time, opened the door and heard Loretta say, "You've got it!"

"How can you tell?" I asked.

"You're smiling," she said.

As I sat down to write, once again I heard Clay's words, "I want you to tell it as it happened."

I began typing:

Pancake pushed back into the cushiony seat on his side of the booth and grinned, a black face taunting me. Super Casual, that's Pancake. "Come on," I said. "Get on with it." His lips twisted to a mock scowl, his eyes feigning hurt. With exaggerated seriousness, he scolded, "Now hold on, fella. If I'm gonna prove how all them doctors don't know nuthin', I gotta contemplate."

My investigation into black-market methadone in Westchester

County was, for the time being, nearly complete. There was just one small piece of proof I needed, and Pancake could deliver it. So there we sat, a few days before Christmas, huddling in a corner booth at the Beehive, a comfortable soda fountain and restaurant on Mount Vernon's dilapidated Fourth Avenue.

Pancake's 34, though he'll tell you he's 24. Except for his massive lips ("In the Army they'd tell the other guys to suck in their guts. Me, they'd say suck in your lips.") his face is impossibly flat. It looks as if somebody had stepped on his head, which is exactly what happened on a Harlem sidewalk in the fifties. The nickname was inevitable, and in an odd way honorable: "It made me look bad. Brothers would say the Pancake's comin' and kinda step aside." Today, he lives in New Rochelle's downtown district with a woman and two children, one his. Heroin found a home in Pancake over the years, but he handles it pretty well, sometimes working, sometimes selling.

"Maybe we oughta talk about twenty dollars," Pancake bargained, giving me the bad-guy glare. A put-on.

"Hassle some other fish," I said, starting to squeeze out of the booth. "Five bucks and the cost of the junk, and then only if you can demonstrate what you promised." My half of the put-on.

"Siddown!" he ordered. I did.

From his left breast pocket he withdrew half of a Lilly Disket, a methadone pill, then dropped it into his quarter-full water glass. We both looked around, *Mission: Impossible* style, checking for observers. All clear. Pancake dipped a handful of surgical gauze into my half-full water glass. The Disket had already dissolved into a tangerine Jell-O-like glob, which he poured into the gauze and squeezed over the ashtray. Several drops quickly formed a small puddle away from some ash. "See," he said. "Believe me now?" I nodded. Pancake had proved that the Diskets could be broken down and injected into the bloodstream to produce the desired "rush." He stuffed the still-wet gauze into his pea-coat pocket, then moved the ashes around to destroy the evidence. We left.

As I continued I described the newspaper articles I had written. I recalled my research findings, my interviews with doctors and with police. I discussed the autopsies I had viewed to gain a better understanding of drug abuse and how the Westchester medical examiner's forensic findings helped me to prove what was believed to be the nation's first methadone death, one of nine that I discovered. I finished the article a few minutes before seven Monday morning.

"What happens now?" Loretta asked.

"I take the subway to Manhattan and turn it in," I said.

"Then what?"

"Then," I said, "we pray they accept it."

I had called Jack Anderson, *Parade*'s Washington bureau chief, earlier and asked him if I could use his private office for a meeting with my friend Elmo Zumwalt III, a North Carolina attorney who was a Vietnam veteran a couple of years younger than I.

"I'd be *honored*," Jack said, "and, if it's at all possible, I'd like very much to take the two of you to lunch. I think that young man is one of our country's most courageous people, Walt, and I sincerely hope he makes it."

It was about 11:00 A.M. on a frosty morning a few days before Christmas, 1984, when Elmo Zumwalt and I stood near a set of windows overlooking Sixteenth Street, North West, in the nation's capital. Jack Anderson's chief assistant, Opal Ginn, who had also asked to meet my guest, had just closed the door behind her.

"You're getting popular," I teased him, "but I can't figure out why."

He laughed heartily, a deep, friendly, throaty laugh. "That's what happens when you put somebody on the cover of *Parade*," he said. "Let's sit down."

As I listened to his laughter I recalled our first meeting the previous June. Elmo and his wife, Kathy, had arrived together at my New York office one Friday morning about fifteen minutes early for a nine o'clock appointment. He had black hair and pale hazel eyes; his build was as trim as that of a tennis buff who plays frequently and obeys his diet; his posture was erect, his spine straight, almost with a military bearing. Kathy was slender with classic even features, wide-set green eyes and thick blond hair that fell to her shoulders. He, I thought, would have been elected class president; she would have been captain of the cheerleaders. In fact he was struggling to live.

"I would like to write," he had suggested during that first meeting, "about the misperception, the misunderstandings about Vietnam veterans in America, the difficulties and the complexities of the problems facing these men and women."

"And," I said, "you don't want to write about yourself and your relationship with your father?"

"That's right," he said, relieved.

"No," I told him, "that's wrong."

His eyes widened. "Walter," he argued, "I'm not comfortable writing about myself. Frankly, I'd be self-conscious and I don't think I can do it. I'm a lawyer and I'd rather stick with the issues."

"Elmo," I said, "your story is so compelling that it must be told. Americans, veterans and nonveterans alike, will be touched by it. It is important that you share what you've experienced. If you truly want to make a difference, if you really want to help your fellow veterans—and I know you do!—you must tell your story. It is their story, too. I understand your reticence. I know how difficult it is to write about yourself, to have yourself as part of a report, to tell it, if you will, as it happened. However, you are uniquely qualified. You have already been told by doctors that you have terminal cancer—" Kathy placed her hand over his. "—and you probably contacted it in Vietnam from Agent Orange, which was ordered there by your father, the admiral."

"I don't know if I can do this," he said.

"Yes, you can," I told him.

As we sat in Jack Anderson's office months later, I could still recall word for word the beginning of his article, which he submitted to the magazine a few weeks later: "Other Vietnam veterans are more articulate than I; certainly others are better writers. Many have had far more tragedy in combat. But because I have a disease that was possibly caused by the military orders of my father, I feel that I have been singled out to tell our story."

He described what he felt when he was told that he had non-Hodgkins lymphoma, how it had spread throughout his lymphatic system, had invaded his spleen, his bone marrow, probably his liver, how the doctors advised him that surgery was useless, chemotherapy questionable, that median survival was eight years: "I thought about my family," he had written, "and its uncertain future. My son Russell, now seven, from birth has had a sensory dysfunction which caused developmental problems. I thought about Agent Orange, which I had been exposed to as a young naval officer in Vietnam. . .

"My father, Admiral Elmo Zumwalt, Jr., was a strong advocate of the use of Agent Orange in the Vietnam war. That doesn't mean I hold him responsible for any disease I may have incurred. He did what he felt he had to do to reduce casualties; I did what I felt I had to do. I volunteered for service in Vietnam because I felt, whatever the risks, that was where I belonged. Even now, at the age of thirty-eight and confronting undoubted perils, I'm not sorry I went.

"My object in telling my story is not to create sympathy for myself but to help draw attention to Vietnam veterans in general—a group of worthy Americans who I feel have been ignored and neglected by their fellow citizens. I'm not trying to raise a statue to anybody, to hold a parade or pass a bill. My whole purpose is to make you, the reader, understand a little better who we are and what we went through."

After his article was published by *Parade* on October 7, 1984, he and his father were asked to appear on national television, to speak to groups across the country, to be interviewed by newspapers and magazines, to contribute to an important biography of their lives. There was even talk of a made-for-TV movie. Elmo, much to his surprise, had become famous. Now, seated in Jack Anderson's office, I hoped to gain from my friend some insights he had not shared.

"Elmo," I asked, "do you remember when you first became aware that people die?"

"Yes, I do," he said. "I was twelve, exactly."

"What happened?"

"I had survived a bout with polio when I was younger," he said, "but I also had a cardiac condition and the surgeons finally scheduled me for open-heart surgery. In the hospital in the bed next to me was another twelve-year-old boy, a boy named Leroy who also had a heart problem. He was dying, and I remember vividly how he suffered because his parents refused to visit him. Pleas to them didn't help; they had abandoned the boy. My mother and father, and some other parents of children at the hospital, tried to comfort Leroy. They'd bring him presents, hold him, talk to him. It helped some, but, of course, it was not enough. I'm sure that Leroy's parents could not face their son's death, but their insensitivity, their refusal to accept their loss, constitutes the most callous, cruel, inhumane act I've witnessed in my life. His suffering ended only when he died. Thus, very early I became acutely aware of the possibility of death and the importance of others in the process."

"Elmo," I asked, "what do you fear most?"

"When I found out that I had a terminal illness," he said, "I realized that being told you're going to die is not the worst thing in the world, but living miserably, because you have that knowledge, could be. Later, when I'm receiving intensive treatment or in severe pain or close to my last hours, I may feel differently, but I hope not. My most agonizing moments now are when I weigh the uncertainty of the time I have left with the needs of my family."

"Is fear itself frightening?"

"I don't think I've ever been afraid of being afraid," he said. "Fear is natural, and unless you let it overwhelm you, it's healthy. I've experienced fear many times in my life—and usually at the right times."

He paused, looked down at his hands, then back toward me. "A client of mine, a brilliant professor at North Carolina State, was originally misdiagnosed, only to eventually discover that he actually had terminal cancer. I told him of my condition, and I asked him, 'How tough is it on the mind?' His answer was devastating. He told me, 'Elmo, it *destroys* the mind.' I left his bedside understanding the battle I was facing. I couldn't let the disease destroy my mind."

"Do you think you're unlucky?" I asked.

"Not at all," he said, his voice firm. "Had I been born a hundred years ago, I probably would not have survived polio; I certainly would not have lived longer than my teen years without open-heart surgery."

"Elmo," I said, "could you share with me what you would say to a friend who is dying?"

He nodded.

·   ·   ·

With my fellow students applauding, my throat seemed to thicken and I struggled not to cry. As I stepped down from the podium I saw my wife trying to squeeze her arms through the lines of people to take my picture. It was the June 1972 commencement of Mercy College and I had just received the gold medal for psychology, which was my major, and, as valedictorian of the graduating class, I had been awarded the president's Medal for Preeminent Scholarship.

When I reached my seat, a fellow student, a mother in her forties who had taken all her courses at night, pinched my arm and told me, "You did good, kid."

My eyes filled.

Across the crowds, over the heads of students and well-wishers, I saw my wife. We both smiled. I knew that Loretta, more than any other person, understood what it had taken to meet that moment. She had shared it all, the scrimping, the strain, the loss of evenings and weekends.

She nodded.

I nodded back.

How much my life is changing, I thought. I had only a few days earlier spoken to Clay Felker, the editor of *New York* magazine, to seek his advice. He had encouraged me to become an editor, though that was not what he had originally intended to do.

"The methadone article was an important success," he reminded me, "and it had impact nationally. I want you to do more investigative work for us—"

"Clay," I interrupted, "do you think I could become an editor?"

"What?"

"Do you think I can be an editor?"

"What brings this up?" he asked.

"Gannett is going to give me the chance to be managing editor of the news bureau in Westchester. If I do it well, if I succeed, I could end up editor of a newspaper."

"How old are you, Walt?"

"Twenty-seven."

"It's not to my advantage to answer this question," he told me, "but

I'm going to. *Bet on your talent.* The truth is that you'll succeed whether you go on writing for *New York* or whether you continue to work for the newspapers. I think that you'll make a fine editor, Walt. In any case, you should try it. You know the telephone number here if it doesn't work out."

"Thank you, Clay," I said.

Sitting under a large tent at the Dobbs Ferry, New York, campus of my college, watching row after row of students rise to receive degrees, silently sharing thoughts with my wife, I told myself that I'll worry tomorrow whether I can make it as an editor, not today.

"What's important to understand," Elmo Zumwalt told me, "is that anyone who learns that he has a terminal illness is never the same. More, the lives of his family and his associates are forever changed. I don't know how many sincere, intelligent, well-meaning people have advised me that because I don't know precisely when I'm going to die, I should simply think the way I did before I found out that I had cancer. That's well-intentioned support, but it is meaningless to the person with a terminal disease. I cannot pretend. I *have* cancer.

"What would I say to a friend who's dying?

"I'd first find out what makes him comfortable. Each person is different. One patient will want to talk. Another will not. If he wants to talk, I'll listen. If he wants me to leave, I'll leave, and my feelings will not be hurt. If he wants to cry, I'd encourage him. I would not allow him to be embarrassed about his feelings. The key to what to say lies not within you—there's no magic phrase!—it lies within him. What does he want to hear? Understand that a terminally ill person, no matter how many friends and loved ones surround him, is alone. Death is personal.

"At the cancer institute last week, I spoke with a woman in her forties whose family was upbeat, forever pretending that she was not ill. For their sake, she said, she went along with it. I reminded her, though—and cancer patients are incredibly honest with each other— that she pretended for herself too. She enjoyed being upbeat. She agreed.

"What would I say to a friend?

"I'd recognize he's learning more about his life than he ever suspected and I'd encourage him, if he was inclined, to talk about it. I
can't believe how much time I wasted away from my family, how busy
I allowed myself to be, how distant, if only for minutes, I was from the
people I care about. It's not that I love them more; it's that I appreciate
them more.

"What would I say?

"I'd try to remind my friend that hope is a successful, pragmatic way
of life in the real world.

"Why would I say that?

"For me, life is an adventure, the challenge of facing adversity,
whether polio, heart surgery or Vietnam. Please don't misunderstand
me. There are times when I'm sad, deep-down sad, depressed, in pain,
self-pitying, when I think the adventure's over. But, all in all, the truth
is that I have a good life. I've known love and I've seen honor and
integrity and idealism in people close to me. I'm blessed with a loving
family, friends, joy. I *love* life"—he smiled—"and I value it."

I parked at a metered space near the corner of North Avenue and
Huguenot Street in New Rochelle, New York. It was a brisk Sunday
morning in the late fall of 1973, and as I looked through the car window
at the narrow, two-story concrete block building across the street that
held the offices of an 18,000-circulation newspaper, the *Standard-Star*,
I considered the irony.

Next door to the *Standard-Star* was the post office where I had met
the gunnery sergeant who recruited me into the Marine Corps almost
thirteen years earlier. I remembered how nervous I was when I signed
the papers. I was sixteen. In my mind I watched that boy, who was both
thrilled and frightened, leave the post office and, after taking a few
steps, turn back to stare again at a marine recruiting poster—he then
seemed to stand a little taller, and his chin jutted out as he walked away.
He tripped at the curb, which ended his swagger and sent blood to his
neck and cheeks. I laughed and looked again at the *Standard-Star*.
Anderson, I wondered, are you going to trip again?

In a few weeks I would be editor *and* general manager of this daily newspaper.

"Elmer Miller is retiring," Thomas P. Dolan, who was the president and publisher of the Westchester Rockland Newspapers, had told me, "and I want you to succeed him as editor and general manager in New Rochelle. You'll run the whole paper, do both jobs. I know you can do it."

At twenty-nine I would be the youngest general manager and one of the youngest editors in the newspaper group. I exuded confidence when I spoke with Tom Dolan, but inside I was as frightened, as unsure as that sixteen-year-old boy when he had just enlisted in the Marine Corps. I withdrew my wallet and removed a small wrinkled piece of paper on which I had written Clay Felker's telephone number. Maybe I should call him again, I thought. This promotion is a real opportunity and I should be happy, but I'm not. I'm nervous. No, I'm *scared.* What if I fail? Who am I to take a job like this? Let it go, I heard myself saying, *let it go.*

I squeezed the piece of paper into a ball, rolled down the window and dropped it.

The elevator doors opened at the fifth floor of 598 Madison Avenue in Manhattan to a crisp, modern reception area, its gray marbleized floors reflecting in the block-mirrored ceiling above. To the right was a sitting area and in its center a table through whose glasstop I counted fifty-three books by such authors as David McCullough, William Safire, David Frost and Jackie Collins. I recognized several current best-sellers: *Moscow Rules,* by Robert Moss; *The Good News Is the Bad News Is Wrong,* by Ben J. Wattenberg; *Mistral's Daughter,* by Judith Krantz; *Go for It,* by Dr. Irene Kassorla; *Changes,* by Danielle Steel. Directly ahead was a gray cloth wall interrupted by silver lettering that read, "Janklow & Traum Law Offices" and "Morton L. Janklow Associates Inc. Literary Agents." To the left was a broad door of honey teak, which I expected to swing open at any moment and reveal the ebullient man whom I had come to visit, Morton L. Janklow himself.

His was indeed a compelling story. From modest roots he had risen to become one of America's most successful attorneys. It was Mort Janklow who had introduced me to John Ehrlichman and who had represented more than a score of free-lance writers and at least six contributing editors to *Parade* magazine. A graduate of public elementary schools in New York City, Syracuse University and Columbia Law School, he had, among other achievements, become a visiting lecturer at Columbia Law School and at Radcliffe College, an adviser to the Solomon R. Guggenheim Museum and to the New York University School of the Arts, a member of both the Council on Foreign Relations and the President's Independent Committee on Arts Policy, a member of the City Center of Music and Drama, a director of the Film Society of Lincoln Center and a director of and counsel to CTW Productions, a subsidiary of the company that produced *Sesame Street* and *The Electric Company.*

I knew that Mort Janklow's achievements were all the more remarkable because years earlier he had conquered a deadly illness that no other patient had ever survived, a disease with no known cure—a revealing story that I hoped he would share with me on a winter afternoon in 1985.

The broad wooden door opened.

"Walter, my friend!" Mort Janklow greeted me. "How are you?"

Slightly taller than six feet, he wore gold-rimmed glasses and, at fifty-four, he was slender. Smartly dressed in a conservative gray plaid suit, maroon tie and tailored white cotton shirt, Mort Janklow was a man of gestures, his energy bursting in continual movement. He thrust his hand forward enthusiastically, which I shook, returning his greeting, and followed him to a conference room, where we were able to sit comfortably, privately, and where I asked my first question.

"Mort," I said, "how did you acquire and survive the disease that nearly took your life?

"After passing the New York bar exam," he answered, leaning back in his chair, "I volunteered for induction and joined the Army as a private in 1953. In the middle of combat infantry basic at Fort Bliss,

Texas, we were out on maneuvers in the desert when I became desperately ill. I was rushed to the hospital with a raging fever, which was diagnosed as bronchial pneumonia, but I remember thinking that I was dying. I had this incredible weakness. Finally I seemed to recover. I returned to basic training, was eventually assigned overseas, did my time in the military, was discharged and began my career as a young lawyer in a large firm."

Mort was normally a rapid-fire speaker, but I noticed that now his words were softer, subdued.

"Then one day in 1958 I went for a checkup and had a routine chest X-ray. My lungs were riddled with lesions. By running tubes into my lungs and drawing out fluid, the doctors were able to identify exactly what they were dealing with, a rare fungus called coccidiodomycosis. They told me that it was *incurable*."

As Mort Janklow uttered one of the most dreaded words that a patient can hear, I recalled an earlier conversation with him and an insight he had shared with me from his childhood.

"Walt," he had told me, "I never had doubt that my parents loved me, but I also never had doubt during those tough times that we had no money. I still remember getting into a fight with another kid in a car as we rode to the beach and my father scolding me that although I was right, I was a guest in his family's car and I should behave differently. I did not like the constant frustration, the too frequent reminders that I was a guest, that someone was doing me a favor or doing us a favor. We seemed always to be at the disposal of someone else and very early, *very* early I determined it was not going to happen to me. I started to work at eleven. The Depression had conditioned a lot of us. Then the war made people realize that life was tenuous."

"After the diagnosis," I asked, "what did you do next?"

"I checked into the Kingsbridge Veterans Hospital in the Bronx," he said, "because the condition was military-related. Also, Kingsbridge was the only hospital that had any experience working with this illness."

"How were you treated?"

"My doctor discovered that the Squibb company had been working experimentally on a drug called Amphotericyn B, which seemed to work on fungus diseases, but nobody had tried it on a human being. Nobody knew its toxicity or whether it would even work. They told me, though, that this was the only chance I had. They leveled with me: I had a life expectancy of six months to a year and it was going to be a pretty tough death. When the disease reached my brain and became meningital, it would be excruciating. I was the first patient to receive the new drug, so my case is part of medical literature. They started me on intravenous infusions of the drug; they didn't know how to administer it. It was extremely toxic, so I ran fevers of 106 and 107. They packed me in ice. I became convulsive. I lost about eighty pounds in two to three months.

"Every other day I received one of these 'cocktails.' I grew progressively weaker, not from the disease but from the medication. Although the drug was causing a terrible reaction elsewhere in my body, like my kidneys, they could tell it was helping from the blood-test results. Nevertheless, it became a tremendous psychological challenge to take the drug. It was destructive, nauseating, worse than cancer chemotherapy. They were giving it in far too intensive concentrations, one hundred milligrams per liter of glucose. It was dropped, finally, to twenty milligrams.

"One day a doctor, a specialist in the disease, flew in from California, where the disease was more common. He said, 'Look, this drug is never going to help you. You are either going to live or die and all you are doing is weakening yourself. You should not stay with this drug.'

"My personal physician disagreed, saying, 'Mort, it's your only hope. Stick with it.' "

My wife, who was seven months pregnant with our second child, had to walk more slowly than most of the other hockey fans streaming out of Madison Square Garden. It was an unusually warm spring night in 1974, and the crowd had thinned by the time we turned the corner a block from our car and I saw danger.

Ahead of us was a group of four or five teenagers who were throwing karate kicks and punches at one another. They crowded the narrow sidewalk; they seemed oblivious to any passerby who could be hurt by their noisy horseplay. As we neared them, I began to hear my heartbeat. I glanced at my pregnant wife—then I heard nothing. No one, I thought, no one is going to touch my wife. The heat rose along my spine and into my neck. My heart pumped faster, my breathing quickened, my jaw tightened. No longer was I a thoughtful newspaper editor. I was a seven-year-old boy who, with blood flowing down his face, wouldn't surrender his Bonomo's Turkish Taffy to two street bullies; I was a fifteen-year-old who knew how to throw a straight right hand; I was a Marine. I would protect our unborn child. Within a few feet of the teenagers, I stepped forward quickly and placed my hands on the shoulders of two of them, tightened my fingers, drew them to me, then spread them apart. "Cool it," I said, my voice hard and ugly. The teenagers looked at one another, said nothing, stepped aside and let us pass.

When we reached our car and entered it, my heart continued to pound, my forehead stayed moist. I started to tremble.

Loretta reached across the seat, clasped my hand and told me, "We could have crossed the street."

"What?" I said.

"We could have crossed the street."

I sat quietly, my hands falling loosely from the steering wheel. I was confused. Did I do the right thing? It had never entered my mind to cross the street. I watched the teenagers pass by and they no longer looked threatening; they were just kids. *We could have crossed the street.* Had I endangered my wife and myself? Why did I *choose* violence?

A few minutes later, as we drove in silence up the FDR Drive in Manhattan, I said softly, "You're right."

It was as if an idea had been tugging at me for years, one that had always stayed just out of reach, and in that instant I was able to grasp it. I remembered sitting at a typewriter three years earlier, recalling the shudder of Anthony Colombo, a son whose father had just been shot, the scene at the hospital, how it seemed somehow to sum up the utter futility of all the violence I had witnessed in my life, from the explosions of my childhood to the Marine Corps to the drug abuse, the cruel, silent deaths I had reported in the article for *New York* magazine. *I had to let my past go.* My most difficult struggle would not be with the world; it would be within myself. I had to be larger than what I had taken a lifetime to learn. My fists tightened on the steering wheel in determination. I *could* change. Somehow I'd learn to use my anger, my anxiety, my fear more constructively.

"Yes," I said, "you're right."

"What did you decide?" I asked Mort Janklow.

"I stuck it out eight months," he replied. "I had entered the hospital in February 1958, and I was released in October 1958. I weighed one hundred five pounds. It turned out I had made the first complete recovery."

"How did it affect you, Mort?"

"It has been all these years since that experience," he said, "and it still has an impact on my life. I had been in confrontation with death, although not in an instant as you sometimes are when a car whizzes by or like a soldier in combat. This was slow. I had six months to think before I came out of the woods. Now I try to do the things I really want to do. My own experience with death put things in perspective for me. Who can scare me? If a client, for example, threatens to leave my firm, what does that mean in the context of my whole life? Something else: I came to the conclusion that the payoff in this world is not on brilliance, or even genius. *It's on courage, the capacity and willingness to take risks.* This is true of personal relationships—whether it's getting married or having children—or risk in business or investment decisions.

"Did you ever hear someone ask, 'Why is so-and-so successful? He's such a fool.'

"Well, 'so-and-so' is successful because he took a hundred-to-one risk without even knowing it was risky. He thought it was a sure thing! He lucked out. For every one like him, there are ninety-nine who went over the side. The people to admire, I have discovered, are the ones who have the subtlety of mind and the analytical capacity of mind, the intelligence, to know precisely the risk they're taking—and to take it anyway!"

As his voice rose he leaned back and stretched his arms wide behind him.

"Mort," I asked, "how would you advise someone who is facing death?"

He paused. "The confrontation with death comes to everybody," he said, leaning forward again and speaking slowly. "You have to make up your mind that whatever time you have left—whether it be a month or a year or a day—you must go on living. Whatever you *can* do, you *must* do. Even if you're in a hospital room, as I was, or a convalescent home, you have to keep interested in life, in family, in friends. It's easy to become self-pitying, especially if you're in pain.

"When I was on that damn medication and my fever was raging and I was uncontrollably nauseated, there came moments when I really wanted to quit. Another patient who started on the drug therapy after me—his name was Warner and we used to commiserate—started to get the disease in meningital form. He was more advanced in the disease than I was. He couldn't tolerate the medication. It was too large a psychological hurdle for him, and he left the hospital under cover of night. He disappeared and died. In fact he was saying, 'I would rather die than face this.' This left me the only patient on this drug with a form of disease no one in the world had survived."

Mort Janklow paused, reflecting. When he continued, his voice was firm. "However long life is," he said, "it *is* life. You might consider, for example, the article Elmo Zumwalt wrote for *Parade* revealing his own disease, his Vietnam experience and the extraordinary relationship he has with his father. It is not only an alleviation of his own pain, but also a great lesson to others. You don't know how you're going to act until you're there, but *survival has to do with a lust for living.* I think that the confrontation with death and the living of life are one and the same. People who do one well will do the other well. *The people who confront death the best,* in my opinion, *are the people who confront life the best.*"

I turned off my tape recorder and reached across the table to squeeze Mort Janklow's hand. I had no questions left.

When I asked John Ehrlichman why he had not committed suicide, he said, as I reported in Chapter One, "I had to decide for myself whether to live or die. If I wanted to live, I had to quit my depression. I had to say my life had value, and I had to mean it. I chose life." Mairead Corrigan Maguire, after her sister's tragic death, saw even more clearly the need for peace. She made a choice, as did Alex Haley when he loosened his fingers from the stern rail of that ship. They, too, chose life. "I think," Mort Janklow said, "the confrontation with death and the living of life are one and the same." Mortimer Levitt told us, "I remember taking off my stocking and discovering what I thought was melanoma, the most deadly form of skin cancer. *In that moment I knew I wouldn't change anything.* I would go right on doing what I was doing." When I asked John Glenn why he risked his life in a rocket, he replied, "I have always felt it was more important how you live your life than how long you live." Sherry Lansing remembered that when she woke up in intensive care and was told that her leg might have to be amputated, she thought: At least I am alive. Jerry Lewis recalled that he had always suspected that people who almost lost their lives became different, but "now I understand . . . the same world's still there. Maybe that's the lesson." Elmo Zumwalt said, "Being told that you are going to die is not the worst thing in the world, but living miserably because you have that knowledge could be."

Courage, as is apparent in the lives of these people, *is* a three-letter word—and that word is *yes*. Yes to life. "You'll see," I wrote in the first chapter, "how successful men and women have learned to do more than simply cope with their most agonizing fears by actually turning those feelings into assets. You'll learn how they, and you, can summon courage, once you understand what courage really is. But I promise you no easy formulas. This book is about real life, real people, real problems."

Real life, *real* people, *real* problems. You have read how I finally began to overcome the violence I learned in my earliest years. That's one kind of farewell. It's letting go of what we have learned, what we cling to, and it's difficult. Even more difficult, though, is saying good-bye to someone we love.

As I stood at the edge of my sister's grave the minister's words rolled by me. I remembered not the woman he described but a blond girl seven years older than I who had tattled to our father about something I had done after I had tattled on her. I remembered how afterwards we had made a pact: neither would ever divulge secrets about the other —and, throughout our lives, we never did. I remembered the Rockettes, a group of teenage girls who named themselves after the famous Radio City Music Hall dancers and how they wore satin jackets to high school and how they were led by my sister, one of the tiniest of the Rockettes. I remembered a fight she had with a much larger girl— weighing only ninety pounds, she was outsized in every contest—who said that my sister bleached her hair. The girl, her nose bloodied and her blouse torn, ran home.

I looked across the mourners assembled that September morning in 1974 toward my brother, Bill, who was thirteen years older than I. He was our big brother, always larger than life to the two of us, a fighter, a motorcycle racer, always, it seemed, an experience ahead of each of us. His memories, I knew, would be different from mine. Carol was his little sister; she was my big sister. I watched my mother standing quietly, and I understood that I could not comprehend her pain; I could only suffer *with* her. We had lost a sister, but she had lost a daughter. Carol's husband had lost a wife. Her three children and a foster child had lost their mother. How differently we'd all remember the small blond lady with the large blue eyes.

I remembered two letters I saved that she wrote to me when I was in Vietnam:

September 21, 1965.

I've been thinking about you all the time. I just finished watching the news on television. I hope you take care of yourself. We all love you and we want you home safely. The kids are in school now . . . so I have some peace and quiet. Daddy comes up here more and he talks about you a lot. Even though he doesn't say it to you, he's proud of you. I will write soon. I love you, little brother. Please be careful.

Love, Carol.

November 21, 1965.

I pray every day that you are safe. You're my little brother, you know. Mommy called me up to tell me your picture and your letter were in the *Daily Argus*. She read it to me. It is so hard to describe how I felt. It was perfect the way you put it, Walter. Not even a writer could do it better. I'm so proud of you. When you get out of the Marines, I hope you go to college in New York State. I don't want you to move far away. You've been away from all of us so long already. Please be careful.

Love, Carol
P.S. I weigh 105 pounds!

I remembered how, during a posh political fund-raising party at the White Plains Hotel two years earlier, my sister—who was then a suburban housewife and a district leader from northern Westchester—held my arm tightly and asked, "What do you think all these people would say if they knew where we came from?"

"They'd ask for your autograph, sweetheart," I told her.

"I'll bet," she said.

"Would you like me to introduce you," I asked, "as the former leader of the Rockettes?"

"I'll break your neck," she told me and pinched my forearm.

I remembered my sister in a hospital bed, her breast and ovaries removed, a doctor confiding that she might live only a few months. Cancer, he said, was killing her. I remembered more than a year later how Carol and I had talked in the living room of her home.

"I don't know about this chemotherapy," she said. "It makes me sick."

"Are you going to let them operate again?" I asked.

"No," she said, "what I have left is what I'm going to die with. I'm not going to let them bury me in pieces."

181

"Why do you pretend with almost everyone that you don't know what's happening to you?"

"That I'm dying?" she said.

"Yes."

"Because," she said, "it's easier on them. I have only one regret, and I can't do anything about it."

"What's that?"

"I'll never see my children become adults."

"Carol," I told her, "I love you."

"I know that," she said. "I've always known that. I love you too, little brother."

I remember making a promise to myself at my father's grave: "I will not," I said, "attend another funeral." As I, a young Marine sergeant at the time, bitterly perceived it, this, the first such ceremony I attended as an adult, was barbaric—a cold corpse in an open casket, with misty-eyed friends and relatives milling about, the same people solemn later as a pastor who hardly knew the man extolled his virtues and, on behalf of God, accepted his soul into heaven. It chilled me.

"The old man," my brother whispered, "would not go for this."

"Amen," I said.

Within a few months, of course, I was attending other funerals—however strongly I felt, I could not hurt my family or friends with my absence, but secretly my feelings had not changed.

It was years before I was able, with great relief, to grasp the truth that had eluded me as a younger man. The confusion, the conflicting emotions that I felt began to clear up when I heard a widow a few years ago sincerely thank me for being at her side. I saw her face relax, her eyes brighten as she discussed her late husband, their love, their children, their plans, their joys, their disappointments, the suddenness of his death. "Thank you," she said and she meant it. *I* felt better. Funerals, whether it's two atheists shaking hands over the grave of a friend or the most elaborate religious ceremony, may be, I slowly began to suspect, a necessary catharsis for the survivors.

It was the death of another friend, though, that forever altered my view. Her name was Cappy, and she died of cancer at fifty-one in June 1983. She and her husband, Bud Greenspan, who has been accurately described as America's foremost producer of sports films and possibly the world's leading sports historian, shared a firm, touching love. They were, in fact, inseparable, living together, working together, producing award-winning movies like *Jesse Owens Returns to Berlin, Wilma* and the *Olympiad* series, but Bud and Cappy were also individuals. Bud was an early riser; Cappy liked to sleep late. Bud enjoyed shopping; Cappy hated it. Bud loved to cook; Cappy would rather not. Bud was explosively creative; Cappy could calmly administer. "It was," Bud once told me, "like good cop, bad cop."

When Cappy died, Bud ordered a celebration of her life, not a funeral. "It's what she would have wanted," he said. We, her friends, toasted Cappy and embraced Bud. The outpouring was important, but one particular act had special meaning to Bud—a letter he was handed two weeks after Cappy's death by Dr. Sammy Lee, a United States Olympic gold medalist in diving in 1948 and 1952. He told Bud, "I know it's not possible for me to miss Cappy as much as you do, but I'd like to share with you a story that might help," which was Strickland Gillian's *The Dark Candle,* about a father who becomes reclusive after the death of his daughter. One night the father dreams that he's in heaven, watching a procession of angels, each carrying a lighted candle. One angel's candle, though, is dark. The angel is his daughter.

"How is it that your candle alone is unlighted?" the father asks.

"They often relight it," she tells him, "but your tears always put it out."

When the father awakes, the message is clear. No longer will his daughter's candle go unlighted.

When I saw *Sixteen Days of Glory*, the official film of the 1984 Olympics, which was produced by Bud and dedicated to Cappy, I thought about a lighted candle. I remembered how Bud had shared the story and the letter with me, its meaning to him, and its significance to me. Dr. Sammy Lee, I knew, had committed a most appropriate act; he had been a friend.

What I had to learn, and was too wounded, too consumed by my own sadness, to perceive at my father's funeral, was the value of a mourning period and how to conduct myself comfortably, appropriately and with love during that time.

I've since discovered three don't and three do's that have served me well:

• *Don't pretend.* Don't make believe you're there for some other reason; do not divert conversation to other, what *you* consider "less painful," subjects. Survivors usually want to talk about their loss, so this should be encouraged.

• *Don't try to make the bereaved feel better.* Although this may seem at first like a contradiction, it is not. I don't know how many funerals I've attended where well-meaning people have advised, "Don't take it so hard." It leaves the bereaved no response and encourages them to conceal their grief. The last time, which was the *last* time, I said, "Don't take it so hard," a survivor asked me, "How hard *should* I take it?"

• *Don't fear tears.* The expression of sorrow is normal, and it's better expressed than suppressed. Tears of grief are healthy tears. If stifled now, they'll erupt later, and more painfully.

• *Do let them talk.* Be a good listener. The most helpful conversation may be the one in which we listen far more than we talk. Be sensitive. Again, don't discourage talk about the deceased.

• *Do reassure.* When someone close to us dies, it's normal to feel guilt: Why didn't I say this or do that? How many times have we all wished: If only I had the chance . . . Reassure the bereaved. A kind word goes a long way here.

• *Do call again.* The best friends are there the next day. Remember that Dr. Sammy Lee's letter to Bud Greenspan was received two weeks after Cappy's death. There's a widely held belief that the bereaved need time to themselves. I don't think that's true. I've found that the survivors need support more after all the early attention than during it.

It was a few minutes after five o'clock Monday afternoon, February 10, 1975, and I was working on the last column I would write as editor and general manager of the *Standard-Star*. No words seemed appropriate. I was walking away from people I really liked and a community I really enjoyed. How could I express what the last year had meant to me, what I felt about the journalists I had worked with, men and women with enough dynamic passion, energy and integrity to be recognized with more editorial honors in fifteen months than in the previous fifteen years? I looked at some of the awards in the hallway, as if in some magical way I'd find guidance there. I read the names of my friends on the citations from the New York State Publishers Association, the New York State Associated Press Association, the Public Relations Society of America and the most prestigious corporate honor a Gannett newspaper could receive, the Frank Tripp Medallion for Public Service, but I came away empty. That's what other people said about the *Standard Star*. It wasn't what *I* felt.

Finally, I heard my own words. *What I felt.*

I began typing:

New Rochelle. My father was born here in a Finnish ghetto along Mechanic Street. Both my parents lived here and my brother was born here. I enlisted at 16 in the Marine Corps right next door to the *Standard-Star* building. Five years later, after Viet Nam, I was assigned to the Navy and Marine Armory as my last duty station . . . and eight years later I returned to New Rochelle to succeed a great man of journalism, Elmer Miller. An honor in itself.

I had been entrusted with what seemed to me an awesome responsibility—to be editor and general manager of this newspaper.

Now, somehow, it seems to have been longer than a year. My daughter, Melinda Christe, was born and my sister, Carol, died of cancer at 36. The joy and sadness I have experienced personally during the last year have been paralleled professionally.

The *Standard-Star* has had success and it has had failure. As has the city. As have you.

And today I have been appointed editor of the *Reporter Dispatch* in White Plains, a position I have been asked to assume and have accepted . . . Yet, though I will be leading the newspaper on which I started my career eight years ago, I leave New Rochelle with a special sadness. I doubt that I will ever work with a better staff than the people who bring

185

you the *Standard-Star.* I doubt that I will make as many friends or come to respect as many people in one community as I have here . . .

When I completed the column, I placed it in the "in" box to be published the next afternoon, folded the day's edition of the *Standard-Star* into my briefcase, looked slowly around my office and said, "Goodbye." I was going home.

Chapter 9

WHY ME?

Her Park Avenue home was spotless, with no wipe marks across table tops or windowsills, none of the dust that in Manhattan seems always to invade even the tiniest and most hidden crevices. It was not that the apartment was higher than where dust usually settled; rather, it was that great effort had been expended quietly, as it always had, I suspected, in the life and career of the woman who lived here. She was nothing if not a hard worker. She had begun by crafting material for stars like Dick Van Dyke, Will Rogers, Jr., and Jack Paar when Dave Garroway, then host of NBC's *Today* show, hired her as a writer in 1961. Three years later she got the chance that would propel her to a level of recognition that few people, even the leaders of some nations, achieve. Following years of more than thirty *Today* "girls," including celebrities like Helen O'Connell, Florence Henderson, Betsy Palmer and Maureen O'Sullivan, she, Barbara Walters, was asked to appear on camera. More, she was encouraged simply to be herself, to be what she was, an educated woman. Two decades later, as we sat together in her New York living room, I was aware that Barbara Walters, who at fifty-three had already received three Emmy awards for her television reporting and had consistently been described as one of the world's most admired women, had *earned* her fame. I also knew that she'd

survived some very cruel criticism and harsh experiences, which, however painful, I hoped she would share with me.

"Barbara," I asked, "what was the worst?"

I suspected that she'd tell me it was that awful year of 1977, when
she and Harry Reasoner unsuccessfully co-anchored the *ABC Evening
News*, an unhappy and uncomfortable partnership for both. She left
the anchor spot after eighteen months and returned to reporting on the
same network, her $5 million five-year contract still in force, but Bar-
bara Walters, who had become America's highest-paid journalist, had
plummeted professionally, pushed by her critics.

She nodded and leaned back in her beige couch. "During the first
year I was with ABC," she began, "along with all the terrible publicity
about Harry Reasoner and me, I'd read that I had limousines lined up,
that I insisted that bookcases be specially delivered to me, that I
demanded a pink typewriter, that I was, purely and simply, a spoiled
brat. It hurt and I would bleed over every word. Broadcasting was my
livelihood, my sole means of support. I *had* to work. I was not independently wealthy. I worked hard, very hard; I was not a prima donna.
Actually, I took taxis or walked to work, had no limousines and none
of the rest of it either. What I did have was a makeup person, which
was widely reported, but less reported was the fact that *every* network
newscaster was made up by a professional makeup person. It was that
sort of near truth that, perhaps, burned the most."

I remembered, as she spoke, that when we first met, nearly two years
earlier at the Four Seasons Restaurant, she had hailed a taxi when we
left. I also remembered that she was smaller than I had expected,
almost petite, *softer* in person, with flawless skin, light brown hair and
hazel eyes. Now, as she sat across from me in her home, I noted again
that the woman who had skillfully interviewed kings and presidents and
scientists and entertainers, whose phone calls had been accepted in the
most important corridors of power, seemed, as David McCullough had
described her in an article that appeared in *Parade,* vulnerable. She
was, despite her brilliant skills, ordinary in the best sense of the word;
she was normal.

"I reached the point," she continued, "when I'd ask my secretary to read the clippings first. If it's going to hurt me, I told her, please don't show it to me. Reading it will do me no good and I'll just feel terrible."

"What sustained you?"

She leaned toward me.

"Common sense, finally," she said. "I *couldn't* fall apart. For years I'd managed to a large degree to keep my personal life and my professional life separate. Photographers might gather downstairs at the door, but here, in my home, I had a daughter who was seven. That tends to keep things in proper perspective. It's critical, especially when you're under stress, to know what your priorities are. Family and friends helped to sustain me, people I knew who would be there whether I succeeded or whether I failed, and I was encouraged by letters and messages that were sent to me by viewers. One, in particular, touched me. It was from John Wayne, whom I had never met, though years later I would conduct the last interview he'd give. He sent me a telegram. It read, 'Don't let the bastards get you down.' " She laughed as she repeated John Wayne's message.

I asked, "How confident are you today?"

"Professionally," she said, her voice again in that familiar staccato, "I've managed to work my way back with nine more years of interviews and special reports, so I feel confident. Also, co-hosting *20/20* on ABC with Hugh Downs is where, finally, I think I've found a home. In my personal life, on the other hand, I still don't have the confidence that I have in my work. I can rise to deliver a lecture to five thousand people, but I can't walk across a dance floor to try any of the dances of the last twenty years. I just can't do it. I can't stand there alone without feeling that everyone is staring. My nervousness is private, Walter. It's not speaking to a large audience that worries me. It's entering a room and wondering whether I really belong or whether 'they' really want me; it's being on the outside looking in."

I wondered, as she spoke, if this sensitive woman who had endured criticism had also learned how to give it.

"Barbara," I asked, "can you tell me how *you* would criticize someone?"

"I can try," she said.

. . .

I saw a familiar editor across the wide, brightly lighted newsroom, the modern home of the *Reporter Dispatch* in Harrison, New York, but I approached him slowly, quietly. I wanted the moment to matter. No longer were there the ragtag rows of splintered, stained wooden desks that I remembered, no pneumatic tubes overhead that whisked stories to teletypesetters, no boiling lead cooled and punched, letter by letter, into type, no familiar, moist odor of ink that seemed forever to pervade the White Plains building. No, it was now 1975 and there were shiny metal desks firmly planted in precise rows and *carpeting* and little screens with typewriter keyboards. I laughed to myself, recalling how a City Hall reporter once dusted off his desk at the old building with his tie as he remarked, "I wanted to see what would float up into the air," and how a female county bureau reporter once stripped off her blouse on a hot summer day when the temperature inside reached the temperature outside. No, not here. I knew that somewhere in this glass and concrete structure a mammoth computer operated by people called programmers electronically translated the reporters' messages into long, even paper columns that were later sided with hot wax, cut and pasted, then formed by compositors into the pages that were published daily.

The man I had come to see was studying a single sheet of typed notes —a familiar pose, his back to me—as I stepped carefully into his office. I did not want to disturb him, not yet; these seconds were precious to me. Once he had been editor of a newspaper, but now he was an editorial writer and a columnist. I noticed that his hair had silvered more and he wore stylish metal-frame glasses that rode higher on his nose, but I recognized him. I'd always recognize him. His name was Bill Bookman, and eight years earlier, when I was a high school dropout, he'd given me my first opportunity.

"Would you like me to edit that for you?" I asked.

Startled, he turned, smiled widely, then said, "I guess you're looking for a job."

We both laughed.

"Welcome home, Walt," he said, rising and clasping my hand.

The reunion was warm and genuine, and a few minutes later, as we reminisced, I noticed some reporters and editors starting to gather across the newsroom outside my new office.

"Bill," I said, nodding toward the group, "I'm about to be introduced to these people, and many of them, I'm sure, would rather lynch me."

"Why?"

"They're not my team, Bill," I said. "To them, I'm the outsider. My predecessor assembled that crew. I only know a few of them."

"You'll do fine," he told me.

"I hope you're right," I said as I stepped out of his office. I could feel my pulse rising as I took my first step across the newsroom. The moment to reflect, the joy of reunion, was over. I was thirty years old, and I had just become the fourth editor in only a few years of what had been carefully described to me as a demoralized newspaper that had undergone considerable turmoil among its staff. Many reporters and editors, I knew, distrusted me. I was acutely aware that critics described me as overbearing, blindly ambitious, impetuous, skeptical and argumentative, to all of which I said phooey. However, like Ebenezer Scrooge forging the links of the chain in life that he'd have to carry after death, I had earned every criticism. It was not my competence that critics questioned, but my personality. My temper, fueled by my insecurity, was volatile. I intimidated people. Simply put, I had become a bully, and I was about to bully someone again.

Why me?

Have you ever wondered why someone else seems to handle criticism better than you? *I* have. In fact, by the time I was in my late twenties I had more defenses against legitimate criticism than, as my grandmother used to say, Carter's had little liver pills. My favorite, of course, was to make the critic, no matter how sincere, feel stupid. I would shamelessly wield any successes I had in my career as a weapon in this arsenal. "Let me ask you this," I'd say, "if I'm so wrong, why am I here?" Another defense was gobbledygook. Because I had grown fluent in the language of the social sciences through my college studies, I also

became polished in the art of attaching a false psychological significance to my bumbling human relations. I could "objectively" explain
away my absolute mishandling of another human being: "You're criticizing me because of your own blah, blah, blah" (pick up any textbook
to fill in the blahs). Looking back, I'm sure I convinced no one, least
of all me, but it was like running down a steep hill; I couldn't seem to
stop. I can blush today when I consider the long years of unnecessary
and agonizing embarrassment I experienced before I finally understood
that handling criticism is a skill we can really learn, that criticism itself
is an opportunity to improve ourselves and to strengthen our relationships, that criticism can be, as we're about to learn from Barbara
Walters, a sincere testament to friendship.

"My specials," Barbara Walters told me, "are produced by a brilliant,
wonderful young woman named Beth Polson. After an interview is
filmed, we'll usually do the first edit together. Then, what we have
saved is transcribed into a manuscript that is always too long. Beth may
edit the manuscript herself. If, for example, we have thirty minutes of
interview but only fifteen minutes of broadcast time, she'll trim it to
fifteen minutes and I'll review the result. So what do I say if I hate it?"
   "You keep it to yourself?" I asked, laughing.
   "Not quite," she continued, also laughing. "Beth and I are both
strong personalities when it comes to work, and each of us wants the
best possible interview to be broadcast. So what do I say?"
   I nodded.
   "First," she explained, "I've learned that if I'm not rushed or tired,
my criticism is kinder, which is fair to Beth and much more productive
for the two of us. I remind myself to respond only to our work, not to
any other discomfort I might be feeling. I know it's better if I examine
my own mood *before* I suggest any changes.
   "Second, I start with the constructive, like good news–bad news.
I sincerely praise what I like: 'I love the opening' or 'I love what you
did with . . .' I'll mention, 'I have a few small nitty-gritty things,' then
make my suggestions. If I'm in total disagreement, I might say, 'Beth,
I know you've worked very hard, but it just doesn't seem to me to fit

together. Can we go at it again? We might start here . . .' "

"Is Beth aware," I asked, "of what you're doing?"

"Aware?" Barbara replied. "She does the same thing with me!"

"I have a tough question," I suggested.

"Yes," she said.

"Barbara, how do you recover when you *don't* handle it well, when it all blows up?"

"We need a way back," she said. "Let me give you an example. After I interviewed Johnny Carson for a special, he asked me to appear on his program. Beth, who had arranged and scheduled my appearance on his show, thought it was a wonderful idea, an opportunity to promote our own report.

" 'It will enable you to talk about the special,' she said, 'and, besides, because he was nice enough to appear with you, you *should* appear with him.'

"I became anxious. I worried that I'd be expected to be funny or that he'd ask me some of the same questions that I had asked him, questions I had no answers to.

" 'No,' I told Beth, 'I don't want to do this.'

"As the day of the appearance grew closer I became more and more upset, until, finally, I lashed out at Beth, 'You're a steamroller and you push me into everything. You're just too strong. I don't want to do the Johnny Carson show. Stop steamrolling me!'

"The blowup occurred in the office, and Beth became cool, distant, tight. We stood apart like two prizefighters. I felt awful, just awful. I care about her, and, I thought: This is going to destroy our relationship. I left the office and I walked for blocks with a knot tightening in my stomach. Finally, I returned, found Beth and put my arms around her. 'I feel terrible,' I told her. 'I still don't want to appear on that program, but I feel awful that I did this to you.' She told me she felt the same way. Well, two things happened. First, I did the *Tonight Show* with Johnny Carson and it was fine. Second"—Barbara Walters reached behind her and withdrew a small needlepoint pillow which she held up for me to see—"this came about a year later."

Embroidered on the pillow was a question, "Have you hugged your steamroller today?"

"Beth Polson has style," I said.

Barbara Walters smiled and nodded. "Sometimes, Walter," she continued, "the only thing left to do after an outburst is to admit you're wrong and say what you feel. The other person probably hurts too. It's hard to find a way back sometimes, but I think it's important that we try."

"One last question?" I said.

"Sure," she agreed.

"What would you ask Barbara Walters?"

"In my interviews," she said, "I often ask, 'What's the biggest misconception about you?' It gives people a chance to reveal themselves, to speak what's really on their minds."

"Please go on," I encouraged her.

"When a writer attacks me personally or caustically, I really want to say, 'Don't you understand that I have feelings, that I bleed too?' When I walk down the aisle of a plane and I hear, 'There's Babawawa,' I try to tell myself that maybe it's not so terrible, that if I wasn't successful, no one would impersonate me. So, to be a good sport, I smile, but, inside, I know I'm being made fun of. I'd say the biggest misconception about me is that I'm unflappable, that I'm bold, that I'm always in a position of authority. Well, I know who I am. I'm a person who, like anyone else, can be hurt."

On the wall directly facing my desk at *Parade* magazine is a single photograph of an immense outdoor sculpture erected at the University of Pennsylvania. Entitled "Covenant" by its creator, Alexander Liberman, the dimensions of the mighty work are staggering. Welded steel columns, uniformly painted red, measure forty-eight and a half by fifty-one by thirty-four feet. Like ants bustling under and about a large fallen branch, students can be seen laughing, talking, passing through the art itself. The size of the sculpture, its *energy,* a critic might say, the young people alive within it, the sheer geometric array of the huge cylinders balanced one on top of another were good reasons to choose that particular photograph to face my desk, but "Covenant" was displayed more because I knew the sculptor and respected his optimism, his seemingly endless drive to proceed in the face of criticism, his willingness, despite the scant chance of financial reward, to paint thousands of canvases and craft mammoth constructions over decades. His art, to me, meant hope.

He had been the subject of a documentary movie in 1981 called *A Lifetime Burning* and a book published the same year by art critic Barbara Rose entitled *Alexander Liberman.* It was clear that people far more perceptive than I would inevitably assess the importance of the work he cast over a lifetime; my interest lay solely in the man behind the art, my friend Alex.

He was seventy-two when we sat together on a February afternoon in 1985 in his Madison Avenue office. He wore a gray flannel suit, a light blue shirt with a dark blue knitted tie. He was slim with an erect, almost regal, posture. His thin mustache, like his hair, was white and his eyes were bright blue. His voice was smooth, cultured, but as he spoke I considered a contradiction. Alexander Liberman was a struggling artist, a craftsman who had apprenticed to Cézanne, Picasso and Matisse, but he was also the urbane, tough-minded editorial director of all the Condé Nast magazines, which included *Vogue, Self, Mademoiselle, Glamour, House & Garden, Brides, Gentleman's Quarterly* and *Vanity Fair.* He'd become art director of *Vogue* in 1943, a year before I was born, and though his success in publishing over four decades was extraordinary, it was the criticism of his paintings and sculptures I hoped he would discuss.

"Have you," I asked, "ever lost confidence?"

"Walter, my friend," he replied, "constantly!"

"Alex," I said, "of all the important people you've known, did any of them lose confidence?"

He laughed. "Even Picasso," he told me. "I remember once seeing Picasso deep in doubt as he studied some paintings. He asked anyone, *anyone* present, if his paintings were good. That scene to me has remained an important lesson. Only fools, my friend, have absolute confidence. Every interesting person I have ever known has been filled with doubts and questions."

"When you create a sculpture or a painting," I asked, "how do you prepare yourself for criticism?"

"With fear and trembling," he said, "and with the hope that there will be a surprise, that somewhere, someone will respond in the way that I wanted. When it happens, it fulfills my wildest dreams."

"How do you deal with criticism?"

"I suffer," he said.

"Why not ignore it?"

"Because," he replied, "I believe there's at least a grain of truth in every criticism. Criticism forces us to reexamine our thinking. Even unfair criticism is helpful; while it can be destructive, it can also be stimulating. Criticism is our test. If we can survive these obstacles, we're stronger because of them. Criticism strengthens us."

I reminded myself as I stood before the editorial staff of the *Reporter Dispatch* not to mention my former newspaper; I knew that several of these reporters and editors had probably heard once too often in the last year that the *Standard-Star* was doing something right, which must have meant to them that *they* were doing something wrong. Furthermore, the newspapers were different. The *Standard-Star,* with about eighteen thousand subscribers, focused its attention primarily on one community, the city of New Rochelle, while the *Reporter Dispatch,* with multiple editions and nearly fifty thousand subscribers, covered scores of communities over hundreds of square miles in two counties.

I can't let them see that I'm nervous, I told myself. My jaw tightened.

Anderson, I wondered, now that you're here, what are you going to say? Some of the reporters and editors, about two dozen in all, had started to glance at one another. Well, what *are* you going to say?

"I don't know very many of you," I began, "but I hope to change that in the next few weeks—"

One reporter nodded.

"—so I hope to meet with each of you privately. I'd like to know how this place works—"

Three or four chuckled.

"—so that I can contribute."

So far so good, I thought. The room was quiet. I had their attention. The tension seemed to ease.

"I'm sure you have questions," I suggested, "and I'll try my best to answer them, but remember I've only been here a couple of hours, so you may get stuck with some 'I don't knows.' "

"What," a reporter asked, "do you plan to do with the *Reporter Dispatch?*"

"I don't know," I said, and the room burst into laughter.

The reporter didn't laugh. "What," he asked, "did you do with the *Standard-Star* that you plan to do here?"

I respected him immediately. Although he was nervous, he was determined to have his question answered. This reporter, I thought, would be a star.

"I care," I told him, "about local news. My focus in New Rochelle was on local news, and I'll insist on the same focus here. When the big story comes, and it will, we'll handle it as well as or better than any metropolitan newspaper, but, first and foremost, we'll emphasize local news coverage."

Another reporter asked, "Are you going to be 'involved' in the community?"

"Yes," I said, "I will be because—"

The room was silent again.

"—I believe a newspaper is part of and not separate from the community it serves. The *Reporter Dispatch* has, I've noticed, averaged a local editorial a week. We'll try for one every day. I'll be visible in the community, very much a part of it. Wherever a worthy cause exists, we'll support it with articles and editorials, but if we find corruption, we'll expose that too. We won't seek controversy, but we won't shy away from it either."

A young woman near the door raised her hand.

I nodded to her.

"Are you going to replace Gene Duffy?" she asked.

Several reporters looked immediately at their feet. This was a tough question. Louis A. Weil III, who was called Chip and was the president of the newspapers, and Thomas P. Dolan, who was the publisher, did, in fact, plan to give me the additional responsibilities of general manager, Duffy's job, but they decided to wait at least three months to announce the promotion. Given that time, I'd have the opportunity to explore the communities that we served, discover the issues of importance and gain a better understanding of the newspaper itself. The *Reporter Dispatch* had problems that were more complex than those facing the *Standard-Star*. If I had been named general manager and editor, I would immediately have been in charge of advertising, circulation and administration as well as editorial content. It was too much. "Tell me," Chip promised, "the day you're ready."

Facing the reporter now, I squirmed. How can I answer this question? If I tell the truth, I'll be announcing the retirement of T. Eugene Duffy, which I have no right to do, and I'll be violating the confidence of my superiors, which I can't do either.

"Is it important to you?" I asked.

She nodded.

"Someday," I said, "Gene Duffy is going to announce his retirement, and I suspect that when he does, because I've been a general manager, I will be a candidate to succeed him, provided, of course, I don't retire first." Some laughter followed, and had I stopped there, all would have been well, but instead my anxiety erupted and I lied, "But to my knowledge Gene Duffy is not going to retire for a long time."

It was as if a pin had popped my balloon. I knew I had lied, which was especially hypocritical in someone who had insisted that he was dedicated to the search for truth. Although I undoubtedly seemed assertive, very much in control, what no reporter or editor in the room could suspect was that I had dissembled; I had lost my compass in a storm. I was unsure, and my guilt made me resentful. What else are they going to ask me? I felt my neck reddening; it was as if a belt were being twisted behind my eyes.

"Are you going to bring in your own people?" someone asked.

"No," I replied.

"What if we disagree with you?"

The belt snapped. Why did I leave New Rochelle? Not to lead these brats, that's for sure. Not me! This meeting will end now.

"If," I said, "you don't like it, you can walk."

The reporter, unprepared to quit, looked away and the room fell silent.

"Any more questions?" I asked.

There wasn't a sound.

As I sat alone a few minutes later, I felt defeated before I had even begun. I'm the one who's out of step, I admitted to myself, not them. I have a problem. If I even suspect criticism, I overreact. What is it I'm afraid that others will find out? What's wrong with me?

The sunlight that entered my office at *Parade* during an early spring afternoon in 1985 seemed to emphasize her gentle, demure softness. It added highlights to her strawberry-blond hair and brightened her pale blue eyes and pink, creamy skin. As she sat facing me, petite in an amber knitted blouse and skirt, I had to remind myself one more time that this delicate person whom I had known for years was an author with an unusual resiliency, a toughness, an incisive drive, a woman who had examined the stages of our adult years, who had added a new meaning to a word and an important understanding to our language. Her name was Gail Sheehy, and she had written, among others, the provocative book about the predictable crises we face in our lives called *Passages*, a volume that more than six million people had purchased since it was first published in 1976. She had also contributed several sensitive articles to *Parade*, including one of the most compelling in the magazine's history, the story of how she had been sexually molested by a neighbor when she was a child. Her willingness to examine hurt squarely, even her own, made me confident that she would answer my questions thoughtfully:

"Can you recall an unfair criticism you could not defend against?"

She nodded. "I still remember," she began, "what I felt when I read the first review of *Passages*. It appeared in the *Chicago Tribune* and was a total pan because of what the reviewer called my shocking lack of scholarship. I couldn't believe it! It was like a stab to my heart; my years of research and hard work were blithely dismissed. It turned out that the book publisher, in a hasty effort to get *Passages* quickly to the newspaper for review, had neglected to send fifty pages of notes and sources. It was too late, though. The criticism had appeared."

"Gail," I asked, "can you remember the most stinging criticism of you or your most embarrassing moment as a child?"

She nodded again.

"I'm sure I was embarrassed many times," she said, "but one incident in particular stands out, and that was the day I was supposed to play 'The Skaters' Waltz' on the piano for my whole elementary school. I was a third-grader, and as my class walked two by two to the auditorium, I started yammering away because I was so excited. The teacher became annoyed with my chatter, and before I could tell her that I belonged onstage, she fastened Scotch tape over my mouth. It was like one of those awful nightmares where you're paralyzed and you can't speak. When they announced my name, the piano stool stayed empty and the adults looked at each other in confusion: 'Where's Gail?' My teacher, realizing the mistake, hurriedly peeled off the tape and sent me alone up to the stage. I was so undone I played as if I had twelve fingers. It was simply a disaster for me. I was humiliated from start to finish."

Gail made pointing gestures frequently as she spoke and her voice rose and fell with intensity; her words came with feeling, as if she were reliving the experience in the telling.

"Have you ever felt that helpless, that vulnerable, that devastated as an adult?" I asked.

She paused. "Yes," she said, "I have."

"When?"

"There was to be a book-signing party for me at Brentano's on Fifth Avenue," she began, "and I got all dressed up. What an exciting day I expected! I arrived early and sat on a chair near the front window, a spot I occupied for an hour and a half. No one came. Not a soul. No one asked me to sign a single copy of *Passages*. Passersby could see me sitting there alone. I felt like the biggest blob in the world"—her voice deepened and the words came more slowly—"and it was like being in third grade again with everyone knowing that I was a flop, everyone witnessing my failure. Finally, I cried, which only deepened my embarrassment because my mascara began to run in ugly black streaks down my cheeks. During the worst of it, the absolute worst moment, a friend came"—she smiled broadly, her eyes wide, her words rapid again— "and she was dressed to the teeth and she whisked me away to an expensive French restaurant as if I were the most successful author in the world. That single act of kindness turned my day from disaster to celebration."

"How long was it," I asked, "before you knew the book was a success?"

"The first positive review," she replied, "came in about six weeks, but it wasn't that. You know what it was?"

"No."

"Strangers. People who didn't know me began to tell me what my book meant to them. That was my secret dream. I wanted *Passages* to be appreciated by people I did not know. Those are the opinions I can trust the most. It's not that professional criticism is of little use; it can, on the contrary, be invaluable to the growth of a creative person. Strangers, though, simply want their money's worth. If my book illuminates or falls short, they'll tell me flat out. Readers speak with true authority."

How sensitive have I been to criticism? I even argued when someone genuinely tried to help me. I can still remember a conversation with Chip Weil in 1974, when I was editor and general manager in New Rochelle. Chip was a top corporate executive and my immediate superior, and he suggested to me that I enroll at company expense in a Dale Carnegie self-improvement course, a recommendation I stoutly resisted. I envisioned, in my ignorance, a crowded little classroom with an instructor, probably a well-intentioned salesman, at a blackboard diagraming tidy little formulas for success. After four years of nightly college studies, I was not enthusiastic.

"Chip," I said, "I sincerely appreciate your suggestion, and if I wasn't tied up learning this new job, I'd probably leap at the opportunity—"

"Walter," he interrupted, "you *will* attend the Dale Carnegie course."

Chip had to order me to take a course that would become a valuable learning experience. Why did I resist? I was being criticized, wasn't I? Wasn't Chip's message that I *needed* the Dale Carnegie course? I'd show him, I promised myself. Criticize me, will you?

During the evening of June 4, 1974, as each of us rose one by one to receive our certificates as graduates of the Dale Carnegie Course in Effective Speaking and Human Relations, I considered the irony. Although initially my boss had to order me to attend, I had grown so enthusiastic, and more so with each succeeding session, that my fellow classmates had elected me their leader.

Why was I so enthusiastic?

Dale Carnegie's suggestions were certainly sound, but it was more than that. The course reinforced in me a lesson that I had been taught in the Marine Corps. Leaders, I was reminded, are made, not born. We *can* change.

Almost a year later, a few weeks after my stumbling introduction to the editorial staff of the *Reporter Dispatch,* I decided to read again Dale Carnegie's classic work, *How to Win Friends and Influence People.* It moved me to read Norman Vincent Peale's equally inspirational *The Power of Positive Thinking* and to reread what remains for me one of the most important books I've ever read, Stuart Chase's *The Power of Words.*

I knew I needed help; this time I read to learn. I sought answers, not formulas. I slowly began to grasp, in the stories and the illustrations these talented authors shared, a larger truth that had endured throughout the centuries, an ageless wisdom that I had first heard somewhere in my childhood, a few simple words that I, like millions of other children, had been forced to memorize: *Do unto others as you would have them do unto you.* I realized that for as long as I could remember I had failed to recognize the practical value of this, the golden rule. It was, I finally understood, the essence of leadership.

How can I best encourage someone to correct a mistake, to modify behavior, to perform more efficiently or more effectively, to correct an error?

Pretend he's me.

How would *I* like to hear that I've flubbed?

I'd like my critic to reassure me that the rest of what I've done, I've done well, that I'm appreciated although I slipped, that my mistake was merely human, that I wasn't lazy, irresponsible or careless. That I *can* do it right, if I try again.

He gently patted the Amphora tobacco into the dark bowl of a sculpted briar pipe, his tapping as easy and expert, I thought, and as subtle, as the man himself. His apartment, which he shared with Nancy, his wife of more than thirty years, was five floors above Manhattan's Central Park. Their son, Hugh, who was twenty-three, lived nearby. The living room, which was where we were seated, was wide and bright, decorated vanilla and beige throughout, with floor-to-ceiling smoked mirrors reflecting the fluffy off-white couches that had been carefully placed to form conversation pits. This was a home with a blond cast to the air, as if a hidden hearth were always aflame, a small corner of New York where guests would be encouraged to talk. My host, whose soft, round face was one of the most familiar in America, had been a teacher from a family of teachers, a merchant seaman, an actor on Broadway and in nearly three dozen movies, but one role, *one* role, catapulted him to unimaginable fame. He was the star for thirteen seasons of one of the most popular television series of all time, *All in the Family,* and its successor, *Archie's Place.* He had been Archie Bunker; he was Carroll O'Connor.

"Carroll," I asked, "what's the worst thing you've faced as an actor?"

"Rejection," he said.

"Rejection?" I asked. His peers, I knew, had voted him four Emmy awards, three of them in a row, and a Peabody Award for his classic performance as the often wrong, but never unsure, curmudgeon from Queens, Archie Bunker. Fifty *million* people regularly watched *All in the Family* at its height.

"Rejection," he repeated. He turned quickly in his chair and glanced toward the outer foyer. He raised his eyebrows as if a doorbell had sounded. I looked too.

"The other day," he continued, "a salesman stood there trying to sell us some office equipment, but after evaluating its use, Nancy and I decided not to buy. Now, that young man was a good salesman and he had a good product, but it simply didn't fit our needs. He was gracious and he left cheerfully. Although he didn't make a sale, I'm sure he didn't feel personally rejected. Compare that with an actor. He has no vacuum cleaner, no word processor, no machine to sell. *He* is his product. Most actors must face powerful rejection right from the beginning of their careers, rejection that often lasts for years."

"Did that happen to you?"

"My case was only slightly different," he said. "To begin with, I passed my first professional audition, because I happened to fit a certain character type, at the renowned Dublin Gate Theatre Company. I was lucky, purely and simply, lucky. I was on a roll, as they say, that began in 1951 and ended in 1954. I returned to New York ready to conquer."

"What really happened?"

"Total rejection, and often in the most desultory of ways. Receptionists wouldn't pass me through to agents. The agents themselves, when I managed to actually speak with one of them, would demand of me, 'Who do you think you are?' To them I was a beginner, not a known earner, and they'd inevitably say, 'We don't need you.' It was devastating to hear. Without an agent, I wasn't taken seriously by producers. Nevertheless, I'd make every open casting call I could, try for every role, day after day, week after week, month after month, year after year. I nearly dropped out. Receptionists would ask me to sign my name on one of those yellow legal pads they all had handy. I don't know what magic I expected my name to have on those yellow pads, but I signed them all. Once, though, I wrote, 'Marlon Brando.' The receptionist didn't even notice."

"Carroll," I asked, "you almost dropped out?"

"Yes," he replied, "I was sub-teaching to make money and was about to pursue teaching full-time when I got an offer to act and direct at a repertory theater in St. Louis. I took it, but the venture failed, and once again, in 1958, I returned to New York, to rejection. This time, however, the great actor-director Burgess Meredith, who has been a very dear friend to this day, cast me in a play. I started to get some parts —and got an agent too—and a producer at Warner Brothers, a gentleman by the name of Roy Huggins, saw me on a dramatic broadcast, and invited me to Hollywood in 1960. It had been six years since I left the Dublin theater and I had nearly quit more than once."

"Has there been," I asked, "a moment of greatest joy for you?"

"It was less a moment," he answered, "than a span of time. When *All in the Family* emerged as the country's most popular show for five years, I felt my greatest satisfaction as an actor. The enthusiastic acceptance of the audience was more important to me than the Emmy awards. I had climbed a mountain of yellow legal pads to hear those cheers."

His words were clipped and precise, softly spoken and carefully chosen, as they had been the first time we met in May 1982. We had been introduced by the respected literary agent Scott Meredith, who had assured me, "Carroll is eloquent, articulate and serious about writing."

On Scott's recommendation I asked Carroll to lunch at Peacock Alley in the Waldorf-Astoria. As one of the fifty million who regularly watched *All in the Family*, I eagerly looked forward to sharing a meal with Archie Bunker. When it became apparent—quickly apparent— that my well-spoken guest was not Archie but Carroll, I was, I'll admit, more than a little disconcerted. It was as if I had lost an old friend.

"Bitterness," Carroll told me as we were served lunch in Peacock Alley, "is caused by disproportionate expectations . . ."

Disproportionate expectations?

Cheezit, Arch, I thought, where did you learn those words?

. . .

It's easier to accept criticism, I've found, when we learn not to take it personally and when we realize that it can actually enhance rather than weaken a relationship. We're most often wrong when we think: If you criticize me, you dislike me. In Chapter Five Sherry Lansing wisely suggested that we should disassociate ourselves from our errors: "The biggest mistake that any of us might make may be to think that when something we do fails, *we* have failed." It's also true of criticism. You and it are not the same thing.

Learning how to handle our emotions under criticism is a sign of maturity and is immensely valuable in the business and professional world. Socially it's indispensable. If one spouse continually reacts to criticism with a series of temper tantrums or other disturbing behavior, dangerous silence can result. Criticism ceases, but so does communication. Eventually the marriage ends too.

The most effective way to learn how to accept criticism may be to learn how to give it. Here are six steps that have worked for me:

• *Can it be changed?* If it can't, don't take the next step. Be silent. Never, *never* criticize what cannot be changed. This kind of criticism can only hurt. If it's too late, forget it: "You shouldn't have worn that dress tonight." This is the hardest rule to follow, because it denies us the opportunity to get it out of our system. We have to contain our disappointment with someone else, when what we really want to do is tell that person off. Remember: *Pretend he or she is me.* There is enough in our lives that we can improve, so we ought not to waste time on what cannot be helped.

• *Choose a proper time and place.* No one likes to hear criticism in front of others. Remember to check your mood. "If I'm not rushed or tired," Barbara Walters learned, "my criticism is kinder—and more productive." I'm a mean critic when I'm angry. I'll bet you are too.

• *Reassure.* Begin with praise whenever possible. What good things did the person do? "Start with the constructive," Barbara Walters suggested. This must be sincere, though. Do not say, "This is great, but . . ." Say what is great.

• *Be specific.* If you cannot be specific, do not criticize. If you can't get it straight, how do you expect the other guy to understand? I've heard editors tell writers to make the beginning of their stories "more lively" or "punch up" their conclusions. Can you decipher the criticism? I can't and neither can the writers. What do you mean? Be specific.

• *Express confidence.* You're criticizing something that you've already determined can be corrected. Help the person understand that he can in fact correct it. Then make the change seem easy to achieve.

• *Praise improvement.* Be there tomorrow. To do less, after you've volunteered a criticism, is rude. If you've taken the time to criticize, take the time to praise. Not only will praise speed improvement, further criticism from you will likely be regarded as sincere and will be welcomed.

Once we learn how to give criticism, we can understand better how to receive it:

• *Focus on the criticism only.* Do not focus on the critic, his emotions or your own. *You and the criticism are not the same thing.* Remember that a person must care about you to take the time to criticize.

• *Find its value.* There may be something important that you're being told, even if the message is poorly delivered. "There's at least a grain of truth in every criticism," Alex Liberman suggested. "Even unfair criticism," he said, "is helpful." Try to remember that criticism is an opportunity to improve. Ask for specifics. Be sure you understand the criticism. Don't yes-yes your critic. Try to hear all he has to say. When you clearly understand the criticism, go to the next step.

• *Evaluate.* If you've focused on the criticism, separated yourself from the emotion of the moment and clearly understood what has been suggested, you're prepared to determine whether it is something you can change or want to change. You might ask yourself whether this is the first time you've heard this particular criticism, whether the critic is a competent, if not impartial, observer, whether the critic is venting frustration or making a keen observation. Remember, though, a critic *can* vent frustration and still make a valuable observation.

• *Say thank you.* Enlist the critic's help if possible.

A common fear regarding criticism is that it makes us a doormat, that accepting criticism, particularly harsh criticism, somehow demeans us. With rare exceptions, discourtesy need not be tolerated— and even with the most unkind cut, if you exercise the steps just outlined, you, and not your critic, are in control.

"Carroll," I said, "I remember the first time we had lunch and how we were interrupted—"

He nodded. A large, heavy woman, who had stared and stared at the famous actor across the restaurant, finally walked over, kissed him on the forehead and said, "I just want to thank you for the enjoyment I've had watching you on television."

"—and how gracious you were with the woman."

He laughed.

"She knew," he said, "that might be her only chance to say what she wanted to say to me. I meant enough to her that she took her courage in her hands, ignored her own sense of manners and did something she'd never normally do. I understand. She meant well. How could I be rude? What does it cost me to wave back when someone in a car shouts, 'Hi, Arch!' If you and I step outside and start circling the block, I'm sure that we'll meet four new people with every revolution."

"Do you enjoy it?"

"Nothing," he said, "gives me more joy than being recognized with delight."

"Carroll," I asked, "what about when you're not received well?"

"Bad reviews?"

"Yes."

"I'm too stubborn to cry," he said, "or to admit to myself that they get to me, but of course they do. As an actor I've received as many bad reviews as good reviews. Some actors claim they don't read their reviews. I read them all."

"Were any particularly biting?"

"Yes," he said, "those that were really personal. They hurt me the most. One critic, whom I must have offended in some unknown way, once wrote that I 'had a nerve appearing on-stage.' I'm a professional actor. That's so silly it shouldn't upset me, right? Well, it did."

"How would you," I asked, "advise a friend to handle criticism?"

"Establish a policy," he said firmly, "of taking all criticism as friendly. Now, you know in your heart there will be times when that's not true, but stick to it anyway, because any critic can prove to you how sincere, how well-intentioned his criticism is. This policy is for *your* peace of mind, not your critic's. If you argue about the critic's goodwill, you'll lose. Once you insist to yourself that the other person is well-intentioned, you'll get value from legitimate criticism, if there's any there to get, and you won't be bothered by the rest. No matter how hard it may be at times to stick to your policy, particularly with people close to you, when you concede a critic's goodwill, you disarm an attacker and encourage an ally."

"Carroll, do you ever say to yourself: What will I do when they find out I'm me?"

"Now, listen," he said, "I sure do. You're my friend, Walter, but there are things I don't want you to know. If you knew what I worried about, you'd probably say, 'Cheez, pal, that's nothing! Everybody's done that.' " Archie Bunker's voice emerged in his words and we both laughed. "But I'm not sure. It's often the small things, I believe, that trouble us most anyway."

"For example?"

"I attended a Holy Communion yesterday for the child of a friend of mine. Also there was another young person I've known since infancy. I failed to take notice of her, and it's troubling me as I sit here. It was a terrible oversight. I think I hurt her. It really bothers me."

Later, as I rode down the elevator, I thought about what my famous friend had told me and I pictured a sea of receptionists with yellow pads. His final words were no surprise.

"I think I'm going to call that kid now," he said.

I was an hour early for my luncheon appointment at the Marco Polo Club in the Waldorf-Astoria. Good, I thought, more time to think. I started to walk uptown along Park Avenue past the famous hotel. What, I wondered, will Jess Gorkin ask me this time? I was one of three final candidates for a senior editor's position at *Parade*, which had the largest circulation of any publication in America, and I was sure my rivals were more qualified. Perhaps, I worried, I shouldn't have been so candid in my written review of his magazine. After all, Jess Gorkin had been editor of *Parade* for three decades. Who was I to evaluate his work, even if he had asked? We'd met twice and I had also been interviewed by the president, James McAllister. An executive recruiter named Howard Johnson of Eastman and Beaudine had introduced me to both men. I had decided, for better or worse, that I'd be myself, though, privately, I wished I had more to offer. My work seemed so anemic. *Parade* was a magazine, and my experience, except for an article here and there, was purely newspapering.

It was a sunny May day in 1977, an exceptional afternoon to enjoy Manhattan. For all I noticed, though, it could have been snowing. The more I concentrated and practiced what I *might* say, the more doubt I raised. Block after block, my anxiety grew, and I had no sense that I had traveled far when I looked at my watch. I couldn't believe it! I had walked nearly a mile. I was able to flag a cab and make it back to the Waldorf with a couple of minutes to spare.

Jess Gorkin had already arrived, and I was led to his table in the Marco Polo Club.

"Did you have any trouble finding this place?" he asked.

"No," I said, "it was easy."

He spoke gently. I wondered, as I listened to him, how many people would recognize this slight, balding, unassuming man with the conservative navy blue pin-striped suit as the fellow who had persuaded a president of the United States, John F. Kennedy, and a Soviet premier, Nikita Khrushchev, to create the famous hotline between their two countries. It was *his* idea and he made it happen, just as he helped to achieve another remarkable piece of diplomacy, the first joint space-flight involving the Soviet Union and the United States.

Why am I here? I silently wondered. The *Reporter Dispatch* is one thing. *Parade* is quite another.

My wife had asked me that morning what I thought would happen during lunch.

"More questions," I said.

"Do you think he'll offer you a job?" Loretta asked.

"Probably not."

"What will you say if he does?"

"You'll be the first to know," I promised.

Jess Gorkin and I ordered lunch. He ordered bland food but told me, "Pay no attention. I have to watch what I eat. You order whatever you like." I think I ordered fish, but for all I know, I might have ordered a steak. I was so nervous that I wouldn't have known the difference.

After we had eaten, he discussed the magazine.

"I liked your analysis of *Parade*," he said, "and I particularly liked your ideas. You have a way of seeing through a complicated problem quickly and suggesting a solution"—he paused—"but are you aware you're recommending changing something that's very successful?"

My life had come to this moment. I was thirty-two. I had been a journalist precisely ten years, and during the last two as editor and general manager of the *Reporter Dispatch* I had learned some important lessons, not the least of which was that I had begun to understand, despite many failures, how to criticize without stirring resentment: *Pretend he is me.* I knew that the *Reporter Dispatch* had done well and my contribution was valued by the Gannett Company, but I also knew that I could not turn down a once-in-a-lifetime opportunity to be an editor for the most widely read magazine in America, a chance to learn from a man who brought nations together. How should I answer his question? If I suggest change, won't I be criticizing his work and destroy any chance I might have of being hired? If, on the other hand, I believe change is called for and I remain silent, what am I? How badly do I want this job?

"Jess," I said, "you're a great editor, and, frankly, I'm sitting here thinking: Who am I to evaluate your work? Well, my friend, you asked and I guess I'm going to have to wager you really want me to answer. This is my view . . ."

I spoke for fifteen minutes. Jess didn't interrupt and his face stayed expressionless. I had no sense of what he felt. I explained what I thought was very good about *Parade* and where I thought improvement was necessary. Some of my comments, I knew, struck at ideas he had encouraged for years. In for a penny, in for a pound, I told myself. Let him hear it all. When I finished, I immediately wished I had said nothing.

He was silent.

That's that, I thought.

"Walter," he said finally, "I do not want to hire you to be a senior editor at *Parade.*"

My stomach twisted.

"I want you," he continued, "to be my assistant, though you'll have the title of senior editor. Within a year I will promote you to managing editor, then within another year, if everything goes well, you'll succeed me."

The salary and benefits he mentioned were more than I had planned to ask for.

I was silent.

"Jess," I said quietly, "will you please excuse me for a moment?"

I rose from my chair, walked to the bathroom, checked the stalls to be sure I was alone, faced the mirror, threw up my hands and said, "All right!"

When I returned to the table, I told him calmly, my voice serious, "That's certainly a generous offer and I appreciate it. So that I can discuss this with my employers and give it more thought, may I have a week to give you an answer?"

"Of course, Walter," he told me. His eyes seemed to twinkle, as if he wanted to smile, but he didn't.

After we said good-bye a few minutes later, I ran to a telephone in the Waldorf, misdialed once, then dialed correctly.

"Hello," Loretta answered.

"Guess what?" I asked, my voice cracking.

She laughed.

"I think I can," she said.

Chapter 10

AM I READY?

The note was dated December 28, 1972, and it read, "I am the sweetest of fellows and my agent is hard as nails. I suppose that's the two poles of the truth." The message was signed by the renowned American author Norman Mailer, and it was hung on a wall in the reception area of the thirteenth-floor offices of the Scott Meredith Literary Agency at 845 Third Avenue in Manhattan. To the left of the letter was a locked glass case with shelves that held twenty current books, including the latest volumes by Norman Mailer, Carl Sagan, Arthur C. Clarke, Margaret Truman, Garry Wills, Elliott Roosevelt and Dr. Stuart Berger. As I waited on a June afternoon in 1985 to see the talented man who had created this immensely successful agency, I studied an eight-pronged brass chandelier centered in the ceiling above me. I noticed that three of the electric candles were extinguished, four were steady and one, brighter than the others, flickered excitedly. It was as if that single candle, against the absolutes of natural law, was struggling to prevail. I laughed. If it doesn't dim, I thought, I'll name that candle Scott Meredith.

Jack Scovil, one of the several agents who worked with Scott Meredith, had confided to me over the telephone earlier in the day that there had been considerable speculation among employees about what I might ask the founder of their agency.

"This time," I told Jack, "the boss cannot prepare."

"Not at all?" Jack asked.

"And," I teased, "none of you can guess what I have in mind."

I did not share with Jack an important clue, a comment made to me months earlier by another of Scott's clients, the distinguished television newsman and author David Schoenbrun.

"You and Scott talk alike," David had told me.

"We talk alike?" I asked.

"No," he amended, "it's more than that. You *are* alike. I can hear Scott in your words and you in his."

I recalled, as I mulled over David's observation, the mountainous piles of writer's magazines that I had studied as a teenager, never failing to notice, it seemed, advertisements or stories about the hundreds of successful authors discovered by the Scott Meredith Literary Agency. Several times I wrote long, involved letters to this famous agent, but never mailed them for fear of being rejected. As long as I didn't send a letter, I couldn't fail—though I couldn't succeed either.

Alone now, as I waited to be taken in to see the man who had since become my friend, I looked to my right at the wooden doors that opened to the agency. Almost compulsively I remembered an afternoon five years earlier when that entrance seemed an impenetrable barrier. I could recall every detail from the first moment, at precisely 1:00 P.M., October 9, 1980, when the elevator closed solidly behind me: I faced those two wooden doors, each bearing the symbol of the Scott Meredith Literary Agency, a gold-leaf circle enclosing the founder's initials. I was there to meet Norman Mailer. I had suggested to Scott Meredith that Mailer write an article for *Parade* exploring capital punishment. The author had written a gripping, insightful piece, but I had some suggestions that I mentioned over the telephone to Scott, and so we made an appointment to discuss the article. *I had some suggestions for Norman Mailer.* Fear suddenly, coldly, overwhelmed me as I stood in the hallway. I froze. My palms grew moist. My throat dried. My pulse quickened. What am I doing here? I asked myself, incredulous. I can't edit Norman Mailer! I'm a high school dropout from a tenement in Mount Vernon, New York. Who am I trying to kid? Who do I think I am? He's the greatest writer of our day. The terrifying, hungry creature of a thousand nightmares howled before me; I was the prehistoric cave dweller fearing for my life. I wanted to flee. Those doors seemed to grow larger as my anxiety swelled. The elevator button was only inches away when, for whatever reason, another thought flashed: If I can get through the next hour, I can do anything. I barged in, *barged* in, because if I didn't move fast, if I hesitated, if I thought any longer, I knew I'd choose the elevator.

Now as I sat in the reception area recalling the experience, I nodded, as if I were somehow agreeing with myself.

"Hi, Walter," Jack Scovil suddenly hailed me, as he opened the door to the inner offices. I was back in the present.

"Would you like to see Scott now?" he asked.

"Absolutely," I replied. "Did you guess my questions?"

"No," he said, "but we tried."

Beyond the desk with its curved work surface of white marble delicately veined in gray, the concrete, steel and glass of scores of Manhattan skyscrapers could be seen through the two windowed walls of Scott Meredith's corner office. The floor was parquet and the wallpaper a subdued flowered print of beige and blue. I sat with my back to the windows on a tan couch, one of two around a walnut coffee table. Scott sat across from me, a small bronze bust of John Kennedy to his right. He had a neatly trimmed beard which, like his close-cropped curly hair, was salt-and-pepper, a hundred shades of black and white and gray. His black eyebrows arched at the ends, as if in perpetual surprise. His glasses, with clear lenses, were brown-framed, matching his eyes. He wore a blue patterned silk tie, its knot loose in the collar of his tailored powder-blue cotton shirt, the sleeves of which, not surprisingly, had been rolled up. He slowly twirled a gold ballpoint pen between the fingers of his right hand.

"David Schoenbrun," I began, "told me that we're so similar he had trouble telling us apart over the telephone. What do you suppose he meant by that?"

Scott laughed. "I'm not sure," he said. "Our voices are not the same. Perhaps it's because I'm sincere and honest with him. I don't stall when I have bad news and I'm genuinely happy when I can give him good news. Maybe that's what he meant, the directness, that's how we are alike."

But there was more to it than that, I suspected, for as Scott, my trusted friend and counselor, sat across from me, I thought I saw something that he himself could not see. I hoped the interview would reveal it.

"Do you remember the day I met Norman?"

"Sure," he said.

"Did I look nervous?" I asked.

"No," he said, "and that's interesting because you've since told me how anxious you were and how you lingered outside the door. Actually, as soon as you walked in, you struck me as one of the most confident young men I've ever known. You gave no trace of what you felt. You spoke beautifully, clearly making your points."

The meeting was still vivid to me. Norman Mailer, who had written *The Naked and The Dead, Armies of the Night* and *The Executioner's Song,* was, to my extreme relief, responsive, professional and sincerely interested in what I had to say that might help to improve his essay. Although he looked drawn and was temporarily troubled by back pain, he was gracious. I suspect that he sensed, but politely chose to ignore, my anxiety. An hour stretched to an hour and a half. Imagine having ninety minutes to ask the most important American writer, an author whose work you've studied for years, any question you liked; I had first read *The Naked and The Dead* fifteen years earlier, when I was a lance corporal in the Marine Corps. We discussed writing and editing and Mencken and Lippmann and existentialism and boxing and democracy. I remember that later, when the wooden doors to Scott's offices closed behind me, I stood alone again in the quiet hallway. I also remember how I threw my hands in the air and whispered, "Hurray!"

.   .   .

I stepped off the bathroom scale the morning of August 31, 1983, which was my thirty-ninth birthday, and made a promise: "I will never look like this again." I weighed two hundred and thirty-five pounds; I was at least forty pounds overweight. "You," I told the flabby person I saw in the mirror, "will be in the best shape of your life on your next birthday." Everybody says that, I thought. You can do it, I told myself. Start today.

It was warm and humid. Nevertheless, I laced on a pair of jogging shoes, stepped out of my home and started to run, a heavy, sloppy jog. Ten yards. Twenty. A hundred. My lungs ached and my thighs felt thick. I stopped and leaned forward, puffing and dizzy. This is dumb, I thought. Start tomorrow. No, start today. I straightened up and ran ten more yards, stopped, took several deep breaths and walked home. Well, I told myself, it's a start.

"Scott," I said, "there was a moment in my childhood when I looked into the night and declared, 'I'm going to get out of here.' Did you have a similar experience?"

He paused. "People often laugh," he began, "when I tell them I had six years of hard apprenticeship before I sold my first manuscript at the age of fourteen, but it's true. I began submitting my stories to magazines when I was eight. My family lived on Tenth Avenue and Fifty-third Street in Manhattan, then the worst corner of Hell's Kitchen. Because I couldn't afford postage, I'd deliver my new manuscripts by hand every week, year in and year out, and I'd pick up those that had been rejected. *I was determined to get out.* In addition to writing, I took any other job I could get. For example, although I was a skinny kid, I was hired to carry flowers. I wasn't strong enough, though, to carry the large boxes loaded with vases for very long. I'd work them into my arms, my back bending and my knees buckling under me, until I was out of sight, then I'd pull the boxes stuffed with vases along the ground, which was all I could do. I was so afraid that they'd see me dragging the cartons and fire me."

"Were you ashamed of being poor?"

"Sometimes," he replied. "One day when I was eight, my elementary school teacher decided to check the condition of the footwear of each pupil. That was more than half a century ago, but I remember the incident as clearly as if it had occurred this morning. I felt terror as she came down the aisle between our desks. Some students had holes in their soles, which prompted giggles from my classmates. I thought, Why can't she take each of us privately into the coat closet to check? Finally, she got to me. She lifted my feet. Everyone laughed. I had practically no bottoms at all. I was humiliated. On Saturdays I was the kid who didn't get to go to the movies. There were days when there was no food—not *less* food, *no* food."

"Today," I reminded him, "you own one of the world's most successful literary agencies and, my friend, you have become a millionaire many times over."

"That's true," he said softly.

"How," I asked, "did you start?"

"I almost didn't," he said. "About forty years ago, right after World War II, I was discharged from the Army Air Corps, a veteran with eleven million other young men, and like each one of them, I was determined to make it, whatever *it* was. At the same time, though, I was concerned less with success than with eating. One day an agent, whom I had asked to represent me, suggested that *I* be an agent. That night, as I told my wife, Helen, about his suggestion, I ridiculed it. My experiences with agents had been dreadful. Helen said, 'Now, wait a minute. You've always been fascinated by contracts, and you could do it the *right* way. You enjoy writing and editing, and you love to spend time with writers and editors.' She was right. 'Go ahead,' she encouraged me. Grudgingly I withdrew our life savings, two hundred dollars, and I went into the agency business. I said I'd try it for three months" —he laughed—"and Friday we celebrate the thirty-ninth anniversary of the Scott Meredith Literary Agency."

It was six in the morning, Labor Day, 1983, and I had walked and jogged, mainly walked, about half a mile. Not bad, I told myself as I stepped on the bathroom scale. I had lost a pound in less than a week. I was also relieved, because the previous day the scale had indicated that I had *gained* two pounds.

"Scott," I asked, "what is it that you most appreciate in your life?"

"I've been very lucky," he replied. "I don't think I have a superior mind or a superior editorial talent, but I've had success despite what I don't have. Helen and I have lived in Kings Point, right on Long Island Sound, for seventeen years. It's lovely. There are no sidewalks or streetlights. You cross a little bridge and you see trees hanging over the road and their branches touch each other. It's beautiful. Sometimes I wonder, though: How did I ever deserve this? I think about how lucky I am to live in this house, swim in this pool—*my* pool—and enjoy my life. I have a wonderful wife and children and grandchildren. My grandson, who is eight, told me the other day that dinosaurs lived a long time ago. 'And,' he added, 'so did Beethoven.' Beethoven! Can you imagine that? At his age I didn't even know who Beethoven was."

Scott, I remembered, had stood humbly, nervously, at the Mercy College commencement ceremonies on January 30, 1983, as a collegiate hood signifying an honorary Doctor of Letters degree was placed over his head. Among the thousands in attendance were his wife and children and several close friends, including Norman Mailer and Gerald Green, who wrote *The Last Angry Man* and *Holocaust.* For Scott Meredith, a fellow who had to drop out of school as a child to support himself, it was, I knew, an electrifying moment. I was present because, after being named to the college's board of trustees a couple of years after my own graduation, I had been elected its chairman in 1980. I had nominated Scott for the honor, and as I led him back to his chair on the stage of the Westchester County Center, he squeezed my hand tightly. I had never seen him smile so broadly. Several times he glanced up toward the balcony where Helen was sitting. Seated to my right, he applauded as each of the hundreds of students walked across the platform to receive a degree.

A few days later I received a letter:

When I was a kid writing for the pulp magazines, I was sometimes assigned to write all twelve stories in an issue of a football magazine, or all twelve stories in a Western magazine (under twelve names, of course)—when I'd never even seen a football game and never been further West than Philadelphia. It was a cinch no matter what kind of writing I was assigned to do. I just did some quick research with a library book or two, and then pounded the typewriter until the stories were done. Despite the foregoing, I'm absolutely stumped when it comes to writing and telling you what last Sunday meant to me, and how grateful I am to you. The right words, I guess, haven't really been invented, so I'll settle (like a true agent) for ten percent of what I *want* to say, and tell you that Sunday was the high point of my professional and personal life, that the memory of it will warm me forever. . . .

My heels pounded the cold pavement in a steady rhythm, and although it was seven o'clock on Saturday morning, the day before Christmas, 1983, I was exuberant. By eating carefully and exercising regularly, my weight had dropped eighteen pounds. After three months I was able to run two miles at an average speed of ten minutes per mile three times a week. The first half-mile of every run was miserable, an agonizing and painful period in which I had to continually struggle not to quit. I liked running best in the missing moments, those inexplicable times when my mind would wander and I'd suddenly discover, to my delight, I had traveled several blocks. Also, like banging my head against the wall, it felt great when I stopped.

Before me sat a man, Scott Meredith, who had conceived hundreds of creative projects, had encouraged legions of authors, artists, photographers, actors, world leaders, entertainers.

"What," I asked, "would you suggest to someone who really wants to change his life?"

"First," he replied, "I'd ask, 'Are you willing to take a risk?' I'd explain that not one of the talented people I've known has been truly confident, particularly when changing his or her life. I might cite an example. It would surprise many people, I'm sure, to learn that when

I first met Carl Sagan some years ago, he actually asked me whether I thought he could succeed at writing. I immediately told him he could, because his talent, his ability to articulate, his brilliance were apparent to me. In retrospect, considering his spectacular success, that might seem obvious to anyone. Consider, however, the courage it took for Carl Sagan to commit himself to an *additional* career, because he is still, as you know, a serious professor and a respected scientist. That man was willing to face risk. A person needs conviction, Walter, more than confidence. When half of you insists that you will fail, the other half must argue that you will succeed. Each person really does have the power to start. Sadly, though, too many never begin new lives or careers because they wrongly believe they must be confident. They say things like, 'When I'm ready—' "

I interrupted. "When *should* a person start?"

"Today!" he said, rising forward on the couch, "because there is no better time. Right now! Look, on D-Day you had to wait for clouds before you could land, but in our day-to-day lives there's no real reason to stall. We can always find very good, persuasive reasons not to do something. The world, though, is there for those who *do*. I think we forget sometimes that none of us have a contract that says we'll live ninety years or, for that matter, ninety days. Start today!"

We've explored many questions in this book. One remains. *Am I ready?* None is more important, because without that first step there's no journey. In Chapter One I suggested that you find a small pebble, save it, squeeze it as a reminder of the mountains we can move even if we hoist only one stone at a time.

Consider the lives of the real people whose stories you've read. Have you, as I promised earlier, seen yourself reflected in their pain, their joy, their discoveries?

Each of the people we've met was imperfect. In every case their personalities reflected a *blending* of strengths and weaknesses. However unique they might have seemed on the surface, they shared, finally and deeply, a common bond. Heartbeat to heartbeat, like you and me, they struggled. Each person had potential, but each was limited. What have we learned? As long as we live, we have the power to change ourselves, to improve, to grow in a hundred ways, to experience new adventures. The message is not that you can do anything; it's that you can do *more*.

Are you ready?

Although the temperature was a flat 40 degrees and it was drizzling the morning of February 18, 1984, I had been running for more than three miles. Never, I admitted to myself, had I ever really been an athlete. As a boy, I had played some playground basketball and tossed a baseball in a weedy lot, but that was all; I had little time and less discipline. Running as a sport, I remembered, was out. Kids ran in my neighborhood when they had a reason to. In the Marine Corps, like everyone else, I stayed fit, but I was not addicted to calisthenics.

The light rain, almost a mist, cooled me as I put one foot in front of the other. I daydreamed. *If*, I thought, if what? If I really got in condition, maybe I could finish a race. A race! Me? No, not a chance. On the other hand, what a feeling that must be to cross a finish line. I'd like to feel that. Anderson, I told myself, you're going to be forty years old and you've lost forty pounds. You weigh one hundred and ninety-five now. Don't press your luck. Once, just once, I thought, I'd like to run ten miles. That's it! On my fortieth birthday, I'll run ten miles. *Ten* miles? If I can do that, I *will* be in the best shape of my life.

Can I really run ten miles?
Am I ready?

I followed Scott Meredith into the elevator. As it descended, I considered David Schoenbrun's observation: "You *are* alike."

I remembered a letter I had received from Scott in January 1982. "As you've probably heard," he had written, "it was a pretty bad time, since the melanoma was sufficiently large that, if it had spread, it would have been the end of the road. But, though a huge operation was involved, they got it all and, most important, the slides showed no spreading. So now the recovery period is almost over, and I'll be back to work a week from Monday—the only difference being a big scar and a lot more hair on my face. I was too weak to shave at first, and then too lazy, so I'm now (probably temporarily) one of the bearded set."

The elevator doors opened and Scott stepped into the lobby.

"When the melanoma was diagnosed three years ago," I asked my friend, "were you ready to die?"

He shook his head. "No," he told me. "I'll never be ready to die. I love life too much. Professionally, since I first became an agent, I've never, never had a dull day. I've had terrible days and depressing days, but never a dull day. I enjoy the sunrise and the seasons and I treasure my family—I'm closer to Helen than to any other human being—and I value my friends and all the exciting world around me. I love life."

I nodded. "Me too," I said.

For most of us, the fear of embarrassment is particularly acute in adolescence, but even when we are adults it stings. What is it, though, that we really fear others will discover?

That we are inferior.

That we are vulnerable.

That we deserve to be rejected.

It's true of all of us, isn't it? The astronaut, the priest, the prince, the great sculptor—they all worry. What have we learned? Clearly, that such anxiety is no reason to quit, that it's a reason to act. For performers like Jerry Lewis, Marlo Thomas and Carroll O'Connor anxiety is a friend, a source of energy that helps them focus, gives them strength. Anxiety is not a barrier; it's a ladder.

Anxiety opens the door to our future. We're never as ready as when our pulses are pounding.

It was a warm morning early in the summer of 1980 when Carlo Vittorini, who was the president of *Parade,* and I walked west along East Forty-sixth Street to Madison Avenue, where we were to meet with Samuel I. Newhouse, Jr.

"Be yourself," Carlo advised, "and be prepared to discuss your editorial plans. He'll have questions . . ."

The Newhouse family owns *Parade* and, among other interests, more than twenty daily newspapers, the Random House book publishing company, several cable television systems and Condé Nast, a company that publishes such stylish magazines as *Vogue, Glamour, Mademoiselle, House & Garden* and the recently created *Self.* This was to be my first meeting with Samuel I. Newhouse, Jr., who, despite the vast billion-dollar communications company he manages with his younger brother, Donald, and other family members, was rumored to be an extremely private person.

"What's he like?" I asked Carlo.

"Quiet," Carlo said, "and I think you'll find him easy to talk to. He's very interested in editorial. He's read your review of the magazine and—"

"You showed him *that?*" I interrupted.

"Of course," Carlo said, "and I think you'll find him particularly interested in your comments about quality and the people you intend to have write for the magazine."

It had been three years since the morning of my first day at *Parade.* I could clearly recall how disappointed I was when, six months after I started, Jess Gorkin left *Parade* after three decades and became the editor of a new magazine now called *Fifty Plus.* I did not succeed him. He was replaced, instead, by James D. Head, a journalist who had been my executive editor when I was an investigative reporter with the Westchester Rockland Newspapers. Although Jim Head was a friend and assured me that he'd name me managing editor as Jess Gorkin had promised, I was crushed. I remembered the conversation I had had with my wife the day I learned that Jess had been asked by Jim McAllister, the president of the magazine at the time, to retire.

"I'm going to quit," I told her.

"Why?" she asked.

"I'm embarrassed," I admitted.

"You're going to quit because you're embarrassed?"

"No," I said, "not because I'm embarrassed. I'm going to quit because I won't be editor of the magazine. That's the reason I came to *Parade* in the first place. I have a hundred ideas I'd like to try."

"Walter," she asked, "are you really ready to be editor of *Parade?*"

I didn't answer.

I knew I was angrily responding out of hurt; in truth, I was not yet equipped to be editor of a magazine.

That night I slept poorly, rising three times, the third at 4:00 A.M. Sitting alone in the darkened living room, the air still, I asked: What's wrong with me? I reminded myself, Use your anger. Finally, the mist lifted and I could see. *I wasn't ready.* My neck reddened. I was envious of Jim Head. Despite all logic, I wanted Jess Gorkin's pledge to be honored, and I wanted to be appointed the editor of *Parade.* But in the silence I finally conceded, I'm not ready. I had more to learn. I was, after all, only thirty-three.

Now, almost three years later, as I rode the elevator up to the fourteenth floor of the Condé Nast Building with Carlo Vittorini, I reflected on the last few weeks. Jim Head had resigned to help start up a children's magazine called *Three to Get Ready.* Carlo and Mr. Newhouse had jointly conducted a search among some of the leading editors in the country, but nevertheless Carlo had recommended that I be given a chance to handle the assignment. I was only thirty-five, but *I had been given a chance.* If after a few months I proved myself, I would be "editor." The elevator doors opened. The butterflies began to dance in my stomach. I followed Carlo into the office of Samuel I. Newhouse, Jr.

I wondered: Am I ready now?

I considered some advice I had heard years earlier from Ed Sullivan, whom I had been assigned to interview in 1971 by the Westchester Rockland Newspapers. One of the most popular showmen of all time and the host of what had been the country's longest-running television program, he lived with his wife, Sylvia, in Manhattan's Hotel Delmonico on Park Avenue.

I remembered saying to Sylvia when Ed left the room for a moment: "Often, I notice, as I ask him questions about himself, Ed describes the achievements of others."

She agreed.

"He sincerely likes people," Sylvia told me, "and he projects that sincerity. People aren't easily fooled. He's loyal to his fans—and he enjoys them as much as they enjoy him. One night, when we were eating at Gino's, a fellow asked for ten autographs for his ten children. Though the food had just been put on the table, Ed took the time to sign ten times. Once we were crossing the street to Delmonico's and a man hailed Ed and started to sing right there on Park Avenue. Ed booked him for a summer show."

She laughed. "It's true," she said.

When he returned to the room, I asked Ed Sullivan, "How did you get to be so expert about entertainment and the arts?"

He gently grasped my elbow and led me to a window, where he pointed to the crowded sidewalk below.

"See those people?" he said.

I nodded.

"It is not that I'm so different," he continued, "it is that I'm so much the same. You see, I *am* the man in the third row. If I like it, others seem to. If the show's successful, it's because I am not an expert."

I am the man in the third row.

The message was clear to me. For better or worse, I told myself, be who you are.

Mr. Newhouse was indeed a quiet man, but his questions, which he asked softly, were perceptive.

I found myself discussing quality. "The only medium," I said, "that attracts audiences as large as ours is television. The success of shows like *Roots, Holocaust, 60 Minutes* and *Brian's Song* is no accident. Americans demand quality. If we match the right writer with the right idea, our readers will respond. Americans *demand* quality."

The meeting lasted a half hour. He asked me to call him Si, and he frequently folded his hands before him modestly as he spoke. He had brown eyes and curly black hair. I knew that he was fifty-two, but he seemed younger to me, stronger somehow. Maybe it's his power, I thought. No, it was something else.

"Walter," he asked, "whom do you plan to publish?"

"The widest variety of American authors," I said. "People as diverse as Norman Mailer and John Cheever and Gail Sheehy and Herman Wouk and David Halberstam and Irving Wallace and Erica Jong and Alex Haley and Studs Terkel."

"Walter," he asked, "do you *know* these writers?"

"In a sense."

"In a sense?" he asked.

"I've never met any of them," I admitted, "but I know them from their work."

He was silent for several seconds. "Are you confident you can attract these writers to *Parade?*"

"Yes," I said, "I am. *Parade* will be a receptive environment in which ideas flourish. In other words, Si, it's going to be exciting. No, more than that, it's going to be irresistible. Why will the authors participate? Because the ideas will be compelling, not clever. We'll get their blood rushing. Something else . . ."

"What is that?"

"I believe," I said, "that if I appeal to their more noble motives, we'll get their finest work."

"Can I help you?" he asked.

By the early summer of 1985 he had been appointed the full-time strength coach of the New Jersey Nets basketball team and the New Jersey Devils hockey team; he had been a consultant to the Philadelphia Flyers, the New York Giants and the New York Yankees. He'd trained tennis stars Billie Jean King, Arthur Ashe, Chris Evert Lloyd and Martina Navratilova, movie stars like Karen Allen of *Raiders of the Lost Ark,* baseball players like Sparky Lyle. He was a program adviser to respected corporations like Morgan Stanley, and he even designed physical training programs for major hospitals. A decade earlier he had only a little money and a big vision. Virtually by himself, working out of a small space in a doctor's office, Michael O'Shea started what would become one of the world's most respected fitness centers, the Sports Training Institute in Manhattan, a multimillion-dollar facility with thousands of clients.

He was thirty-eight, two years younger than I. Six feet three, broad-chested, he weighed one hundred and ninety pounds, with wide brown eyes and full, curly brown hair, an even nose and high cheekbones, classic angular features, a face that belonged on a marine recruiting poster. He was, in addition to all else he had achieved, a triathlete, a frequent competitor in those grueling events that required swimming, biking and running in the same contest.

"Mike," I asked as we walked along Park Avenue, "who has been the greatest influence in your life?"

"I was raised in West Philadelphia," he began, "in a neighborhood that seemed to shrink each year, growing rougher every day. My mother decided when I was six that there was nothing but trouble for me to be roaming the streets, so she began sending me during the summers to my grandfather's home in Shenandoah, Pennsylvania. It was a small coal-mining town that had once thrived when coal mining was big. When oil heat replaced coal in the Northeast, most of the coal miners were put out of work. This left small jobs and welfare for many.

"My grandfather was a physician there. His name was Dr. John Monahan, and he was what you'd probably call a small-town doctor. He could easily have moved to City Line Avenue in Philadelphia and he would have been well-off financially. He felt he was needed, though, in Shenandoah, and Shenandoah was where he stayed, despite economic pressures, even as other doctors left for better, higher-paying practices elsewhere."

He stopped speaking.

"Walt," he began again, "my grandfather had something money could not buy. He earned respect, and he earned it the hard way. From the time I was six until I was fourteen and he died, each year confirmed it more. He was the greatest man I've ever known; he influenced my life more than anyone else, and he never left this small town. I remember as a child making the rounds with my grandfather. At least two or three nights a week we'd sleep at the hospital in a different room, whatever was available, so that he would be ready for emergencies. In the middle of the night he'd be summoned, and sometimes I'd go with him. Even as a child I could see how my grandfather was regarded—

respected!—by the hospital staff, other doctors, patients and nurses."

He paused again, as if he were turning pages in an album and had found a photo he particularly enjoyed.

"When he went on calls to people's homes, they'd see him from the window and they'd cheer up immediately. He'd encourage the very poor to give him a pie or cake or mow his lawn for his services. He made the poor see it as an exchange of necessary services, so they never lost their pride, never were allowed to feel they were getting something free, something they had not earned. When he received a cake, he showed such excitement and appreciation, you'd think it was the greatest cake ever made—and for my grandfather maybe it was. He'd visit dying patients and sometimes he'd give them no medication, not even a placebo. He'd sit with them, talk to them, and if they were Catholic, he'd recite a Rosary with them.

"During these rounds with my grandfather, while we were in a car or walking, he'd tutor me. He had ordered books, extremely interesting books like the story of King Tut's tomb, a history of the Air Corps in World War Two, Robinson Crusoe—and we'd read and he'd ask questions. To this day I can remember those books. He taught me math and chemistry also. So much did I enjoy his teaching, so well did he prepare me that in grammar school I *never* made an error on a math exam. Not once. I had a perfect record because he had me two to three years ahead of everyone else . . ."

As Mike O'Shea spoke, the pages turning faster now, I recalled how we had first met. I had stopped by the Fifth Avenue office of one of *Parade*'s contributing editors, Stuart Berger, a prominent psychiatrist, nutritionist and best-selling author. It was March 8, 1984.

"There's someone I'd like you to meet," Dr. Berger told me.

Before I could change my mind, the doctor had me scheduled for an appointment at the Sports Training Institute on East Forty-ninth Street. Within a week I was a client.

"What are your goals?" Mike asked me.

"I'd like to run ten miles on my birthday," I said.

"That's no goal," he argued. "You can do that now."

"I can?"

"Of course," he said. "You're in better shape than you realize. Let's amend that goal."

"To what?"

"We'll have you run ten miles," he promised, "in less than ninety minutes."

I nodded but made no comment. Fat chance, I thought, you train too many athletes, Michael. It's made your brain spongy.

"Something else," he added.

"Yes?"

"Read this."

He gave me a large brown envelope. Inside were three triathlete magazines.

"Why," I asked, "are you giving me these?"

"You'll enjoy reading them," he said. "Meanwhile, concentrate on your ten-mile goal."

That evening, as I rode the New Haven train to Harrison, I noticed other commuters peering at me as I read the magazines: They think I'm a triathlete! Anderson, I told myself, now *your* brain's going spongy. You couldn't swim fifty yards. Of course, none of my railroad companions knew that. I sat a little straighter, and, as I recall, I may have read the magazines a little more obviously.

"My grandfather never seemed to tell stories about himself," Mike continued as we walked. "I learned more about him from other people. For example, my cousins and I were hiking in the woods one day and we became lost. We saw a cabin, knocked on the door and introduced ourselves. The man knew our grandfather. He dropped what he was doing and drove us home, telling us how our grandfather had helped him.

"Also, around the corner from his office in Shenandoah, there was one of those all-purpose candy stores that sold everything, including the day's illegal 'number.' I'd return soda bottles there and receive two cents each. The tough men who hung out there didn't like me at first because of my Philadelphia accent, but when they discovered who my grandfather was, I had carte blanche. More important, they told me stories of how my grandfather had saved lives, sometimes theirs:

" 'He came into the mine and pulled me out . . .'

" 'He carried *my* brother from the mine . . .'

" 'My uncle wouldn't be alive if your grandfather hadn't . . .' "

What if I fail? It's a question, probably more than any other, that tugs at us, grips us, holds us back. After all, if we don't run, we don't stumble. Not today, we say, we'll be ready *tomorrow*. Which of the successful people described in these chapters has not failed?

Scott Meredith once told me, "Good judgment comes from experience, and experience comes from bad judgment."

All of us fail.

Imagine if John Glenn had hesitated in his spacecraft as it fell to earth. Prepare, he advised, but recognize that the unforeseen, like a loose heat shield on a speeding rocket, can occur.

What's the worst that can happen? When we honestly measure consequences, rarely do we find them as bad as we imagined. Worry, we've learned, doesn't stop the future from unfolding; it only ruins today. Once we've examined our concerns, often we know precisely what to do.

Courage is acting *with* fear, not without it. Yes, you *can* dare to be you.

"When I was discharged from the service," Mike O'Shea told me, "I didn't know what I was going to do, but I knew what I was not going to do. And that was to do what my father had done, commute each day to a job he hated. My dad was a stockbroker in New York. When we lived in Philadelphia, he'd rise early each morning and commute to Manhattan to a position over which he had little control."

"What made the choices so difficult?" I asked.

"It was like trying to shop for a hundred-thousand-dollar home," he replied, "by looking at homes that cost four hundred thousand dollars. I had seen my grandfather's life. That was a four-hundred-thousand-dollar home. I wouldn't settle for less, though, honestly, I didn't realize I was so intensely directed. I tried several jobs, including iron worker.

I wasn't happy. I thought about my grandfather and I made a decision: If I don't make a dime, I'm going to do what I enjoy, which is to help people. I started the Sports Training Institute by myself, because I believed in it. Like my grandfather at the hospital, I had to sleep where I worked, but I did because money was tight. An apartment meant no Sports Training Institute.

"I wish I could say that I planned the success of the Sports Training Institute, that there had been various stages and that they had been carefully worked out. The truth is that I'm not that smart. Success happened, period. I did not plan it or expect it. I only set out to do what I really enjoyed. All the rest followed. In fact, a shrewd business-man could undoubtedly show me many ways I could have saved money over the years—or made money differently. We don't sell T-shirts, massages or whirlpools. We're only interested in health and training, and we invest our money in improving those sessions. Maybe that's the best business decision of all, though, because we've never not made our money back. Our clients know the difference, and we do not encourage people who are not serious about their health to join the Sports Train-ing Institute."

"Mike," I asked, "how does this reflect your grandfather?"

"My grandfather," he said, "had a long-term commitment, and I think that is what I've settled into. Instant gratification does not fit into my life. Everything I do is one small step, an hour here or there, at a time. I never leap to the top of the mountain; I walk steadily, one foot in front of the other."

He paused and took a breath. "I received my master's degree part time," he continued, "working a little bit here and a little bit there. I attended *ten* colleges. I have been working nine years—nine years! —on my doctorate. Within a few months I'll receive that Ph.D. I've earned it by rising early and working an hour or two every day, complet-ing my thesis and experiments as I can. Had I said to myself, 'This will take nine years, so forget it!' I would not be in the position I am in today. The nine years would have passed whether I got the work done or not—the difference is that now I'll have my doctorate."

"Do you ever feel like giving up?"

"The initial study for my thesis involved the effects of exercise on pregnancy. It took me months to write it to the examiners' satisfaction, months to get it approved by the research committee, months to get it approved by the human rights committee, months to get each of the doctors to approve it. I had forty-two copies that had to be distributed and initialed. Finally, I had it done."

He paused again. "But I had made one mistake," he said. "Although I had the subject checked by computer to be sure no one else was doing the same study, one was in process, which I discovered after thousands of hours and all this process. That *was* discouraging. I was ready to quit. But I waited a month, relaxed, exercised a lot, and came back to it a little at a time. Four hours one week, then the next—and here I am." He threw his arms in the air and smiled widely.

"How do you handle failure, Mike?"

"When I fail," he told me, "I start again. I've failed many times. But I do everything one day at a time. During the day, I try one hour at a time. Everything big begins in a small way."

We've heard many voices within these pages. Do they sound familiar?

I wrote earlier that hundreds of times I have looked into the eyes of an eminently successful person to ask gently, "When it is dark and you are alone, do you ever say to yourself: What will I do when they find out I'm me?"

I had never failed to make a friend with the question. And I never failed to get a nod. It was as if I knew who they were, that I understood, and because I understood, I could be trusted. I have seen, I said, the cool composure of some of America's toughest business leaders melt.

"How about you?" I asked. "Do you worry that someone will find out that you're not good enough, that you can be hurt, that you don't belong? If so, read on. Your fears, my fears, are shared by millions of sane people."

"We are not alone," I promised. "Truth be told, it is we who are the majority and it is we who are normal. Fear, once you understand it, can be OK. In fact, sometimes it can save your life."

.   .   .

Less than a week after my first meeting with Si Newhouse, I was introduced to the talented photographer Eddie Adams, one of the most gifted people I have ever met. As a distinguished correspondent for the Associated Press, he had received the Pulitzer Prize in 1969 for a picture of a Vietnamese colonel executing a Viet Cong prisoner, a photograph recognized throughout the world as one of the most important of that war.

As I stood in a Manhattan gallery that was displaying an exhibit by the renowned documentary photographer Arthur Rothstein, who was *Parade*'s photo editor, I recognized Eddie Adams immediately; he was the guest without a tie. About ten years older than I, five feet nine inches tall, of average build and balding, he had metal spectacles on a cord draped around his neck. He wore jeans and a safari jacket over a light blue cotton shirt opened at the collar. It was his pale blue eyes, though, that distinguished Eddie Adams. They were *laughing* eyes, bright and joyous.

"Would you like to meet Eddie?" Arthur asked.

"Please," I said.

A few minutes later I told Eddie Adams, "You're going to enjoy taking pictures for *Parade.*"

"I am not," he declared, "going to work for *Parade.*"

"Yes, you are," I promised.

"No, I'm not," he insisted.

"Let's not argue here," I suggested, indicating the photo gallery where we both stood. "Meet me in my office later this week."

"Why should I show up?" he asked.

"That's easy," I said. "You have to find out why I'm so sure you'll be working for *Parade.*"

As I peered out the window of the American Airlines jet heading west to Los Angeles one afternoon in August 1981, I considered what I might say to Julia Child, the popular French Chef of Public Broadcasting fame, an extraordinarily talented and sophisticated woman who I hoped would join *Parade* magazine as a contributing editor.

Her attorney, Bob Johnson, had suggested that I introduce myself to Julia at her condominium in Santa Barbara. My initial contact with her representatives had been discouraging, but I had grown accustomed to hearing "No!" With few exceptions, most authors whom I contacted during my first few months as editor quickly refused to contribute to *Parade.*

Eddie Adams, who had become not only a special correspondent to *Parade* but also one of my most cherished friends, once asked me, "Don't you *ever* give up?"

"Not often," I admitted.

"That's why I'm here," he said, shaking his head. "You were so enthusiastic, I couldn't resist. You believed in me; I had to believe in you."

I remembered the pledge I made to Eddie the day he showed up at my office for our first meeting: "If you take a risk and commit to *Parade,*" I told him, "you'll be our chief photographer. Your pictures will be seen in more than twenty *million* homes and you'll work with the finest authors and the most important subjects in all the world. You're too good at what you do to say no. Say yes."

It was a year later, and as I settled into the flight, I smiled. We had published an important interview with Richard Nixon by Marguerite Michaels, a sensitive review of the Entebbe raid by Herbert Kupferberg, a stunning investigative report by Michael Satchell on animal abuse, and we'd also presented our readers with a variety of articles by Herman Wouk, Studs Terkel, Beverly Sills, John Cheever, David Halberstam, Norman Mailer, Erica Jong, Dick Schaap, Alex Haley, Ernest K. Gann, Lally Weymouth, Dotson Rader, Anthony Sampson, Alistair Cooke and Andrei Sakharov. The President of the United States himself, Ronald Reagan, wrote our July Fourth cover story, with a picture, of course, by Eddie Adams. We were about to publish a compelling report by John Ehrlichman, who had been searching the nation to find dignity among the poor.

This is exciting, I thought, but, still, how do I persuade the French Chef to become part of *Parade?*

Julia Child had a smile that could melt a nation. With two Frenchwomen, Simone Beck and Louisette Bertholle, she had founded a cooking school called L'Ecole des Trois Gourmandes and created the classic volume *Mastering the Art of French Cooking.* Her public television program, *The French Chef,* which was broadcast from Boston, had become an unparalleled success. She had received a George Foster Peabody Award and an Emmy, and, like Alex Haley after *Roots,* she herself had become an institution. When fans said they *loved* Julia, they meant it.

If she could be encouraged to join *Parade,* it would be a huge contribution to the magazine. It would also mean much to me professionally as editor. Julia Child was universally respected.

Bob Johnson, her attorney, had cautioned me that she had no pressing needs to fill, that her life was balanced. "I'll arrange the lunch," he promised, "but the rest is up to you."

It came down to Julia. If, after meeting with me, she wanted to write for *Parade,* she would. Or, I realized only too well, she would not.

When we sat together in her Santa Barbara condominium the day after my flight from New York, Julia seemed, at first, genuinely intrigued with the idea I presented. Ira Yoffe, who was *Parade's* director of design, had created a colorful prototype for me to show, and Julia studied it carefully.

"I wasn't aware," she said, "that you used color."

"We will now," I promised. This is going well, I thought, relieved.

Later, though, when Julia Child asked me about Vietnam, I stiffened.

"I understand you served there," she said. "Is that true?"

I wanted very much to be able to return to New York and tell everyone that Julia Child was joining *Parade.* Would I lose the chance? I knew that passion about Vietnam still ran high. Too many times I had heard, "*You* served in Vietnam? Why?" I had no idea what Julia Child felt about the war. Like many Vietnam veterans, I was sensitive, possibly too sensitive, to the attitudes of others toward those who had served there. I *could* say nothing. Fifteen years earlier, though, I had made a promise that, no matter what, I would never deny my service.

"Yes," I said, "I was a Marine sergeant in Vietnam."

Julia, showing great interest, asked me several questions about my time in the military, particularly about the reception veterans had received in the United States. I thought: Well, that's that. You've blown it now.

Later, when I stood to leave, Julia looked at me silently for a few seconds.

"Walter," she said as she gave me a hug, actually lifting me to my toes, "we'll love working together!"

"Wallace Wolf is on the phone," Gida Ingrassia, who had been my assistant for seven years at *Parade*, told me.

I took a deep breath. It was Tuesday afternoon, August 21, 1984. The following morning I was scheduled to fly to Des Moines, Iowa. The *Register*, which was the newspaper there, was generally regarded as one of America's best, and its decision to begin to distribute *Parade* in a few weeks was important to the magazine. I had been asked to speak to the newspaper's circulation executives. When I returned from Iowa, I would be in the office only one day, then I planned to start my vacation. I was pressed for time.

"Gi," I asked, "could you ask Wally if I can call him tonight?"

"I told him you were really busy," she said, "but he insisted that it was important."

I had met Wally Wolf, who was an attorney in Los Angeles, almost four years earlier. He had represented Irving Wallace, his daughter, Amy, and his son, David Wallechinsky, in discussions to create the feature called "Significa" for *Parade*. He had since introduced me to film producers Bud and Cappy Greenspan and to Dr. Leroy Perry, an author who was a respected adviser to world-class athletes. Wally Wolf and his wife, Carolyn, had become close friends of my family. Wally once held a world swimming record and he had competed in four Olympics, winning a gold medal in 1948 as part of the 200-meter relay team. A few weeks before this phone call he had instructed me how to breathe and swim so that I could complete that part of a triathlon, an event my friend Mike O'Shea had persuaded me to enter. If Wally needed me, I'd be there.

"Walter," he said, "I need your help."

"What can I do?" I asked.

"On the evening of August 30," he began, "I have a meeting of the United States Gymnastics Team in New York. Can you please attend? It's very important to me. I need you there."

I'd have to come off vacation to attend. *He said it was important.* Wally, I thought silently, you're the only person for whom I'd give up a vacation.

"Sure, Wally," I said. "Where will it be?"

"At Tavern on the Green," he answered, "and Carolyn will be with me. Can you bring Loretta?"

"I'll ask, but I'm sure she'll want to go."

"By the way," he asked, "how's your training coming and when is the triathlon?"

"I'm working my tail off," I said, "thanks to you and Michael O'Shea. It's September ninth in Westchester."

"What are your goals?"

I laughed. "One to sign up," I replied, "two to show up, three to finish, and four not to finish last."

He laughed. "Which is the toughest?" he asked.

"Two," I said.

On Monday, August 20, 1984, I had lunch with Jason Epstein, the editorial director of Random House, to discuss a book he had asked me to review.

Toward the end of the lunch, though, he volunteered a curious comment.

"I would like," he said, "to be *your* Walter Anderson."

"What do you mean?" I asked.

"I'd like to see you write a book revealing your own philosophy and life experiences," he said, "and I'd like to be *your* editor."

"Have you been talking to Scott Meredith?" I asked.

"Why?"

"For more than two years," I told Jason, "Scott has been encouraging me to write that book. I've said no. I really don't think I'm ready."

"Why don't you try an outline?" he suggested.

"I'll think about it, Jason," I promised.

"Will you talk to Scott?"

"Yes," I said, "I'll call Scott."

A cramp stiffened my leg near the quarter-mile marker of the triathlon's half-mile swim in Long Island Sound. I had a quarter of a mile to go, then fourteen miles by bicycle, followed by a four-mile run.

I swallowed some water. Stay calm, I warned myself. This is no place to panic. I couldn't seem to right myself in the water. My strokes were getting ragged. I gasped. It became more and more difficult to breathe.

"Are you in trouble?" another swimmer asked.

I was bobbing in the path of scores of triathletes.

"Yes!" I blurted.

"Do you want a lifeguard?" he asked.

"Not yet," I said. "Can you push me to the side? I can float, I think."

He stopped his race, losing precious seconds, to pull me a few yards out of traffic.

"Thanks," I said.

A lifeguard in a wooden boat rowed near me.

"Do you need help?"

"Not yet," I said. "I think I have a cramp, though."

"You want me to pull you out?"

"No!" I insisted, my voice sounding a lot more confident than I felt. "I'm going to try to backstroke . . ."

It was slow going, but I was able to move a few feet with each stroke. In a few minutes I never felt more alone. I knew I was the last swimmer of hundreds that had started. *Stroke, stroke, stroke.* This was so slow. I looked into the powder-blue sky. I wondered: Why am I doing this? All I have to do is raise my hand, a lifeguard will scoop me out and this pain will end. *One more stroke.* I strained my neck to see the shoreline. I had begun to swim in circles! I straightened out. Utter silence. I knew the swimming portion would be the toughest for me, but I hadn't expected a cramp. I knew I could bike fourteen miles twice if I had to. On my fortieth birthday nine days earlier I *had* run ten miles, and as Mike O'Shea had predicted, I completed the course in eighty-seven minutes and nineteen seconds.

What a feat that was, I thought. The night before, my friends, brought together by Gida Ingrassia, surprised me with a birthday party at Tavern on the Green. Wally Wolf had tricked me! There was no United States Gymnastics Team dinner. Think about the party, I told myself. Make this a missing moment. *Stroke.* It was, simply, the best night of my life. Jess Gorkin, whom I had asked to return to *Parade* as an adviser to me, was there, and so were Si Newhouse and Scott Meredith and Carl Sagan and Barbara Walters and Hugh Downs and Carroll O'Connor and Lisa Birnbach and Dotson Rader and Dr. Stuart Berger and Earl Ubell and Roy Cohn and Dick and Trish Schaap and Cleveland Amory and Eddie Adams and Barbara Gordon and James Brady and editors like Herb Mayes and Art Cooper and Clay Felker and Sey Chassler, and the cartoonist Bill Hoest and many more writers and friends and co-workers, perhaps a hundred people in all. Think about it. *Stroke.* Carlo Vittorini introduced Jess, who made a toast: "As your waist grows thinner," he said, "may your horizons grow wider." I turned in the water. The shore!

As I neared the end of the race an hour and a half later, the announcer called out my name and my age. I had reached my goal; I had found a finish line! My time was two hours, twelve minutes and nineteen seconds. The young man who won the event had a time of eighty-four minutes, forty-four seconds. I was number one hundred and seventy-seven of the one hundred and ninety-four competitors who completed the second annual Westchester Triathlon. I felt like a champion.

In the middle of September 1984 I drove alone to the neighborhood in which I was raised. I parked my car across the street, walked over and touched the building where I once lived. I closed my eyes and tried to imagine my father's voice. I listened for my brother and my mother and, of course, my sister.

Could I tell this story?

Nothing, I was sure, could ever be as difficult for me. I had put away so many memories. I'd have to remember events I'd rather forget.

"I don't know if I can do this," I had told Scott.

"You can," he said, "and you should."

I sat down on the stoop of the building. Then I knew I would.

ACKNOWLEDGMENTS

The writing of *Courage Is a Three-Letter Word* was a long journey, a challenge I could not have completed alone. Now I'd like to thank those who walked with me:

First, the people who read this book as I wrote it, my friends at the Scott Meredith Literary Agency, especially Scott himself and Jack Scovil, who encouraged me when I needed support most; Herbert Kupferberg, a gifted editor, and Anita Goss, a tireless and talented researcher, both of *Parade;* and, of course, Loretta, to whom this book is dedicated, and our children, Eric and Melinda.

Jason Epstein proved to be a skillful, creative editor, a trusted adviser who never lost confidence in the project. His contributions were invaluable, as were the suggestions and advice of the publisher of Random House, Howard Kaminsky, a man of endless enthusiasm.

I'm especially grateful to those friends whose stories appear in these pages and to three psychologists, Joyce Brothers, Sal Didato and John McNulty; Si Newhouse, whose support and confidence I cherish; Irving Wallace, David Wallechinsky and Amy Wallace; Wallace Wolf, author Barbara Gordon, who wrote *I'm Dancing As Fast As I Can;* my copy editor, Sono Rosenberg; Carlo Vittorini; my friends Peachy and Manny Santos; editors David Starr and Steve Newhouse; Sylvia Schur, the respected president of Creative Food Services; Jay Burzon, an advertising executive of indomitable spirit; Catherine Hemlepp and the editors, authors, photographers and artists of *Parade* who encouraged me as I wrote this book: Eddie Adams, Cleveland Amory, Jack Anderson, Chris Austopchuk, Stuart Berger, Lisa Birnbach, Sara Brzowsky, Jacqueline Burns, Fran Carpentier, Sey Chassler, Julia Child, Haskell Cohen, Bob Colacello, Paul Cook, David Currier, Ovid Demaris, Joseph DiBlasi, Anne Edmondson, John Frook, Elizabeth Gaynor, Opal Ginn, the late Jess Gorkin, David Halberstam, Bill Hoest, Larry L. King, Elinor Klein, Peter Maas, Norman Mailer, Gael McCarthy, David McCullough, Marguerite Michaels, Mary Murawinski, Willie Morris, Roger Niles, Jean Noble, Brent Petersen, Robert L. Peterson, Arlene Pueschel, Dotson Rader, the late Arthur Rothstein, Carl Sagan, Bonnie St. Clair, Al Santoli, Michael Satchell, Dick Schaap, Doris Schortman, Marvin Scott, Tom Seligson, Lloyd Shearer, Gail Sheehy, Larry Smith, Tad Szulc, Martin Timins, Al Troiani, Earl Ubell, Lally Weymouth, Hank Whittemore and Ira Yoffe.

And, always first with me, Gida Ingrassia.

This book could not conclude properly, though, without mentioning Gene D'Ambra, a retired restaurateur who married my mother a few years after my father died. He is one of the most gentle and sensitive men I have known, and I'm happy to report that he and my mother have found a joyous life together.

Neither would the story be complete without remembering the Becktoft, the Thiele and the Artz families—my aunts, uncles and cousins—and, again, my brother Bill. They, with my grandmother, Lillian Crolly, taught me to say *yes.*

Thank you.

About the Author

WALTER ANDERSON is editor of *Parade* magazine, the country's most widely circulated publication. Before joining *Parade* in 1977, he was a reporter and an editor with the Gannett Newspaper Group.

A former Marine sergeant and Vietnam veteran, he is a graduate of Mercy College in Dobbs Ferry, N.Y., for which he now serves as chairman of the Board of Trustees. He is also a director of the New York Vietnam Veteran Leadership Program.

Mr. Anderson lives in White Plains, N.Y., with his wife, Loretta, and their children, Eric and Melinda.